Michael Baumgardt

Adobe Photoshop 6.0 Web Design

with ImageReady 3 and GoLive 5

Adobe Photoshop 6.0 Web Design
Michael Baumgardt

ISBN 0-201-72146-5
9 8 7 6 5 4 3 2 1

Printed and bound in the United States of America

Design by Mito Media, Inc., New York

FOR MARC SHEERIN

A few years ago, I made the transition from desktop publishing to Web design without anyone to show me the ropes. Now I hope this book can serve as a guide for anyone making that transition today. I wrote it to provide information that goes beyond the software manuals, answering questions and offering insights you won't find anywhere else.

You know the old saying, "Give a man a fish and he will eat for a day, but teach a man to fish and he will eat for the rest of his life." My goal with this book was to give you the knowledge to be a better Web designer, and knowing Photoshop is only one step. You also need to know how to export graphic elements and bring them back together in GoLive, plus how to design attractive Web elements in ImageReady. And every good designer should be well versed in the basics of navigational design and information architecture.

This book is broken down into four easy-to-follow parts that will teach you all that and more:

Basics: The first section focuses on Web design, so anyone making the leap from desktop publishing should read these chapters.

Photoshop and ImageReady: The second part features the Photoshop commands and techniques that are most important for Web designers. It should help all Photoshop and ImageReady novices.

Optimizing Images: The third part deals with compressing and optimizing image file size—one of the most important tasks in Web design. There's plenty of new information here, even for pros.

GoLive: The last section shows you how to bring Photoshop designs into GoLive to make a fully functional Web site. Even for those with prior GoLive experience, these chapters offer tips on how to set up your site more efficiently.

Finally, let me clarify what this book is not. It doesn't show you all sorts of special effects like chrome or water drops, because these elements are not used in professional Web design. And even though it includes many step-by-step explanations and tutorials, it was never my intention to show you 100 ways of creating buttons, because that knowledge would not make you a better designer.

I tried to make this new edition one of the most comprehensive guides available. I hope you find it useful and enjoyable. If you have any questions or feedback, mail me at

MBaumgardt@Mitomedia.com

Visit the companion Web site for this book
www.mitomediabooks.com
to download tutorials and updates.

I want to thank the following people
for their help and support.

● **Jolene Woo, Jill Merlin, Grace Abbett** Adobe ● **JB Popplewell** Alien Skin Software ● **Mark Patton** NetObjects ● **Matt Cupal** S-Vision ● **Lori Izabelle, John Geyer** Terran Interactive ● **Bonnie Mitchell** Casady Greene ● **Christopher Stashuk** Aristotle Little Rock, Arkansas ● **Paul Ehrenreich** Blickpunkt Fotostudio Munich ●

This book was faced with many challenges and difficulties. I am really gratefull to the people at Peachpit Press who supported me, even though it meant a lot of extra work on their part. My thanks goes in particular to Marjorie Baer (for organizing everything at the end), Anita Dennis (a great editor who contributed a lot), Linda Gaus (for doing such a great job fixing my "Denglish") and Becky Morgan (who helped so much at the beginning). A big thanks goes out to Gary-Paul Prince and all the others at Peachpit Press who helped to market this book. Last, but not least, I want to thank Nancy Ruenzel for her trust and support. It is a great pleasure to work with such a great team.

Thanks to ...

Florian Allgayer; Florian Anwander; Sabine & Christopher Bach; Friedericke Baumgardt; Heike Baumgardt; Hermann and Renate Baumgardt, my parents; Annette Baumgardt-Thormälen; Nina Bergengruen; Marion & Reimund Bienefeld-Zimanovsky; Karen Bihari; Tim & Jenn Bruhns; Ulrike Brüser; Claudia Brütting; Hajo Carl; Angela Carpenter; Mark Dolin; Albert Dommer; Tim Dorcey; Paul Ehrenreich; Ramsey Faragallah; Cordula Fischer; Andreas Florek; Susanne Flörsch; Sabine Frischmuth; Anja Gestring; George Geyer; Isabelle Girard and Allonzo; Alejandro and Christina Gjutierrez Viguera; Fritz Goßner; Christine Graf; Harry Greißinger; Silvia & Armin Günther; Tammi Haas; Juliet Hanlon; Mirko & Agniescka Hauck; Carol & Terry Hoare; Ernst & Kathie Hofacker; Peter Hoffmann; Nina Jakisch; Wolfgang Keller; Christopher LaRiche; Theresa Lee; Katja Lerch and Günther; Roger Libesch; Anja Maurus; Laurie Anne McGowan; Shari Mitchel; Julia Moreva; Meagan Murphy; Tom Nakat; Sabine & Joseph Plenk; Mark Rodgers; Manfred Rürup; Stephen Salters; Wieland Samolak; Andreas Schätzl; Marc Sheerin, I enjoy hanging out with you; Anja Schneider-Beck; Michael Seipel; Gia Stemmer; Lisa Tran; Katja Verdier; Lars Wagner; Ilona & Vera Waldmann; Corinne Werner; Udo Weyers; Uli Wiedenhorn; Klaus Wittig; and last, not least, my friend Steve Zierer.

The first edition of this book was written (June to October 1998) in New York, Munich, Verona and Istanbul; the second edition (the first English edition) was translated and updated in New York and Port Chester (July to November 1999). The current edition was written in New York, Roveretto and Munich (September to December 2000).

TABLE OF CONTENTS

PHOTOSHOP TECHNIQUES

DESIGNING WEB ELEMENTS

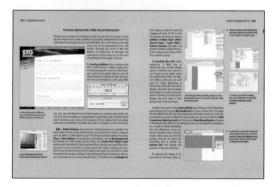

WORKING WITH IMAGEREADY

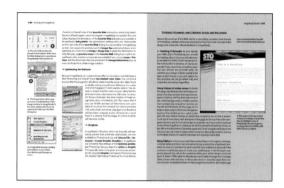

GIF ANIMATION

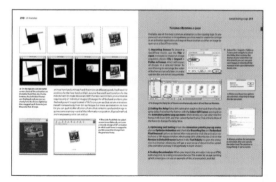

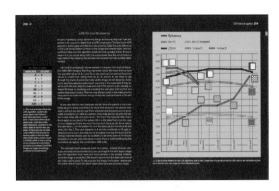

GIF

JPEG

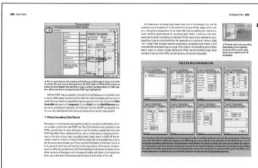

PNG

GoLive Basics

Video and Audio

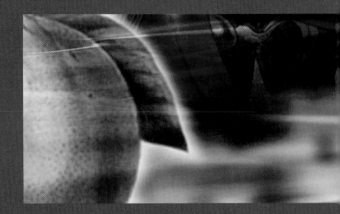

Illustration: Michael Baumgardt

THE BASICS OF WEB DESIGN

From Desktop Publishing to the World Wide Web: The Basics of Web Design

Just as California has Silicon Valley, Manhattan has Silicon Alley—a stretch of Broadway that runs from 28th Street in midtown to Spring Street in SoHo. The Alley is home to a huge number of Internet and Web companies. In fact, New York has experienced a boom from the Internet like no other city. Jason McCabe Calacanis, editor of the Silicon Alley Reporter, considers the city to be the new media capital: "In a short time," he notes, "Silicon Alley has grown from being almost nonexistent to employing 100,000 people and 5,000 companies. Though Silicon Alley is still in its infancy, it has already become the center of the Internet media world."

That success is partly based on the variety of ideas and trends in advertising, music, content, software, and services that are available in New York. The city offers an ideal ecosystem for an Internet company because it is home to many of the world's entertainment leaders: Viacom, Time Warner, Sony, NBC, CBS, ABC, NBA, Columbia Records, and RCA. In fact, most Northern California agencies have to open New York branches because this is where the big money is made. For example, the Web agency Organic had 80 employees in San Francisco when it started its New York subsidiary with a staff of 4. A few months later, the New York office had grown to 35 employees, and now Organic New York employs more people than the home office in San Francisco!

But regardless of where you live, the opportunities to design sites and content for the World Wide Web are tremendous. And if you have print experience, it's only natural to move into Web design as well. But while just a few years ago Web design skills could be mastered in a week, the field has grown exponentially in complexity—and thus so has the need for specialization. This book focuses on three important aspects of Web design: design itself, graphic compression, and conversion into HTML using Adobe GoLive.

Although I will give you some basic information on HTML, it's not the book's prime focus. Still, some basic HTML knowledge can be helpful, which is what this chapter is for.

HTML Basics

HTML is the language that allows information on the Web to be displayed in a browser. One advantage of HTML is that it's written in ASCII characters, so it works on multiple platforms. (ASCII stands for American Standard Code for

Information Interchange and has been a standard in the computer field for many years.) This means that a Web page created on an IBM-compatible PC can be read and interpreted by a browser running on another platform, such as a Macintosh.

Incidentally, it is quite easy to see the HTML source code that defines a Web page in your browser. If you choose Source from the View menu in Explorer or Navigator, a window opens and displays the HTML code. It looks something like this:

\<B>This is bold text.\</B>.

HTML generally consists of a beginning and an end tag, both of which are placed in angle brackets. The end tag sports a slash ("/"). In the example above, the text between the two tags will be displayed in bold in the browser.

Despite the long list of HTML tags, such as for headers, paragraphs, justification, and so on, the language is relatively easy to learn, and you can create a Web page by writing HTML code in an ordinary text editor. In the beginning, this is exactly how most HTML authors worked, since the WYSIWYG HTML editors available at the time generally produced incorrect HTML code. These days, you can choose from many WYSIWYG HTML authoring applications that work quite reliably.

```
                                 HTML: www.nny.com/nny/index2.htm
            <!--MORE FILLER-->
            <TD WIDTH="54" HEIGHT="62" VALIGN="BOTTOM"><IMG SRC="Art/1x1.gif" WIDTH="54" HEIGHT="62" BORDER
</TR>
</TABLE>
<!--********************************************************************-->
<!--LINES AND TITLES TABLE-->
<TABLE BORDER="0" CELLPADDING="0" CELLSPACING="0" WIDTH="525">
<TR>
        <!--GREY BAR-->
        <TD WIDTH="1" HEIGHT="51" VALIGN="BOTTOM"><IMG SRC="Art/greybar.GIF" WIDTH="1" HEIGHT="14" BORD

        <!--GREEN LINE-->
        <TD HEIGHT="51" VALIGN="TOP"><A HREF="about_us_intro.htm"><IMG SRC="Art/linea.GIF" WIDTH="131"

        <!--BLUE LINE-->
        <TD HEIGHT="51" VALIGN="TOP"><A HREF="talents_intro.htm"><IMG SRC="Art/lineb.GIF" WIDTH="130" HI

        <!--PURPLE LINE-->
        <TD HEIGHT="51" VALIGN="TOP"><A HREF="clients_intro.htm"><IMG SRC="Art/linec.GIF" WIDTH="131" HI

        <!--RED LINE-->
        <TD HEIGHT="51" VALIGN="TOP"><A HREF="contact_us_intro.htm"><IMG SRC="Art/lined.GIF" WIDTH="131

        <!--GREY BAR-->
        <TD WIDTH="1" HEIGHT="51" VALIGN="BOTTOM"><IMG SRC="Art/greybar.GIF" WIDTH="1" HEIGHT="14" BORD
</TR>
</TABLE>
<!--********************************************************************-->
<!--NICHOLSON NY TABLE-->
<TABLE BORDER="0" CELLPADDING="0" CELLSPACING="0" WIDTH="525" HEIGHT="125">
```

▲ **Viewing the HTML code of a Web page in a browser is easy: in Internet Explorer, choose View > Source.**

"Internet" describes the actual data highway; for example, the fiber optic cables and other physical links that connect servers around the world. The Pentagon created this infrastructure more than 20 years ago with the intention of decentralizing its computer communication system and being able to operate after a first-strike scenario. To achieve this, the Internet was designed with a unique capability: rather than following a predetermined path, data is split into small packets, each of which carries information about sender and receiver that allows it to find its own way through the system. Because universities also had access to it, scientists and students were the earliest non-military users of the Internet. But in those early days, Internet operations were very complicated. Things changed when the World Wide Web was developed. In 1989, Tim Berners-Lee and Robert Cailliau created a special communications system. It allowed all the researchers and scientists at the Swiss research center CERN to access data on the CERN computer from anywhere in the world. Part of this development was HTML, Hyper-Text Markup Language. This relatively simple language makes it possible to place structural "tags" in the text, which, for example, tell the browser to display text as a header or a listing. The boom of the Web went hand in hand with the success of Mosaic, a browser developed by Marc Andreessen, the founder of Netscape.

THE HTML SOURCE CODE OF A PAGE

HTML documents are ASCII files; therefore, you can open and edit them in any word processor. HTML tags are identified by angled brackets. Every HTML document needs to contain at least the <HTML>, <HEAD>, and <BODY> tags. Most tags need to be paired; a tag that opens a block of text (<HEAD>, for instance) needs a companion tag to close that block of text (</HEAD>). Closing tags are identical to opening tags except for the "/" character.

<HTML>: This tag identifies the document as a Web page.

<TITLE>: The TITLE tag identifies the text that will be seen as a headline in the browser window.

<BODY BGCOLOR="#ffffff">: The BODY container holds all the text and graphics of the Web page between the start tag and the end tag. A tag often has several attributes. In this example, BGCOLOR defines the background color of the browser window.

<P><CENTER>: This is a paragraph tag. The embedded CENTER tag means that the paragraph is centered.

<MAP NAME="maintop">: MAPs are picture files, parts of which are defined as hot links. You can click a hot link to connect to another Web page.

<IMG SRC="images/maintop.gif" WIDTH="301" HEIGHT="27">: The IMG tag places a picture on the Web page. The attributes WIDTH and HEIGHT tell the browser the size of the picture. This way, text and layout can be displayed properly before the image elements finish downloading.

```
<HTML>
    <HEAD>
        <META NAME="GENERATOR" CONTENT="Adobe PageMill ">
        <TITLE>Eye2Eye Mainpage</TITLE>
    </HEAD>
<BODY BGCOLOR="#ffffff" LINK="#ff0000" ALINK="#0017ff">
<P><CENTER>
    <MAP NAME="maintop">
        <AREA SHAPE="rect" COORDS="211,2,300,26"
          HREF="press/indpress.html">
        <AREA SHAPE="rect" COORDS="148,0,205,25"
          HREF="bio/bioindex.html">
        <AREA SHAPE="rect" COORDS="69,1,144,25"
          HREF="tour/tourindx.html">
        <AREA SHAPE="rect" COORDS="2,1,61,27" HREF="cd/cds.html">
    </MAP>
    <IMG SRC="images/maintop.gif" WIDTH="301" HEIGHT="27"
    ALIGN="BOTTOM"
    NATURALSIZEFLAG="3" USEMAP="#maintop" ISMAP BORDER="0">
</CENTER></P>


<P><CENTER>
    <IMG SRC="images/e2e_main.gif" WIDTH="301" HEIGHT="211"
    ALIGN=„BOTTOM" NATURALSIZEFLAG="3">
</CENTER></P>

<P><CENTER>
    <MAP NAME="mainbttm">
    <AREA SHAPE="rect" COORDS="94,3,167,26" HREF="exit.html">
    <AREA SHAPE="rect" COORDS="12,2,68,26" HREF="map.html">
    </MAP>
    <IMG SRC="images/mainbttm.gif" WIDTH="176" HEIGHT="27"
```

```
    ALIGN="BOTTOM" NATURALSIZEFLAG="3" USEMAP="#mainbttm"
    ISMAP BORDER="0">
</CENTER></P>

<PRE><CENTER>Click on CDs to listen to check out Eye2Eyes two
available records or ... To get on our mailing list, please send your address
and telephone number to
<A HREF="mailto:email@erols.com">email@erols.com</A>
</PRE>

<H6><CENTER>
    <A HREF="cd/cds.html">CDs</A> | <A
    HREF="tour/tourindx.html">TOUR</A> | <A
    HREF="bio/bioindex.html">BIO</A> | <A
    HREF="press/indpress.html">PRESS</A><BR>
    <A HREF="map.html" TARGET="_top">MAP</A> | <A
    HREF="exit.html">EXIT</A>
</CENTER></H6>

</BODY>
</HTML>
```

<A HREF="mailto: email@erols.com">: **A link is a connection to another Web page. It is identified by an "A."** Links are not restricted to the addresses of other pages or files; in this example, the link tells your e-mail program to create a message and sends it to the specified address.

<H6>: **There are six different headline sizes and categories, numbered H1 through H6. H6 is the smallest headline size, and is often smaller than body text. The most common use of H6 headlines is for text links at the bottom of the page.**

◀ This is the page generated by this particular HTML code.

There are several reasons that a book concerning Web graphics and im-ages needs to discuss HTML. On the one hand, it is important to know the limitations and possibilities of HTML when designing a Web page. On the other hand, many design solutions are based on special HTML features. So there is (almost) no way around having some basic knowledge of HTML. Let me now address some of the design issues that are inherent to HTML.

THE DESIGN LIMITATIONS OF STRUCTURAL CODING

HTML is primarily a structural code. While there are some formatting tags, the main idea of HTML involves defining structures. Let's take a header, for ex-ample: in HTML it is embedded between two "H" tags. Accordingly, the brows-er is told only that the text is a header, but not which font to use or how large the characters should be. Each browser sets those parameters independent-ly, based on user preferences. Therefore, the same header may be displayed in 16-point Arial in one browser and 14-point Times in another. Obviously, this is a nightmare for designers, and many designers sidestep it altogether by avoiding the use of structural tags (like "H") in favor of the FONT tag with the FACE and SIZE format attributes:

<font size="2" face="Arial,Helvetica">This is text in size 2</font>

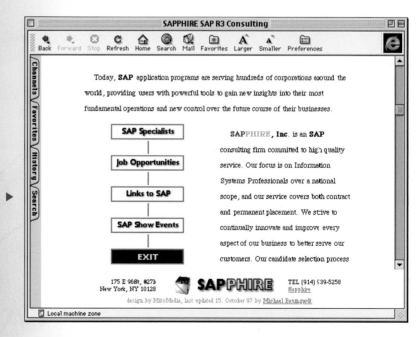

A Web site can look good in one browser but be your worst nightmare in another. This could be due to incompatibilities of the HTML implementation in the browser or to the fact that the visitor's preferences override the settings of the Web site. In that case, the color and size of links or text is beyond your control.

◄ This is the same page in Navigator; if the user has changed the browser preferences to override, all the formatting of your fonts might be lost and the design can look very different than what you intended.

You should not, however, avoid structural tags altogether, because if you do so you sacrifice one of the main advantages of HTML—its ability to mark content. Fortunately, there are other ways to deal with the font issue. HTML has been steadily improved, and it currently allows you to set the definition for structural tags via cascading style sheets. You can even transmit a chosen font to the browser using dynamic fonts. This technology was created to solve a basic problem: every font you want to display in your Web site must be installed on your viewers' computers. Since there's no guarantee of this except for basic faces like Helvetica, Times, and Arial, dynamic fonts send the fonts along with the HTML file. For licensing and legal reasons, fonts can't be transferred in their entirety (and they are converted into a special format). Therefore, dynamic fonts embeds only the characters that are actually used in your design—which makes it less likely that someone can capture and convert them back to a PostScript or TrueType font. But dynamic fonts have their own set of problems. For one thing, it's not easy to get them to work properly. For another, older browsers can't handle dynamic fonts at all, and will display text in the standard font.

If you want to experiment with dynamic fonts, check out WebFont Wizard from Bitstream. A demo version for Windows and Macs is available at Bitstream's Web site (www.bitstream.com). That demo even allows you to create a limited number of PFRs (portable font resources) for free.

THE DESIGN LIMITATIONS OF EARLIER BROWSERS				
	Background	**Foreground**	**Tables**	**Frames**
Navigator 2	Color + Image	Image	no Color	no Frames
Navigator 3	Color + Image	Image	Color	(only visible Borders)
Explorer 3	Color + Image	Image	Color + Background Img	invisible + Color
Navigator 4	Color + Image	Layers	Color + Background Img	invisible
Explorer 4	Color + Image	Layers	Color + Background Img	invisible + Color

▲ This Web site is based on a table in which a background image is loaded, which makes it incompatible with Navigator 3.0.

▲ While Internet Explorer and Netscape Navigator 4.x offer relatively similar features, the 3.x versions were quite different from one another. For example, Explorer could set a background color and image for a table or even make a frame invisible. If you want to design for backward compatibility, stay away from tables with colors and background images and avoid frames, since these will not appear in Navigator 3.0. But then again, not many people are still using those old browsers.

HTML DESIGN LIMITATION: ABSOLUTE POSITIONING

The font problem is not HTML's only design obstacle. HTML offers virtually no way of specifying absolute positioning. When HTML was created, the idea was to display information regardless of what platform and what size monitor viewers were using. In that context it makes sense that text should flow differently on a 14-inch monitor than on a 21-inch unit. Moreover, if the site visitor changes the window size of the browser, the entire page will be re-arranged. Because images are embedded in the text (as inline images), every time the Web page is reformatted, the position of images also changes in the browser. Especially given the fact that HTML did not originally support layers, you can imagine how limited design possibilities were in the beginning. When HTML introduced tables, however, many Web designers worked around the limitations by placing text and images in table cells; this proved particularly helpful for positioning images.

While graphics applications allow you to arrange objects, graphics, and text as needed, HTML originally provided only two layers—a foreground layer for text and images, and a background layer that could load an image or a color. When Internet Explorer introduced backgrounds for tables, the creative potential expanded tremendously. Newer browsers offer cascading style sheets, an extension to the HTML standard that finally offers designers all the features they could desire, including layers that can be positioned with absolute precision. This is even true for positioning on the z-axis, allowing images to partially overlap, an effect that wasn't possible before.

WYSIWYG AUTHORING APPLICATIONS

Write HTML by hand? Only hard-core HTML programmers find this appealing. But there are now numerous HTML-authoring applications that work much like a layout program, where all you need to do is place your elements on a page. It is safe to say that Cyberstudio, which was the predecessor of GoLive, had a big impact on the way today's HTML authoring tools look, feel, and work. And for a long time, that software produced the best HTML code. A statement like this might sound odd because HTML is a standard. How can there be good and bad code? But you'd be surprised if you had some experience with other HTML-authoring tools. I won't name names, but a certain major software company published an HTML-authoring tool that only worked well with that company's browser. To be fair, publishers of HTML authoring tools have their work cut out for them in keeping up with the continuously evolving HTML standard, and browser support for various HTML features. Indeed, browsers often support more features than authoring applications can provide. Adobe GoLive addresses this problem by storing the HTML implementation in a database known as the Web Database. This allows programmers and designers to incorporate new tags even before a new version of GoLive is available. No wonder GoLive has become the tool of choice

GoLive, back then called Cyberstudio, was originally developed and marketed by a German software company. Adobe bought the company and its product and renamed it.

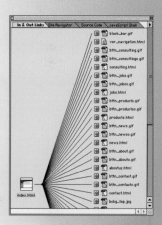

▲ In Adobe GoLive's Link Inspector, you can see all the items on your page. You can fix broken links easily here.

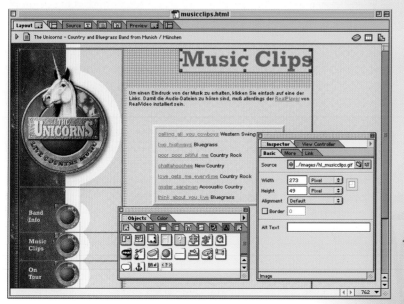

◄ GoLive supports the positioning of objects using a layout grid. All HTML elements can be placed in this grid, which is essentially just an invisible table.

▲ GoLive offers a Preview mode for checking your work. This preview is pretty close to what the page will look like in the browser, but you will still need to double check it.

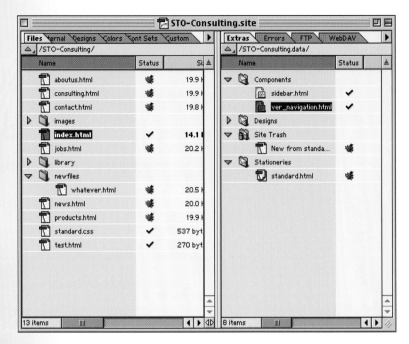

▲ GoLive has a single window for managing the whole site. From files to page hierarchy to colors, everything can be managed in one place.

for many Web designers. Even hard-core HTML programmers like to work with it since it has one of the best (if not *the* best) HTML code editors. Adobe even completely rewrote the HTML parser for GoLive 5.0 to ensure that the code that you enter will not be changed. This seems like a minor thing, but anyone who has done HTML authoring for some time knows that early generations of authoring tools would radically change any foreign code.

Along with the rewrite of the parser comes a feature that will be increasingly important for Web designers in the future: the ability to insert database access routines and application server scripts in the page. GoLive only supports Active Server Pages thus far, but considering that this comes free as part of a regular update while you have to pay for this functionality in other HTML authoring tools, this is a good deal.

There are many more reasons to work with GoLive: dynamic HTML, cascading style sheets, and support for ActiveX and WebObjects, to name a few. GoLive even offers many JavaScript functions as modules that can be inserted just by dragging them onto the page. All these features are also offered by other HTML authoring tools, but not always to the same extent. And Adobe

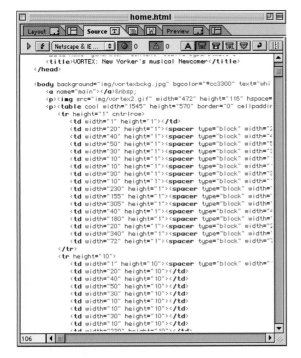

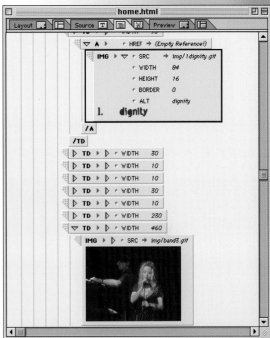

has done a marvelous job of having GoLive and Photoshop work together. Smart Objects, which let you place Photoshop, Illustrator, and LiveMotion files on a GoLive HTML page, is just one of the innovative ideas that Adobe has added to GoLive 5.0. Tracing Images is another feature that can help you achieve a smooth workflow (read more about these features in the "GoLive Basics" chapter).

▲ GoLive offers two excellent HTML code editors, which is one of the reasons why it's so popular with professional Web designers.

Photos and Graphics on the Web

If you're making the leap from desktop publishing, you're probably accustomed to using image and graphic formats like TIFF or EPS. On the Web, these formats are largely irrelevant. JPEG, GIF, and PNG prevail here. As you probably know, bandwidth is a big issue with the Web. Even at 6.7KB/sec (which is what you get with a 56k modem), large data transmissions are out of the question. And images make up usually 60 percent to 80 percent of the data on a page, which makes file compression a significant issue. JPEG and GIF are popular on the Web because they employ effective compression algorithms that can compress graphics into relatively small files and—in case of GIF—allow for things like animation.

For designers, the bandwidth problem means that you should avoid painfully slow downloads for visitors to your Web site, so 40KB to 60KB should be the maximum amount of new transferred data per page. "New transferred data" refers to the fact that browsers store downloaded text and images in a local cache on the user's hard drive; stored data can be recalled from the cache much faster than content that has to be downloaded fresh from the Web.

So when you develop the design concept for your Web site, it's a good idea to use the same image elements as often as possible across your pages. For example, a company logo placed on multiple pages will be downloaded

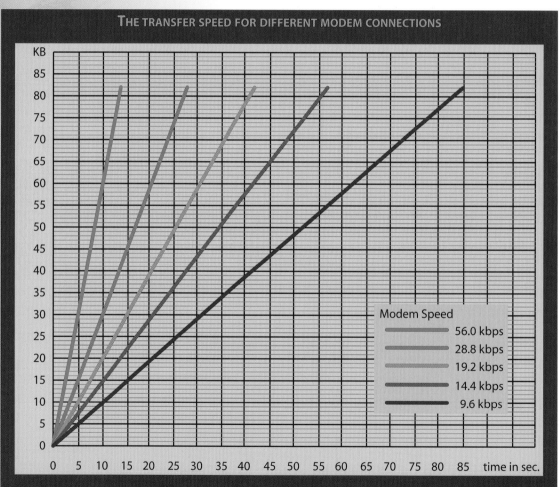

THE TRANSFER SPEED FOR DIFFERENT MODEM CONNECTIONS

Modem Speed
56.0 kbps
28.8 kbps
19.2 kbps
14.4 kbps
9.6 kbps

▲ The transmission speed is never linear, as it is presented here. When designing your page, don't use the best-case scenario; even if the visitor has a 56k modem, it is more likely that he will end up with a slower transfer rate.

and stored in a visitor's cache after they've visited the first page, speeding browsing on other pages. This way, you can add new graphics to other pages on the site while minimizing download time. For instance, you can use an introduction page and load pictures for the next page in the background. You can do this with JavaScript, which is the more advanced method, or simply by placing the image on the text page and scaling it down to 1 pixel so that it becomes virtually invisible (an old HTML trick).

But let's go back to the different image formats. JPEG, GIF, and PNG all have their advantages and drawbacks, which pertain mainly to their different compression algorithms. Generally, JPEG is used for photographs; GIF is used for graphics with solid-colored areas; PNG straddles both worlds. The image formats are explained in detail in their own chapters, but to help you get started designing right away, here's a brief explanation of each:

➤ JPEG—Joint Photographic Experts Group

JPEG can store up to 16 million colors but is not well-suited for text or graphics since its block-by-block compression algorithm introduces a blurring effect. Within each block, differences in brightness are retained, but subtle color changes are lost. Despite the loss of color information, it is amazing how good the image quality is even at maximum compression. Compression factors range from 10:1 to 100:1, meaning that at the highest compression rate, a 1MB image can be compressed into a 10KB JPEG file. That is ideal for the Web, but because JPEG compression is not lossless, always keep a copy of the original file. Also, JPEG lacks transparency, a feature offered by both GIF and PNG.

➤ GIF—Graphical Interchange Format

GIF uses a compression algorithm based on pattern recognition: if several adjacent pixels have the same color, GIF can compress them. Here's a comparative example: if a block of text contained the word "Yellow" 20 times, it could be shortened significantly by writing "20xYellow." Obviously this approach can be used with repetitive color combinations too; each kind of pattern makes it easier to compress the image. While JPEG compresses block by block, GIF compresses line by line.

GIF is not as successful as JPEG at compressing photographs, but it compresses large areas of flat color extremely well. GIF's compression factor with photographs is only around 4:1, but it has the advantage of lossless compression —aside from reducing color information to 256 colors through indexing.

In this case, lossless means that after decompression the picture looks exactly the same as it did before, and that repeated saves don't degrade the image like a JPEG does. GIF has two more handy features: it supports transparency and animations.

In order to produce transparency, one color is defined as "chroma key color" during storage. The browser then disables this color and replaces it with the background—the clipping paths of the Web, so to speak. This feature, along with GIF's capability for animation, is one reason for the format's popularity. With animation, foreground images are layered over background images, and switching them creates the impression of movement. You can even set the duration of each image and define whether the animation should run once or in a continuous loop (learn more about this technique in the "GIF Animation" chapter).

➤ PNG—Portable Network Graphic Format

PNG, a response to the restrictions of JPEG and GIF, was supposed to be the next step in image formats for the Web. PNG combines the best of both worlds: lossless compression with up to 16 million colors, and 256 levels of transparency, which make semi-transparent color areas possible. This is particularly important if you want to let the edges blend smoothly with the browser background.

But PNG is not well supported by browsers; some browsers still require a plug-in to view it. So the upshot is that you probably won't be working with PNG for quite some time. This is unfortunate, since PNG also sports a great Gamma correction function that guarantees images will be equally bright on all platforms. (Since Windows monitors are inherently darker than Macintosh monitors, Web sites created on a Mac look too dark when viewed on a Windows browser; and pages designed on a PC look pale on a Mac. PNG's Gamma correction feature solves the problem, so images display with the correct brightness on both platforms.)

PNG has one other major drawback: the files can be much larger than comparable GIFs or JPEGs, plus PNG does not support animation. As transmission speeds rise, PNG may well become interesting for Web designers.

➤ Vector Graphics

There's one image format I haven't mentioned yet: vector graphics. What worked so well in desktop publishing should also make sense online, right?

How do Browsers Compensate for Missing Colors?

Dithering describes a technique that mingles two main colors together to create the optical illusion of an intermediate color. This is basically the same procedure as printing with process colors; all the colors of the spectrum can be created by mixing different amounts (or dot sizes) of the four basic colors (cyan, magenta, yellow, black,-or CMYK). The dots are printed at different angles to one another, and are so small they can hardly be discerned with the naked eye.

Browsers use a similar process—if a desired color is outside the range of the available color depth, the browser tries to create that color by mixing colors that

are available. Two techniques are used—pattern or diffusion dithering. With pattern dithering, the intermediate color is created by using a regular pattern of pixels, which can produce unpleasing, unaesthetic effects. The second technique, diffusion dithering, simulates the intermediate color by placing pixels in a random pattern. Of course this only appears to be random; it is actually based on a mathematical model that can differ from one application to another.

If an application doesn't simulate a color by dithering, it only quantizes the color, which means it is rounded to the next available color and the color shifts become even more apparent. So 99 percent red, for instance, becomes 100 percent, while 84 percent red becomes 80 percent.

The original image was saved as a 256-color GIF with an adaptive palette and also as a JPEG. Both images were then viewed in the browser with the monitor set to 256 colors. You can see the results in the following images.

Explorer (top) dithers the GIF using diffusion dither, Navigator only quantizes the color value (bottom image). *Pictures are scaled to 120 percent.*

The same image saved as a JPEG (best quality) is displayed in both browsers with diffusion dithering. Explorer (top), in my opinion, yields the better result.

▲With PNG it is no problem to create objects with a drop shadow and have it integrate seamlessly with the design. As you can see in these images, the drop shadow blends with any background loaded into the browser.

That is exactly what Macromedia's Flash and Adobe's LiveMotion do. Flash and LiveMotion are vector-based illustration and animation programs that produce sensational results; you can create animations with text and geometrical shapes with color gradients in files as small as 20KB and of excellent visual quality. Since each item is rendered with optimum resolution, text can fly towards the viewer without appearing jagged.

Another format that supports vector illustrations for the Web is Portable Document Format, or PDF. Developed by Adobe before the Web became popular, it was primarily intended for distributing documents in a cross-platform environment. Inspired by the success of the Web, Adobe developed a plug-in that allows browsers to display PDF files. This has enormous advantages, because once you have created a brochure or flyer, you can export it to the Web without much additional hassle. To create PDF files, you need Adobe Acrobat. Anyone can view PDFs, however, with the free Acrobat Reader, which you can download for Mac or Windows from www.adobe.com.

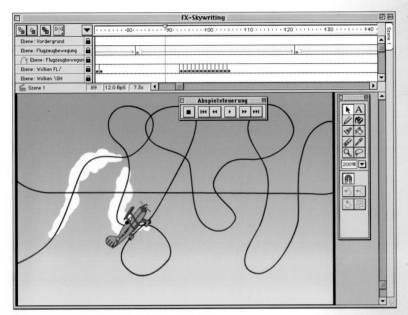

◀ The Flash interface resembles the Director interface—not surprising, since both programs are made by Macromedia. This is where the similarities end; if you are an experienced Director user, don't expect an easy transition—the learning curve is pretty steep.

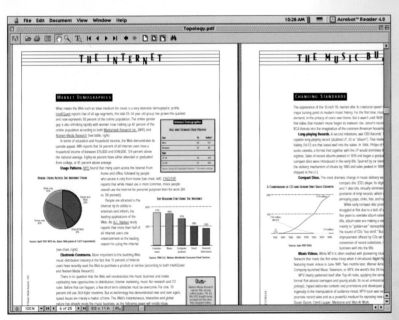

▲ Adobe Acrobat allows you to store layouts with text and graphics in a platform-independent file format (PDF) that can be opened with the free Acrobat Reader. You can even embed those files in a Web page since Adobe offers a PDF plug-in for all the browsers.

Adobe LiveMotion

Flash technology has become quite popular in the Web design community and made the Web—for better or worse—a much more animated place. Until recently, Macromedia's Flash software was the only authoring tool available for creating Flash-based animations or interfaces. That has changed with the release of Adobe's LiveMotion.

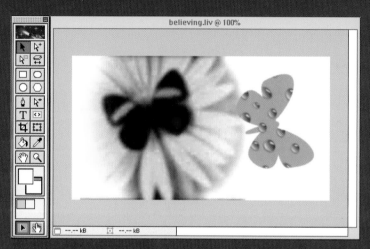

The main difference between the programs is that LiveMotion lacks the Macromedia Flash's programming language and that application's vast constellation of third-party developer resources. LiveMotion does provide behaviors like stopping or starting Flash movie playback (behaviors are similar to actions in Flash), but it's not comparable to Flash, which makes it—at least for now—less suitable for creating advanced Flash projects. But LiveMotion makes up for that short-coming with versatility and ease of use: creating simple rollovers, GIF animations, and interactive Flash projects is much easier in LiveMotion than in Flash. And where Flash is frame-based, LiveMotion is time-based: any object or element can be placed in a timeline, which makes it a snap to change the frame rate (in Flash, this process requires that you adjust the length of frames—a tedious process). Anyone who is familiar with Adobe products will soon feel comfortable with the LiveMotion interface, especially motion-graphics designers who have worked with After Effects.

LiveMotion works with shapes that can be placed either directly using the rectangle, ellipse or polygon tool, or by importing shapes from Adobe Illustrator. These shapes can be filled with images or patterns and can even have effects like emboss or drop shadows assigned to them. When you're done, LiveMotion will create an HTML page along with all the images and JavaScript functionality such as rollover effects.

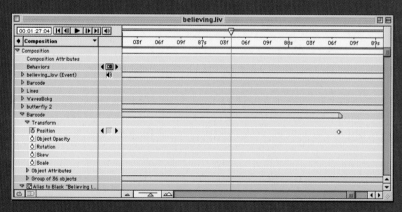

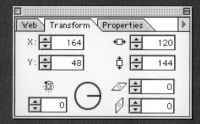

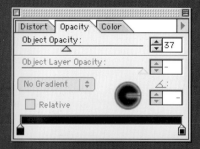

▲ You can set the Transform and Opacity attributes conveniently from a palette.

To animate an element in the timeline, click on the triangle that is displayed before every track name. The triangle rotates 45 degrees and reveals three tracks: **Transform**, **Object Attributes**, and **Layer**. The **Transform** track controls the position, opacity, rotation, and skew and scale values for the object. Changing any of these is simple: click on the stopwatch button to insert a marker (or "keyframe") in the track underneath the object's timeline. Then move the current position to the time where you want to end the animation and set another marker by clicking on the stopwatch button. In the **Transform** palette, you can modify these settings. To animate the object in relation to its anchor point, click on the **Object Attributes** timeline, or change the color and offset of an object by clicking on the **Layer** track. But LiveMotion's animation capabilities go even farther: you can nest animation loops in a timeline so that they play within one another (for example, you could loop a spinning globe and then animate it in the timeline). LiveMotion even shows the length of the loop so that while you are modifying the timeline, you can see how many loops will fit into it.

LiveMotion's strength is the ease with which it lets you create animations, but it also allows you to create some interactivity: mouse-over, mouse-down, and other rollover states can be assigned to buttons and saved as a styles. A style, plus a behavior, can then be applied to navigational elements such as buttons to control the play head. Another great feature is that LiveMotion supports Photoshop filters. These can be applied nondestructively, so if you change your mind, just disable the effect in the Photoshop Filters palette.

Exporting and embedding a LiveMotion project in an HTML page as a SWF file is done automatically. LiveMotion even has a batch-replace feature that makes it easy to add LiveMotion-generated elements to existing HTML pages: the **Batch Replace HTML** command searches for HTML elements and then replaces them with LiveMotion-generated elements.

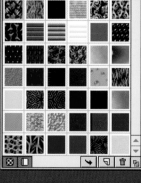

▲ Applying textures is a great way to enrich an object while keeping the data demand low.

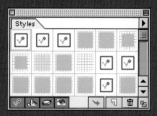

▲ Creating rollover buttons is simple and convenient because the Styles palette can save rollover states.

▲ Aristotle's promotional Fourth of July Web site shows off Flash's capabilities (www.aristotle.net/july4th/). Visitors can choose background music (a MIDI file), the location of the fireworks, and finally, they can launch multicolored fireworks using the Launch buttons.

▲ Visit www.aristotle.net/july4th/ to see a well-designed Flash demonstration.

Click on one of the Launch buttons to trigger a rocket that explodes in one of four colors. ▶

COLOR PROBLEMS WITH IMAGES

Using color in desktop publishing is a snap compared to the challenge it represents in Web design. The 5 percent dot gain that DTP designers have to deal with seems like nothing compared to the color variables on the Web: monitors that display 256 colors to 16 million colors, varying Gammas values across platforms, and competitive browsers that display images differently. But since these factors are all out of your control, you have to learn to learn to live with them: when saving a JPEG image, adjusting the brightness to compensate for the Gamma differences is about all that you can do. GIF images behave a little more predictably, especially when the colors are limited to the Web-safe palette that displays consistently on all browsers and platforms. But using the Web-safe palette is settling for the lowest common denominator: visitors with high-quality color displays will see the same "low quality" picture. That's why few Web designers use the Web-safe color palette; most save GIF images with an adaptive or selective color palette and then test the results in multiple browsers, on multiple platforms, at 256 colors. If colors are acceptable, you can rest assured that the image will look even better on monitors that display thousands or millions of colors (more on this in the GIF chapter.)

▲ Optimizing an image for both computer platforms requires finding a middle ground. Otherwise, images optimized for the Macintosh will appear too dark in Windows, as you can see in this example. The top image is the Macintosh version, at the bottom, the same image as it appears in Windows. Optimizing images for both platforms is much easier when you use View > Proof Setup in Photoshop to switch between the different computers' Gammas.

OTHER IMPORTANT TECHNOLOGIES FOR WEB DESIGN

So far you have read mostly about the design limitations of HTML and the advantages and disadvantages of certain image formats. Here is some basic information about other important technologies for the Internet:

Dynamic HTML: this is not a different HTML syntax than the one you are using to create your Web sites. Dynamic HTML (or DHTML) is simply regular HTML used in conjunction with cascading style sheets and JavaScript. The goal of DHTML is to let designers create, well, more dynamic Web pages. If you would like to get your feet wet, try GoLive's animation editor by clicking on the film button in the upper right corner of the document window ("Open DHTML Timeline Editor"). The animation editor resembles those found in 3D animation packages. To create an animation, place your elements in a layer (only layers allow absolute positioning through an x and y value). If you are at all experienced with 3D applications, you should have no problem creating your own animation, because working with the Timeline Editor is very similar.

XML: this abbreviation stands for Extensible Markup Language, which has been hyped quite a lot because it is important for anyone who is working with databases. Since more and more Web sites are built on a database that displays the content dynamically, sooner or later Web designers will have to understand and learn XML. The idea behind it is simple: instead of marking the content directly with HTML markers (for example, H1 for a headline), you can create your own markers. If you had an e-commerce Web site, you could create a marker for the price of the product. In order for a browser to translate this into HTML, the formatting of this marker is stored in an external document that is linked to the HTML page. XML is not important for Web designers—at least not in the context of this book.

QUICKTIME VR

With e-commerce being so important these days, chances are that sooner or later you'll have a client who is interested in new ways of presenting his products online. Companies offering special plug-ins for the virtual presentation are numerous and some of these technologies are very promising (check out www.metastream.com). One of the best technologies however has been around for some time and is available on over 50 million browsers: Apple's QuickTime. This means that there is a large audience already equipped to see a QuickTime VR movie, which stands for virtual reality. These movies allow a 360° panoramic view of a location or the presentation of an object: dragging the mouse while clicking on the movie is enough to change the angle of view or zoom in/out and, if available, even link to different VR-Movies if the mouse is over a hot spot.

You can use the free QTVR Make Panorama 2 program of apple, that can be downloaded from www.apple.com/quicktime/developers/tools.html (only for Macs), to create QuickTime VR movies. This free tool has its limitations however: it is not able to stitch several images together with this program. That means that you either have to already have a panorama shot (which can be done with some special cameras) or you have to stitch several photos together in Photoshop—a tedious process, because you have to adjust the transparency in the Layers palette to align the overlapping parts. The more professional solution is Apple's QuickTime VR Authoring Studio. Creating QuickTime VR movies is a snap with this program and if you need to do more then two QTVR movies, this software is worth buying (creating a QTVR panorama movie with Photoshop and QTVR Make Panorama 2 can take between 2 to 4 hours; with QTVR Authoring Studio it can be done in less than 20 minutes).

▲ The most important step in creating a QuickTime panorama in QTVR Studio is telling the program what lens was used and the angles between every shot. QTVR Studio then aligns the images automatically.

To create a QuickTime VR panorama movie, all you need is a digital camera and a tripod. When mounting the camera in an upright position on the tripod, make sure that the tripod is level with the horizon and that the nodal point of your camera is directly over the rotation point of the tripod. A common misunderstanding is that the nodal point is the same as the film plane, which is often marked underneath 35mm cameras, but the nodal point is the point inside your camera where the light rays converge and flip over.

For most 35mm cameras and lenses, the nodal point is located somewhere near the center of the lens barrel. When shooting a QuickTime VR panorama, you must rotate around this point to eliminate the image mismatch caused by parallax error. You'll understand parallax error if you do a simple experiment. Close one eye and hold your index finger about six inches away from your open eye. Turn your head side to side and you will notice that your finger moves with respect to the background. This relative movement is due to the fact that you are not rotating your head around your eye's nodal point, which is somewhere in the center of your eyeball. Instead, you're rotating your spine, which is several inches farther back and to one side. It is this relative side-to-side motion that you'll want to eliminate when setting up a camera for VR panoramas.

▲ The KiWi+ from Kaidan is a great utility for shooting panoramic movies. It allows you to adjust the camera to the nodal point of the lens and it comes with detent (indexed) discs to rotate the unit in set degrees. For more information, check out www.kaidan.com.

Finding and adjusting to the nodal point of a camera is tricky, because each camera and lens combination has its own nodal point. With a standard tripod this is virtually impossible, because there is no way to adjust the camera correctly. For less then the price of Apple's QuickTime VR Studio, you can buy Kaidan's KiWi+, a tripod head that lets you mount the camera in an upright position and adjust the nodal point. It also has a twin axis bubble level for adjusting the tripod's horizontal position. The KiWi+ also ships with four detent (indexed) discs that provide click-stops for a variety of lens combinations. Check out www.kaidan.com to find the right product or even see some great examples of what you can do with QuickTime VR.

▲ If pictures are not taken in regular increments, the images have to be aligned manually in the Pair Alignment window. Even though this process goes quickly, it will take 10 minutes longer per panorama than if you use Kaidan's KiWi+.

After shooting a series of pictures, you need to combine them into one large panoramic image. If you are using Apple's free QTVR Make Panorama 2 software, you have to use Photoshop to make your panorama from individual shots. With QuickTime VR Authoring Studio, you can do everything within the program: the Authoring Studio even has an auto-modus that adjusts the images automatically. All you need to do is to enter the angle and the lens, and the Authoring Studio will stitch the individual pictures into one

▲ You can set the display settings for the final VR movie before it is saved.

panorama in a matter of seconds. It does an amazingly good job, but you can also adjust images manually. All you have to do is export this image as a QTVR movie and Apple's QTVR Studio will automatically crop the panorama, sharpen it, and adjust the brightness. This software even blends the individual images at the edges to ensure a smooth panorama. If you set everything up correctly, the whole process will take only a few mouse clicks and the software will do the work for you while you have a cup of coffee.

OBJECT MOVIES

QuickTime VR also allows you to create object movies, which are great for showing an object from every angle, even with some animation. Creating an object movie is as straightforward as creating a panorama movie: after shooting several pictures, just import the images into the QTVR Authoring Studio's Object Maker. To enhance the experience, you can even allow a vertical rotation so that the object can be moved in all directions.

1. Planning the movie: we are so accustomed to movies as a linear sequence of frames that understanding how an object movie works can be a little challenging in the beginning. Think of a QTVR object movie as a grid: the pictures are arranged in sequence but instead of just being able to move forward and backward on the horizontal axis, you can also move an object movie vertically. Since this is a bit complex, it is a good idea to sketch it out so that you can visualize how to organize the project and shoot the frames (the sketch doesn't have to show all the frames, a 3x3 grid will suffice).

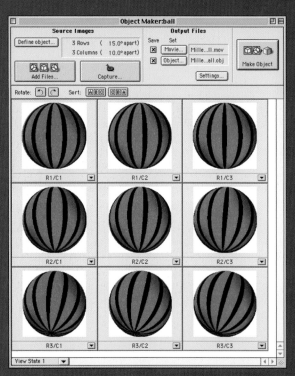

▲ This object movie was created with a 3D animation program: you can clearly see how every picture shows the object at a slightly different angle.

2. Choosing a capture device: the best way to capture images for an object movie is with a digital camera. Not only does this produce digital pictures, but it also makes it easier to align the images when they're stitched together. (Have you ever been able to mount a photo or film on a scanner without a slight angle?) In addition, digital camcorders and cameras let you preview results so that you can check the lighting, alignment, and positioning of the object. This is more important than you might realize: imagine that one picture in a series of 27 is not perfect. It is almost impossible to redo this single shot. Digital cameras are getting cheaper every day. For my shoots, I use a Sony PC-100 camcorder that can also take still images and save them on a memory stick. You can insert this memory stick with an adapter in the PC slot and mount it like a hard disk on the desktop. Transferring images could hardly be easier. Camcorders like the Sony PC-100 come with a remote control, which ensures that you never risk shifting the alignment between the camera and the object platform.

3. Setting up the scene: the most difficult part of shooting an object movie is

rotating the object around one axis. Doing this by hand is almost impossible. For budget-minded hobbyists, a lazy Susan spray-painted black should be enough. If you want a more professional device, I recommend the PiXi from Kaidan. This high-end object rig is specially designed for QuickTime VR shoots and can rotate even heavy objects in increments of 15 degrees.

▲ The Kaidan PiXi is a professional object rig that is specially designed for QTVR object movies.

▲ To create a VR object movie that can be moved along the vertical and horizontal axis, you have to create several rows and columns.

4. Shooting the frames: decide how many shots you want to take per row and

column in your grid. Don't use too many grids, otherwise the movie will become huge. For example: rotating an object 360 degrees with 15-degree increments requires 24 pictures per row. If you plan on rotating the object along the vertical axis 90 degrees with 15-degree increments, you will end up with 144 pictures (6 rows with 24 pictures each). Since you are planning to use the object movie on a Web page, use 30-degree increments for the rows for a total of 12 pictures for the row. When using only three rows, the total number of pictures is 36, which will still be quite big for low bandwidth connections, but is still acceptable.

▲ The final result in QTVR Studio: while holding the mouse button down, the user can spin the ball in any direction. Using a 3D program is a nice way to experiment with object videos. Most animation programs can export an animation as an image sequence.

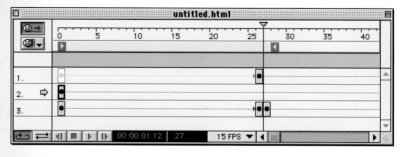

▲ Since the advent of 4.x Browsers it has been possible to place text and images in layers and even animate those layers. This can be easily done in GoLive's Animation window.

▲ GoLive features a couple of ready-made modules that can be implemented via drag-and-drop. For example, the very popular rollover feature is as simple as importing the three images. The required JavaScript is handled by GoLive.

JavaScript: JavaScript is a scripting language that can be inserted into HTML code and interpreted directly by the browser. Many interactive elements (such as rollover buttons) are created using JavaScript, and Web designers should have some JavaScript knowledge. As in many other areas, Microsoft has managed to make the world more complicated by introducing its own version of JavaScript called JScript. And yes, you guessed it: JScript is not totally compatible with JavaScript! But if you just work with the ready-made JavaScripts that come as modules in GoLive, you don't need to worry; they all work across platforms. Since JavaScript is really easy to learn, it is something you should get into at some point.

Java: despite their similar names, Java has little to do with JavaScript. Java is a high-class (and relatively advanced) programming language, similar to C++, which allows you to create platform-independent applications—at least theoretically. Sun Microsystems, which developed Java, has been in the crossfire because Java hasn't truly delivered on its promise of cross-platform compatibility. This is partly Microsoft's fault since it extended Java's functionality and made the two products incompatible again. Nevertheless, Java can open many new worlds because Web site developers aren't limited by the functionality of Shockwave, Flash or any other specific technology. Java is powerful enough to create complex solutions, but it is certainly not something a Web designer has to learn. Leave it to the programmers, but inform yourself about how Java can be used for a Web site.

PERL: sooner or later you will encounter PERL and CGI. Though both terms are used frequently in one breath, they are two different things. PERL is a programming language; CGI is a protocol that handles the data transfer between a browser and a server. The reason they are frequently mentioned together is that PERL is free and works on every server, so many people use it to work with the data that a user has sent. If you sign up for an e-mail newsletter and press the Submit button, the information will be sent to the server. Chances are that a PERL script is triggered to save the data that was just submitted— that is, to store it in a database or text file. PERL, which stands for Practical Extraction and Report Language, is relatively easy to learn. The biggest challenge you'll encounter when learning it is the process of debugging and installing a script; this can be tricky because it depends on the server and how it is set up. But aside from that, it is worth learning the basics of PERL so that you can modify and adapt one of the many PERL scripts that are available for free on the Internet.

CGI: the Common Gateway Interface was created to handle the interaction between a browser and a server. If, for example, you click on a link, a page request is sent from the browser to the server, and the server then transmits the HTML page. But CGI is also used when data is submitted from the browser to the server. Information that a user enters on a form is sent either via POST or GET. These two methods tell CGI how the information was submitted and where to look for it (GET will append the data to the URL, while POST sends one text file).

ASP: Active Server Pages is Microsoft's application server technology. Application servers were developed to make it easier to display content dynamically. For example, if you want to display the day of the week, you could embed an ASP script in the page. When a user requests the page, the application server recognizes the document as an ASP by the extension ".asp" and processes it first before displaying it. This means that the application server will execute the ASP script and insert the day of the week into the HTML code. This is a simple example that could be accomplished with JavaScript too, but application server provides much more. If you are interested in creating database-driven Web sites, you should look into application server technologies like ASP, ColdFusion or PHP.

ColdFusion: Allaire (www.allaire.com) created ColdFusion, another popular application server technology. It works like ASP, but has different commands.

WebObjects: the idea behind WebObjects is to be able to put the functionality of a Web site into one program that resides on the server. Instead of having many little CGI scripts, everything is in one large program, which makes development and support much easier. The interaction with this software is then handled by WebObjects. These are special tags that are placed in the HTML code. If you have toyed around with GoLive's Preferences, you might have tripped over the Modules folder and maybe even activated the WebObjects module. The GoLive palette then displays an additional tab with

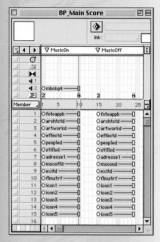

▲ Macromedia Director is a standard program for multimedia designers. It started out as a pure animation program and only later was extended with a language called Lingo, which lets you program complex tasks. Even now, Director's interface reveals its roots—the cast members of a movie (above) are placed in a timeline, or "score," as Director calls it (top).

many new objects that look very similar to regular HTML objects. While creating the GUI with WebObjects is simple, programming the application itself requires knowledge of C++ or Java.

Flash and Shockwave: I've already mentioned Flash in connection with vector graphics (illustrations), but since there is a lot of confusion about Flash and Shockwave, let me make the differences clear. Flash is a technology as well as the name of software designed by Macromedia to create Flash applications. While Flash can also display images and other media like QuickTime videos, its specialty is animating vector graphics. Shockwave, by contrast, is the name of the technology that allows you to embed applications that were created with Macromedia's Director. Director has been around for many years and was popular for creating CD-ROM applications. It works mostly with bitmap images, which result in large files. While the Flash plug-in cannot play Shockwave applications, the Shockwave plug-in can display Flash content. But the difference between Flash and Shockwave lies also in the complexity and ability of the programming languages that both offer. Director's programming language is called Lingo, and it offers you many more commands than the Flash programming language. Learning how to create animations with Adobe's LiveMotion (which can export files in the Flash format) is something you should look into.

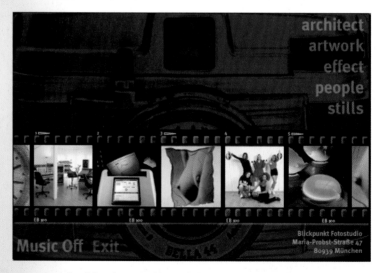

▲The portfolio of the photographer Paul Ehrenreich (this book features a lot of his work) was done in Macromedia Director.

SOME USEFUL SITES FOR WEB DESIGNERS

Do you want to know what's happening in Silicon Alley, the heart of the New York Internet scene, or do you just want to find out more about HTML or JavaScript? You may find the following online sources helpful:

www.wwwac.org
The site of World Wide Web Artists' Consortium (WWWAC) is the best way to locate Web designers, programmers, and Internet fans in New York. The WWWAC holds monthly meetings, and offers special interest groups that focus on a variety of topics, such as interface design and database integration.

www.nynma.org
The New York New Media Association, which also hosts regular meetings and special interest groups, provides job postings on its Web site. If you are looking for a Web design job in New York City, this is a great place to find one.

www.siliconalleyreporter.com
If you want to stay on top of the latest trends in the New York City Internet scene, and you happen to be in the city, you can pick up a copy of the Silicon Alley Reporter on the newsstand; out-of-towners can get a subscription.

www.searchenginewatch.com
This site provides excellent information that will help you to optimize your site to get good results in a search engine.

www.webposition.com
WebPositionGold can optimize your site for better ratings. It generates HTML pages designed to rank your page near the top of search results, and it submits your pages to the major search engines automatically.

www.virtual-stampede.com
One of the first programs available to do batch registrations for Web sites, Spider Software has now been rewritten and released as NetSubmitter Professional. A great (and affordable) tool to register your site with the search engines. I highly recommend it.

ftp://ftp.cdrom.com/pub/perl/_ CPAN/CPAN.html
This is an excellent archive of PERL scripts. It has no fancy interface, but it is very comprehensive.

www.w3.org
The World Wide Web Consortium is the organization that develops and approves new versions of HTML. Check it out whenever there is an abbreviation that you don't know; most likely it is something the W3C is currently working on.

http://developer.netscape.com
Not quite sure which HTML tag was supported in which Netscape browser? This site will tell you. If you want to learn more about HTML, this is a particularly great source.

http://msdn.microsoft.com/ workshop/default.asp
The Microsoft Developer Network is an online source you can use to find out about the HTML implementation in Explorer. It also has a very good introduction to HTML.

www.coolhomepages.com
This site lists some of the best-designed Web sites on the Internet. All sites are listed in categories, which makes this a great source for inspiration or a great way to promote your own Web site.

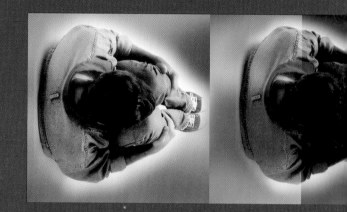

Illustration: Michael Baumgardt

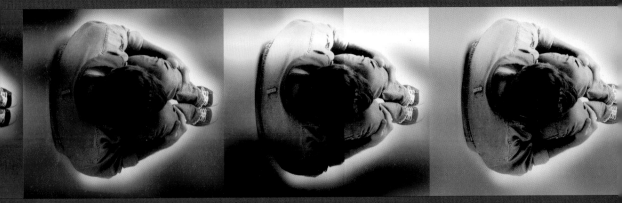

DESIGN CONCEPTS

Developing a Design Concept for a Web Site

Even if you are an experienced print designer, you still need to learn some basics about the World Wide Web before you can start designing sites in Photoshop. This chapter is designed to give you a sense of how the online medium affects your designs.

INFORMATION ARCHITECTURE

"Information architecture" is (or I should say *was*) the major buzz phrase among Web designers in the early days. Clement Mok, founder of Studio Archetype, a well-known San Francisco-based design firm, actually went so far as to rename his company a few years ago; he gave it the subtitle "Identity & Information Architects." The invention of the Web created several new professions, so to speak, and today many Web design companies are looking for new hires who have experience in this field—simply because it can make the difference between a good and bad Web site. What does "information architecture" actually mean? The best way to describe it in one sentence is that it

Left: The main page for DAT's Digital, which distributes digital music (www.datsdigital.com).

Right: Since this Web site requires various plug-ins to hear the music, a dedicated page helps users find the necessary plug-ins. ▼

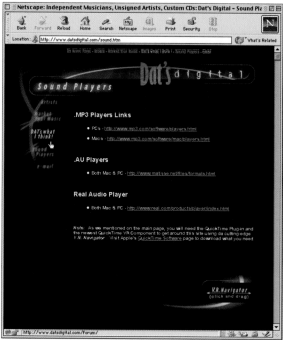

To get a better idea of how to approach the problem, they studied the user model. The typical customer was most interested in tracking the current location of a package, calculating shipping costs, and learning where to drop off packages or how to schedule pickups. Studio Archetype simply reorganized the information and the content around those four central tasks. After the new version went live, phone calls to UPS dropped by 20 percent according to Crumpacker—which shows how much positive impact a well-structured Web site can have on customer support.

➤ Reduction Is Construction

Reducing the amount of information on a Web site and consolidating similar topics into a single topic set are essential tasks for producing a good site. Rikus Hillman from Pixelpark in Berlin, who has worked on the online magazine Wildpark, is familiar with this problem. Wildpark started as a complex site, but the creators soon decided that they should reduce the number of categories from 10 to 4. With this simple change, the magazine's structure suddenly became much clearer, and it became easier for the editors to point out new content to the viewers. But reducing the number of categories was just a start; the information itself also needed to be reworked. Most articles

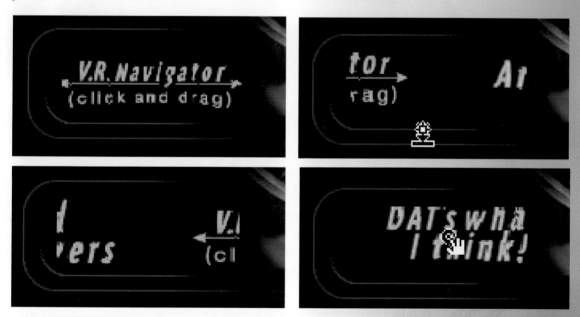

▲ Christopher Stashuk used QuickTime VR to help users navigate DAT's Web site. Because QTVR allows a 360-degree view of a scene, Christopher used it to put text links on the imaginary "wall." QTVR can also embed hyperlinks, which makes for an innovative navigational element. Not everyone will get the concept right away, though, so Christopher also included traditional text links.

COMMON INFORMATION ARCHITECTURE MISTAKES

How do you approach the concept of a Web site and achieve effective information architecture? The easiest way to show you is to point out the most common mistakes:

1. Too Many Categories

Reduction is the key to success. Combine information and avoid too many categories. The rule of thumb is that there should be no more than seven categories; scientific studies have established that this is all that most visitors can remember.

2. Getting Trapped in Established Structures

Does the structure of the Web site make sense, or is it simply based on the company's departmental structure or some other preexisting concept? Always ask yourself if the categories are logical from the visitors' point of view.

3. Inconsistent Navigational Organization

Is your navigational concept simple and straightforward? If not, start over. Your concept should include clear global, parallel, and local navigational structures.

4. Burying Information in too Many Levels

Many Web sites branch out like a tree, but if your tree includes more than four hierarchical levels, it is probably too complex. Creating a visual representation or chart of your design will help you control the site's hierarchy.

and stories in online magazines are too long, says Hillman, a problem that arose early on because many editors came from traditional print magazines. The Internet requires a different approach to editorial.

When Studio Archetype was given the job of reworking the Adobe site, the firm's information architects set themselves the goal of reducing 14 sections to six. With Adobe's help, they regrouped the information to make navigation simpler for visitors. For example, the original site drew a distinction between graphic and prepress products, but for the user, those two categories overlap, so separating them created confusion. "We didn't quite achieve the goal of reducing everything to six sections," says Crumpacker, "but we came close. We ended up having eight categories on the Web site."

▲ The old Studio Archetype Web site was one of the better known promotional sites. Designed by Mark Crumpacker to embody Studio Archetype's philosophy of information architecture, it was a great example of a clean and consistent navigational concept. This shot also shows the concept of content surfacing, in which images are updated regularly and linked to new content within the site.

➤ Navigation in the Information

Many Web designers make the mistake of creating a fancy interface with the expectation that visitors will be able to understand it. Very often this is not the case, and the visitor may have serious difficulties finding the desired information. You can avoid this pitfall by using clear and consistent global, parallel, and local navigation. What does this mean?

● **Global navigation** allows the visitor to move between the main sections of the site. It should be present on every page.

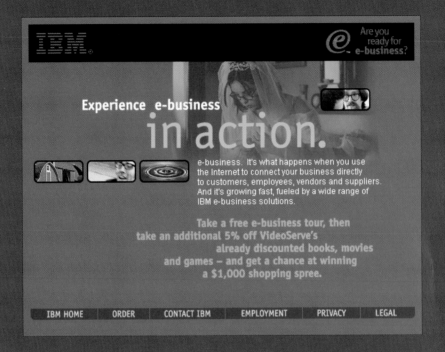

INTERVIEW WITH TOM NICHOLSON

Tom Nicholson is an unassuming man. When he occasionally hangs out with his coworkers and employees after work, he's just one of the crowd. But when he gets into talking about information architecture, both customers and employees are under his spell. No question, he is a man with a lot of experience who can provide highly valuable input.

His company, Nicholson NY, started with interactive media way back in 1987. At that time the Web boom was far in the future, and Nicholson was working on multimedia. Today, the company (now www.iconlab.com) has over 100 employees and occupies several floors in the Puck Building on Lafayette Street in New York's SoHo.

You worked with interactive media back in 1987, when computers were still relatively new technology. What was that like?

We have been in the business for twelve years now, from 1987 to 1999, and we started with interactive media, which was quite different back then from what it is today. Using computers to create interactive media was not as common at the time, and I had to spend a lot of time on core issues, like how do you balance "user drive" versus what we call "editorial drive" in order to get something communicated in this new medium.

Do you remember any particular project from back then? It would interest me to see what you were thinking about interactive media ten years ago as opposed to what you think of it today.

The first project that I did and that really launched my career in that area was a pretty large scale project involving six million visitors to the World's Fair in Knoxville, many of whom had come to the US to learn about energy. I developed six or seven interactive programs using touch screens and computer graphics, and merged them into interactive experiences, such as an energy glossary that listed 500 words—all dynamically animated on screen.

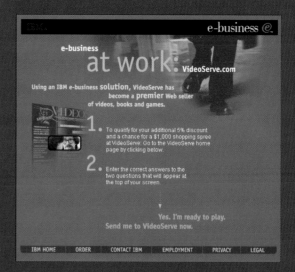

▲ IBM, one of Nicholson's clients, wanted a special Web page for their e-commerce campaign.

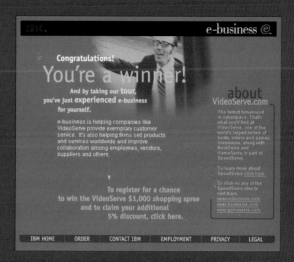

▲ The IBM site also reflects the visual style of Andreas Lindström (see interview on page 72), who acted as art director of the site.

▲ The splash screen of the Sony Web site.

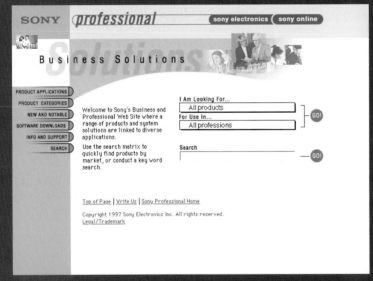

▲ For a corporate Web site, the Sony site is amazingly hip and cool—another Andreas Lindström creation. Tom Nicholson and his team tried to group as many categories as possible to make it easy to locate products and information.

They included videos and a lot of technical terms. We also did projects for IBM and Citibank.

When did you get into Web design?

It was many years after that...around 1991 when Newscorp came in and wanted to create an AOL-killer; it was supposed to knock AOL out of the box. It was our first online experience, and it led to the first Internet Web site developments. That was when the company started to grow from 15 people to 100.

You really watched Silicon Alley rise, so to speak?

We were the first interactive agency in Silicon Alley. When we started, there was basically nothing here.

When you look around on the map there is CKS Modem who were founded in 1987, the same year we were, but that was it.

What would you say is the strength of the agency? I suppose it is the strong background in interactive media?

Yes, I think so. We were leveraging what's possible with interactive media at a time when nobody else was doing it. But we have certainly grown beyond being just a design firm. What is happening in the Internet industry is that it's becoming more and more important to incorporate all aspects of Web design and offer a full solution for the client. Besides working with interactive content and information design or information architecture, we have been building e-businesses for our clients—doing everything from Internet business strategy through creative execution and technology development.

That brings me to my next question. Information architecture is one of the buzzwords of the Internet. What does it mean to you?

Information architecture is nothing more than formatting information in a way that communicates. It's kind of a mental model, where you try to share your mental model with another person by using words, pictures, and so on. The user interface plays a big part in this. For instance, in the print world the information architecture is very much established and fixed; with a book you have three ways of accessing information: from the front with the table of contents, from the back with the index, or by just browsing through the content. But in a flexible environment like Web design there are an almost infinite number of ways of representing the information.

Can you give an example?

Let me tell you about a project that's coming to completion right now. It's a kiosk system for a museum, but it could just as easily become a Web site once bandwidth is not a problem

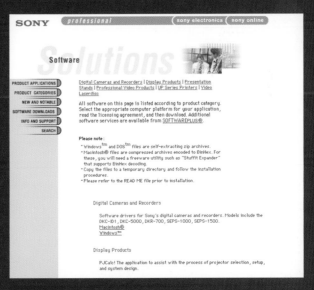

▲ Although the Web site uses a conventional sidebar, the use of different colors gives each section its own identity.

any more. An archeologist discovered something new on this Indian reservation: he found these stains in the ground that he concluded were from a seventeenth-century fort. He started digging, and sure enough he learned that it was a fort, and he found all these components of life in a village.

Instead of content surfacing, the site uses a dedicated news section. ▶

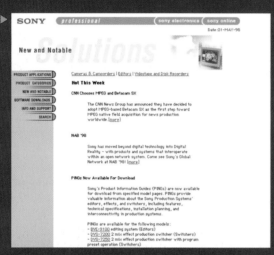

So if somebody came to you saying, "I want to convey this to the public," well, one way to start might be to get an editorial person to figure out what the content is. It might look like "Tell us everything about the fort: Who lived there? Where? Why were they there?" and then you could present it interactively on the Internet. Somebody else might break it down to the fortification itself: arms and defense mechanisms, daily life, food,

social interactions, and so on. This version of the Web site would probably have buttons labeled "Life in the Village," "Food," "Arms," and so on. That's a lot like what you see on the Web today.

Yet another way of approaching this would be to ask yourself, "What is the closest mental model to the subject?" It happens that in this case it is the fort itself, because that's the artifact that offers all the information. So why not just give the fort to people and let them move through it, and interact with it; eventually you would learn all about life on the eastern seaboard. The key to designing an interactive environment is that you can have many different interfaces, which offers great possibilities for adapting to people's different learning styles. The more you can adapt to those differences, the better.

That example really illustrates the possibilities of interactive media. Instead of simply communicating linear information you can model it around the real world. Do you have any more examples? Or can you make a general assessment about what you think constitutes good and bad information architecture?

There are many basic principles that apply. You have to start by thinking about basics like the graphic user interface, what makes for good graphic design, and how well the information has been put in a hierarchical structure.

Then there is the rule of seven: people can only remember seven independent things. They can hold in their short term memory seven independent entities that have no relationship to each other. Some people can do eight, or maybe nine, but most people are limited to seven. That's why telephone numbers have seven digits; that's not an accident. So when it comes to designing a Web site you should stick to seven groups, and then work out a hierarchy with a consistent interface for those seven.

But what happens far too often is that a company has several different sections and departments, and each of them has its own Web site. Sometimes they put an umbrella site on top, but then you don't have any consistency, and the deeper the people get into the site the more confusing it gets.

There are many sites that have that kind of "bad" information architecture. It's a common occurence, because the Web is changing so fast. Our Sony project is a good example. Under the professional products group they had a number of different marketing groups, all of which were independent and all of which used their own printed material. That

didn't matter, because those customers didn't cross paths with each other. Now, all of a sudden, Sony needs to come together on one Web site—as a Web design agency we were faced with the challenge of reorganizing all this content without getting trapped by the structure of the company.

An e-commerce site must have a dedicated page for customer contact.

Sony had several departments, which was an efficient way for them to run their business, but the customers had no perception of that. All the user cared about was that he wanted to buy a monitor, for example, and he didn't care which products group the monitor department belonged to. So the first thing we had to do was to go in and work across the groups to create consistency, which was essential for the success of the Web site.

▲
In most of his
Web sites, Christopher
Stashuk uses a splash screen
that features a GIF animation
and gives the visitor a summary
of the site's content.

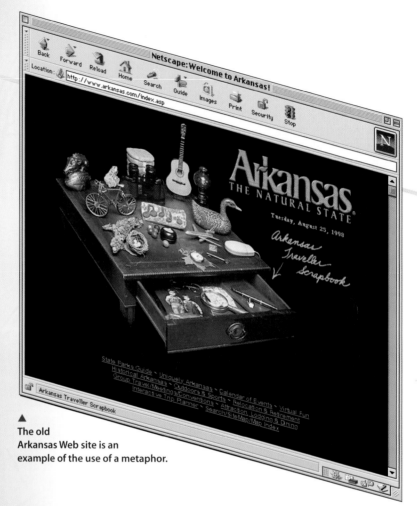

▲
The old
Arkansas Web site is an
example of the use of a metaphor.

● Within each section there are usually subcategories or subsections that also require a consistent navigational structure. Because you are moving in a parallel manner within a section, this is called **parallel navigation**—and it should be present on every page within a section.

● **Local navigation** works like a table of contents. You use it to find information within a page. It may look like a table of contents at the beginning of the page, or it might be a list of links in a sidebar.

For a Web site that uses a classical tree structure, this navigational system (with global, parallel, and local navigation) is the best way to go.

In the future, as Web design becomes more like multimedia design and as the Internet community embraces new technologies, information architecture will have to solve ever more complex problems. With extensions to HTML, information is becoming more dynamic, and the conventional page metaphor, where visitors click from one page to another, will be only one solution among many. Perhaps, as in Clement Mok's vision, future Web interfaces might allow visitors to walk through a virtual world in which they hear ambient sounds, and information is presented in a three-dimensional world. I am intrigued by the idea of using ambient sounds for navigational purposes, but that is light years from now. But wait! Aren't Internet years like dog years? If so, we will be probably amazed at how soon this concept becomes a reality.

DESIGN CONCEPTS

Hopefully this excursion into the underlying issues of information architecture has been helpful. There are some books out there on the subject, but most of your know-how and expertise will come from analyzing other Web sites. However, before you start working on your own site, I would like to take this opportunity to offer some basic design concepts. As you certainly know from

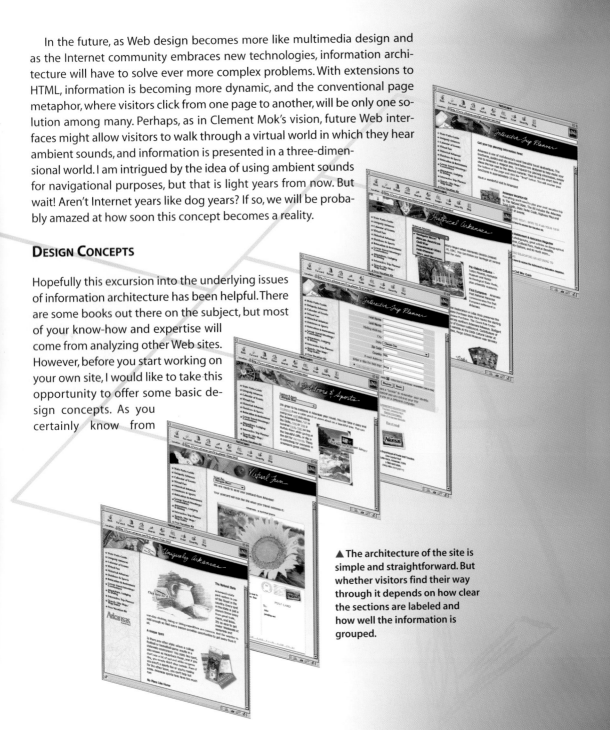

▲ The architecture of the site is simple and straightforward. But whether visitors find their way through it depends on how clear the sections are labeled and how well the information is grouped.

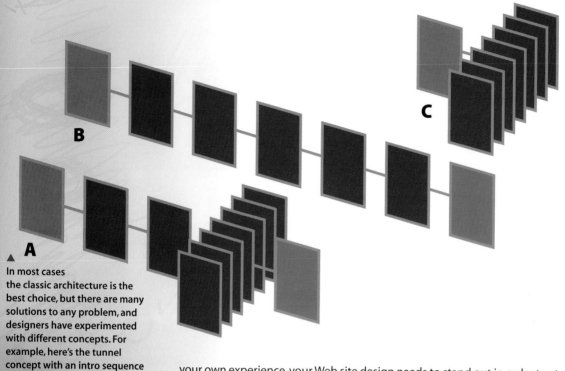

▲ **A**

In most cases the classic architecture is the best choice, but there are many solutions to any problem, and designers have experimented with different concepts. For example, here's the tunnel concept with an intro sequence and an exit page (see example A & B).

your own experience, your Web site design needs to stand out in order to attract visitors and inspire them to return. Here are some tips and techniques:

➤ **Content Surfacing**

Content surfacing is a crucial part of information architecture, since it allows a visitor to locate new content on your site immediately rather than having to look for it. In the same way that a newspaper "grabs" readers with a headline and breaking news, you can pull the reader into your site with something new on your first page.

This might be just a photo and a headline, or it could provide a little summary or the story's lead-in sentences. Either way, it is a great way to grab visitors' attention and tie them to the site. A good example was Studio Archetype's site (unfortunately, since they merged with Sapient, it is no longer live). The main page was built using a modular structure, meaning that the images in the middle of the interface could be exchanged easily. A click on the image brought the visitor right to the story within the site. You should use this

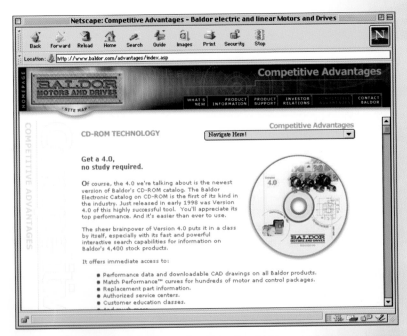

On the Baldor Web site (www.baldor.com), the navigational elements are placed inside a frame that is always visible.

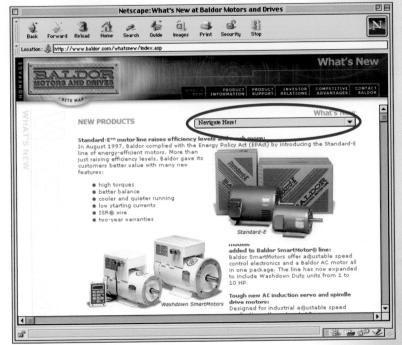

▲ Web sites that use frames should use a splash screen (without frames) so that search engines don't get trapped in a frameset.

◄ A pop-up menu like the one Christopher Stashuk used on the Baldor Web site is another great navigational element.

technique on Web sites with frequent updates, since it is one of the most important ways of motivating visitors to return on a daily basis.

➤ Metaphors

The goal in using a metaphor is to give a site a central and consistent visual theme. Finding and creating a metaphor is not easy, because not every Web site is suitable for this. Very often you see metaphoric icons used for navigational elements, such as a mailbox for e-mail, but this doesn't really qualify as a metaphoric Web site, where all of the graphics and text leverage some appropriate, figurative concept. To see an example of a Web site where a metaphor is used tastefully and effectively, see the example on page 64 of the Arkansas Web site (www.arkansas.com) designed by Christopher Stashuk from Aristotle. This site used a table with several objects to represent the different areas of the site (unfortunately that version is not longer available).

Web sites that use metaphors are certainly more interesting than sites that just use text links, but at the same time, if you overdo it or if you use an inappropriate metaphor, you run the risk of crossing the line between good and bad design. So if you're going to use a visual metaphor, make sure it's something catchy and appropriate.

As with all his Web sites, Christopher Stashuk designed the Arkansas Museum of Discovery site (www.amod.org) completely in Photoshop because it gave him the greatest control and flexibility. Only later do you need to worry about how the design will translate into HTML. For presentations to clients, Stashuk always uses a layer showing the browser interface. ▶

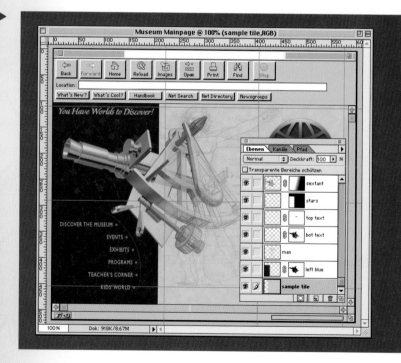

➤ The Tunnel Concept

Printed brochures often use a great-looking cover to grab the reader's attention. The tunnel concept does the same thing by using a splash screen—an attention-capturing image that appears briefly before giving way to another image. Visitors have to click through one or more splash screens before they get to the main screen with the content and the navigational interface. A Web site using a tunnel concept might also use a flashy exit page, which can leave a big impression, but you don't see this very often.

In the beginning of the Web era, many companies were concerned primarily with having a nice-looking site, mostly as a way to show off and provide the company with a cool image. These days, most companies are more sophisticated and they want to use their sites to improve customer service. Forcing visitors to click through a series of pages before arriving at the main page is just not appropriate any more, especially in a time marked by a decreasing attention span. So you don't see many Web sites using a tunnel concept anymore, at least not for corporations. The concept is used mostly in creative fields like design companies or photographers. Instead of several linked HTML pages, many use alternatives like an intro made with Flash.

▲ The Arkansas Museum of Discovery's site looks great without relying on the latest plug-ins. The navigation bar at the bottom is a nice detail; although it's a frame, the background pattern makes it appear curved.

SIDEBAR LAYOUT

If elements are placed over the edge of the sidebar like here in the Arkansas Museum of Discovery Web site (www.amod.org), it's important to consider browser offset. As you can see in the smaller picture, the sextant and the navigational links were saved as transparent GIFs (gray area). Since there is enough room between the navigational links and the edge of the sidebar, they can compensate a browser offset of several pixels in either direction.

NAVIGATIONAL TECHNIQUES AND INTERFACE DESIGN

When building a Web site, you have to come up with a concept for an interface. If this is the first time you are designing for the Web, you probably have only a rough idea of what HTML is, or what it allows you to do, so this section will give you some pointers.

➤ Navigation Concepts

▲ This Web site features typical navigational buttons: Using JavaScript rollovers, each button changes to an embossed state when the mouse cursor is positioned over it.

The most common kind of navigational controls use text or image links to connect pages and information. If you've ever seen a Web site with several buttons, then you saw a set of images that were defined as hyperlinks. This is done in GoLive simply by placing an image and then switching to the **Link** tab in the Inspector: click on the chain icon to make this image a link. By using the point-and-shoot tool, you can then link to a page.

Designers often take the easy route and use 3D buttons as navigational links because it's a simple way of displaying a clickable area, and such buttons are unambiguous. However, there are only a few Web sites where such buttons are actually well integrated and look good. One of them was the Studio Archetype Web site. These buttons used icons as well as text to communicate where they led, and the icons glowed when the mouse pointer moved over them. This interactivity, where a navigational element changes when the mouse is positioned over it, is called a *rollover*. It is achieved by using JavaScript, which most popular browsers can interpret. The only drawback of these rollover buttons is that they require twice as much data to be transmitted (images for both the "on" and "off" button states need to be downloaded). If you are already using a lot of elements on your page, this might be an issue. But if you use GoLive's Rollover Object (on the **Smart** tab of the **Object** palette) this is not a big deal, because the underlying JavaScript loads the buttons after all the main images are in the browser cache.

▲ One of the few Web sites that has tastefully used embossed buttons is the old the Studio Archetype site.

The Studio Archetype Web site was one of the few examples where embossed buttons actually looked good, but most of the time, 3D buttons make a Web site look rather technical. Andreas Lindström, art director of popular sites such as www.carnegiehall.org and www.viagra.com, avoids them whenever possible. He prefers more subtle ways of integrating image links seamlessly in the design. Even though it takes more time to come up with an alternative to 3D buttons, it is certainly worth the effort.

If you want to stay away from buttons and icons, try to find a metaphor in the context of the Web site. The old Arkansas Web site (www.arkansas.com),

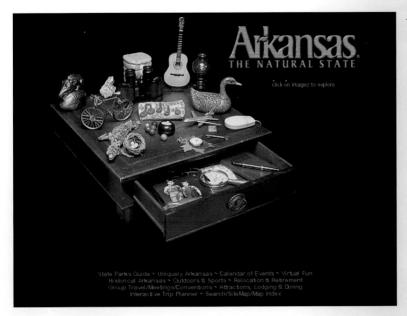

◄ On the old Arkansas Web site (www.arkansas.com), all objects on the table represent an area of the site. When the mouse was moved over an item, text appeared to indicate where the link was leading.

which was designed by Christopher Stashuk, was a good example. On the main page there was a table with many objects, each of which represented a different section of the Web site.

Another good example was the old David Bowie Web site, which was designed by Ben Clemens and Marlene Stoffers. The navigational elements were both artsy and an integral part of the design. To ensure that visitors would know where these links were leading, they displayed a text label when the mouse was passed over them.

Rollovers are not complicated. The only thing you need to know is that if you want to use transparency in a GIF, make sure that the transparent regions are the same for both images. The browser doesn't refresh the entire display each time a rollover button is triggered, it only updates the parts that change. Therefore, in some browsers and under certain circumstances, some pixels in the transparent areas remain visible.

Another thing you should know is that a rollover doesn't have to trigger a change in the same image; it can change a different image somewhere else on the page. In fact, you can have many image changes triggered by just one event. If you want to do this in GoLive, you'll need a good understanding of JavaScript, because the **Rollover** element on the **Smart** tab doesn't allow it.

▲ The 4th of July Web site uses icons for navigation (www.aristotle.net/4thjuly).

INTERVIEW WITH ANDREAS LINDSTRÖM

Andreas Lindström, a native of Sweden who has been living and working in New York for several years now, has achieved something that only a few designers can claim: he has developed a totally unique Web design style. His work for Carnegie Hall and the Viagra site, among others, carry his signature. He is one of the best-known and most in-demand Web designers in New York today.

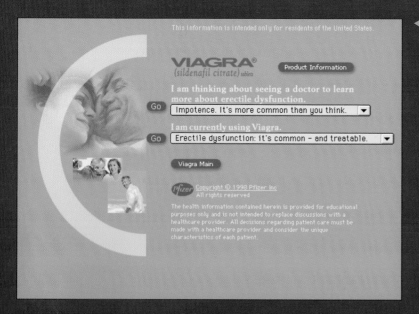

◀ Pfizer, the company that manufactures Viagra, hired Nicholson NY to do a web site for their customers. Andreas Lindström was art director of this site: "the color combination in this Web site is based on the printed brochure, other than that the design is very different. The main navigational element is a pop-up in which the visitor can select the information that he is interested in. This has the advantage that the site can easily be extended and at the same time the design remains very clean and clear. To align the elements on the first page with the background pattern we used JavaScript to compensate for the browser offset.

How did you get into Web design?

I attended a special high school for design in Sweden, and was lucky to get a job offer from an advertising agency in Malma, Sweden, right after my graduation. So instead of going to college I went directly to work, which I think is an advantage. I learned so much at that time that after five years I felt that Malma was a little bit too small for me. I wanted a bigger challenge, so I applied to the Parson School of Design in New York, and was accepted. After I finished there I started to work in the print field. When the Web started to happen, I got in contact with Avalanche, a company that was just starting up in New York. They did cutting edge stuff on the Internet, and I worked there for two years, learning about this new medium and how to push the limits. It was a great experience.

You designed the Lost Highway site, which is a good example of your style, because it used large, dimmed images in the background combined with smaller images in the foreground. What can you tell me about the site?

I think the use of large images in combination with smaller images creates a real dimension and depth to the page. For example, on the Lost Highway site I used a large face that blended into the black background, and in the foreground I placed smaller images of the actors in the series. This created tension and depth at the same time.

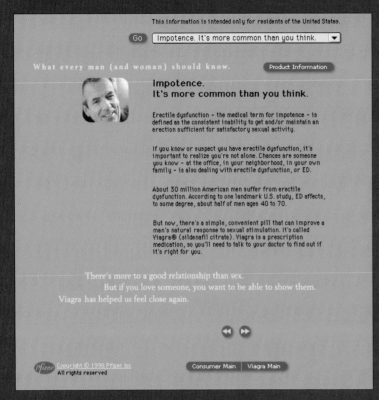

This information is intended only for residents of the United States.

Go | Impotence. It's more common than you think. ▼

What every man (and woman) should know.   Product Information

Impotence.
It's more common than you think.

Erectile dysfunction – the medical term for impotence – is defined as the consistent inability to get and/or maintain an erection sufficient for satisfactory sexual activity.

If you know or suspect you have erectile dysfunction, it's important to realize you're not alone. Chances are someone you know – at the office, in your neighborhood, in your own family – is also dealing with erectile dysfunction, or ED.

About 30 million American men suffer from erectile dysfunction. According to one landmark U.S. study, ED affects, to some degree, about half of men ages 40 to 70.

But now, there's a simple, convenient pill that can improve a man's natural response to sexual stimulation. It's called Viagra® (sildenafil citrate). Viagra is a prescription medication, so you'll need to talk to your doctor to find out if it's right for you.

There's more to a good relationship than sex.
But if you love someone, you want to be able to show them.
Viagra has helped us feel close again.

Pfizer Copyright © 1998 Pfizer Inc   Consumer Main | Viagra Main
All rights reserved

There are quite a lot of Web sites for movie companies in your portfolio, for example the Polygram Filmed Entertainment Web site.

Yes, that was actually the first Web site I created. I used film props to create the tone of the site, and tried to associate various objects with different sections. This is one of the few sites where we had a real photo shoot, and didn't have to use stock photos. I think you end up with a much better result that way, because it gives you control over the outcome and you can get closer to your vision as a designer. The same applies to the Carnegie Hall site, where we had a photographer come in and shoot pictures. It made a big difference in the quality of the design.

You also worked for Nicholson in New York. What are some of the projects you did there?

The first site I did as art director for Nicholson was a site for Sony, a business solutions site. We had to create a site that could handle something like 50,000 products. The important thing was to consider Sony's brand, which has a very clear look, as well as creating a navigational system that could pull all this information together—so whatever search results you would get, it would fit into the template we created. Another project was a Web site that was part of IBM's e-business campaign. We did

What was really neat about this site was the navigation elements that we came up with. The site didn't have traditional navigation. Instead of buttons or any other kind of visual indication of where to click, we based the navigation on how the story of the movie was going. We also linked the pages so that you would get more images if you clicked on an image, and you would get more text if you clicked on a text link. Since every visitor has individual preferences, I thought this was a great way of giving them a choice.

that in conjunction with a company called Video Surf that sells video-tapes online. It was just a demon-stration of how e-business works, an opportunity to see it in action. The site reflected the advertising cam-paign that was going on at that mo-ment, as well as taking you through a couple of IBM pages and a contest.

Another big project was the offi-cial Viagra Web site. I think it has a very unusual and appealing charm. We used a very simple user interface with a very unconventional naviga-tional system. Instead of using tradi-tional buttons and links, the main navigational element is a pop-up menu. I was almost surprised that a customer like Pfizer agreed to do it, since big corporations lean more and more toward standard sidebar navigation.

That indeed is the overwhelming trend. When you develop a Web site, how do you approach the navigation?

Personally, I wish clients would ex-periment with a few more naviga-tional possibilities. I try to break out of that standardized sidebar concept as often as I can by creating naviga-tion elements in different places, or by trying to come up with different page layouts. Usually clients prefer the standardized model, because they have seen it so often, so most of the time it's a battle. My overall goal

is to develop very clear navigation. I prefer to avoid designing with but-tons, although they have become such a standard that sometimes I have to use them. Buttons are not necessarily the worst choice, but I prefer to use them more delicately, maybe as a subtle sub-element.

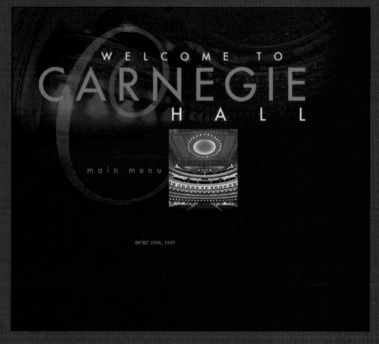

When you start a project and get the outline, how do you come up with a concept and a site design?

Generally I sit with the client and show them different designs and see what they like; it's important to find that out. Then, after we have estab-lished the creative direction, I experi-ment with different kinds of imagery.

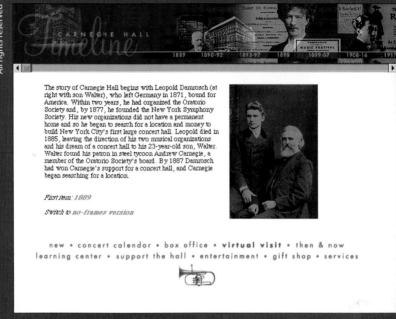

▲ The history of Carnegie Hall is presented on its own page.

I usually do sketches by hand and try to develop two or three different solutions—solutions that might work together, because sometimes you show the client three solutions but they may like certain things here and there, and want to pick pieces from different solutions. At least that's been my experience.

Another thing that's important, particularly when you create a Web site for a location, is to go to that location, which is what Avalanche did for the Carnegie Hall Web site. I walked through the aisles and halls, listening to the noises and trying to visualize sound as a color. Colors and images are my strength, and I try to use these elements for my designs.

How do you think Web design is going to change the development of new technologies?

Since most of my clients are corporations, I really have to keep the low-end user in mind. I still do my designs so they will be compatible with older browsers, because a lot of people are not using the latest versions. Of course I would love to experiment with the high end, but now that I'm mostly working on corporate Web sites, I have to stay away from really fancy design features.

What do you think the future of the Web will be?

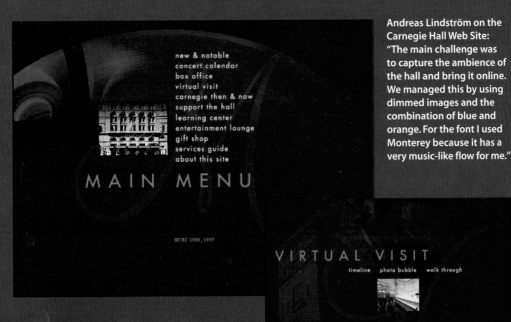

Andreas Lindström on the Carnegie Hall Web Site: "The main challenge was to capture the ambience of the hall and bring it online. We managed this by using dimmed images and the combination of blue and orange. For the font I used Monterey because it has a very music-like flow for me."

I think the Web will merge with television. Interactive TV is definitely where the Web is going, and I'm really looking forward to that, since in the future, bandwidth will allow for different kinds of design and functionality.

What's your vision of a Web site without any limitations?

It would be like interactive video, where everything is in motion all the time, almost like a computer game. I can see that being used in very interesting ways in corporate Web sites, when they finally get there.

The Web is so serious right now, it's not as experimental as it was in the beginning. Now it's all corporate—I'm really waiting for the next step, because at the moment everything looks the same.

(ImageReady can do this, however: if you create a rollover state for a button, but the changes affect a different slice, ImageReady will save the appropriate JavaScript.)

The other way of aiding navigation is to use text hyperlinks: just select the text in GoLive and choose **Special > New Link**. Type the URL into the **Text Inspector** or use the **Browse** button to navigate to a file to which you want to link. Text links let you assign up to three colors: one for the unclicked link (Link), one for every link that has been visited (Visited Link), and one for the moment when the visitor actually clicks on the link (Active Link). To set those colors, click on the **Page** icon in your GoLive document (in the upper left corner), because those colors apply for the whole page and are therefore placed in the BODY tag.

Since Web visitors have gotten used to rollover buttons, a lot of designers want to use the same effect for text. Unfortunately, HTML doesn't offer this option (Explorer does have that feature, but not Navigator does not), so they solve the problem by rendering the text as an image and applying a different color, glow, or other effect for the rollover image.

The last navigational element that I want to mention is a pop-up menu. One advantage of this is that it can be extended without having to change anything in the design and it uses up the least amount of space. It also requires the use of JavaScript, but GoLive offers a ready-to use element for this: open the **Objects** option bar (**Window > Palette**) and select the **Smart** tab (second from the right), then drag the **URL Popup** element to your page. In the **URL Pop-Up Inspector,** enter the text you want to appear and the URL to which you want to link.

> ➤ **Interface Design with Frames**

Using text and images as links has the advantage of being backward-compatible to Netscape Navigator 2.0. The only problem is that navigational elements may scroll out of view if there is more content on your page than the browser can display on a single screen. To compensate for this, frames were introduced after HTML 2.0. Frames let you split a browser window into two or more independent areas, which allows designers to create a sidebar or topbar where they can place buttons and navigational elements. No matter what happens to the main frame, the navigational sidebar and topbar remain onscreen at all times.

▲ What seems to be a regular text link is often text rendered as an image, allowing for effects that would otherwise be impossible.

Frames require an additional document called a *frameset,* which contains such information as the frames' dimensions and which HTML page should be displayed in which frame. Each frame can be addressed using a target attribute; this is essential in creating navigational bars.

Do you want to give this a try? Start up GoLive and open the **Objects** option bar (**Windows > Objects**). Before you can drag a frameset from the **Frames** tab into your document, you need to switch to the **Frame Editor**: click on the second tab from the left in your document. To create more complex framesets, just keep adding additional frames by dragging them to your page. Adjust the size of a frame by clicking in the frame and resizing it.

By default, these frames appear with a 6-pixel border and in gray—two settings that I seriously doubt you want to use for your page. Usually frame borders should be invisible. To ensure that they appear that way in both Netscape Navigator and Internet Explorer, you have to set the **BorderSize** to 0 pixels and the **BorderFrame** attribute to "No." To do this, click on the border (rather than inside the frame) to view the **Frame Set Inspector**, where the options can be specified. If you have several frames, you must repeat this step for each.

Frames are a great improvement over no frames at all, but in the first version you couldn't make the borders invisible. The attributes that I have just mentioned didn't exist when frames were first introduced. Only later did Explorer and Navigator offer these essential attributes, but by then frames had lost popularity among Web designers because they realized that frames have some serious drawbacks. The most important drawback is that Web sites with frames often fail to get good results from search engines. This has to do with the way search engines work: they index the text in an HTML document and count how often a certain keyword appears on a page. Unfortunately, if you use frames, the search engine never gets to see or index the real content of your Web site. The search engine only "sees" the frameset document, which contains only a few lines of HTML code. To make matters worse, the pages with content replace each other in the frame, which makes it virtually impossible for the search engine to list a specific page.

I don't want to go into too much detail on this; all you need to know is that using frames can be counterproductive if you want to create a content Web site. There are ways to use frames and still have your site appear high in the ranking of a search engine, but optimizing sites for search engines is extremely complex. If you want to find out more about how to do so, log onto one and search for the key words "search engine." You will find a number of sites that offer advice or even the service of optimizing your Web site for you.

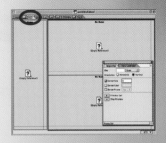

▲ The second tab in the document window hosts the frameset view. Once a frameset is dragged from the Frame palette, click on the frame itself and the Inspector will show its properties, for example BorderSize.

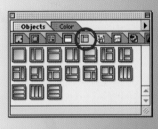

▲ Various framesets are stored in the Frame palette and just need to be dragged over into the frameset view of the document.

WebPosition is a powerful tool for checking the ratings and position of a Web site with the major search engines. You can find more information at www.webposition.com. If the search engine rating is very important to you, avoid using frames—they have a negative effect on search results.

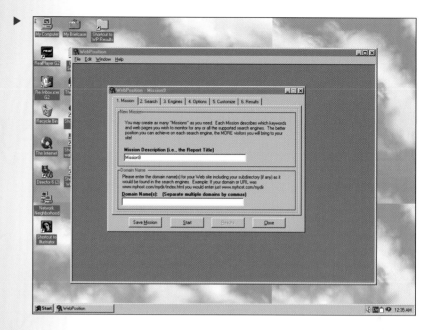

Use careful judgement if you decide to use one of these services, because truly effective optimization for search engine promotion requires someone to monitor the changes that happen constantly among the search engines—they change the way they index more frequently than you might think, because they are constantly trying to improve the accuracy of their results. A good place to get more information about what's happening is www.searchenginewatch.com.

Most Web designers, knowing the importance of a good search engine ranking, have gone back to frameless designs. However, if your Web site is database driven, using frames does not make a difference (a search engine can't index content in a database, so you might as well use frames).

Keying framesets for search engines is not the only problem with using frames on Web sites. There are also design issues: for instance, if there is more content in a frame than it can display, it shows a scroll bar. (You can prevent this by setting the **Scrolling** attribute to "No" in the **Frame Inspector**). While a scroll bar in a frame with content is not an issue, it is a problem if it appears in a control bar. Keep this in mind if you decide to use frames when you design your page.

➤ The Sidebar Design

One of the most popular Web design concepts is using a sidebar that contains all the navigational elements. This can be done with frames, but as I just explained, frames have some disadvantages. Most sidebar designs are based on a background image that has a rectangle on one side, usually the left, which is a different color from the rest of the page (see the chapter "Designing with Photoshop"). The only drawback is that all the navigational elements in the sidebar eventually scroll out of view if there is a lot of content on the page; that's why every designer places a copy of the links as text links at the end of the page. This way, a visitor doesn't have to scroll back up to move to another page.

▲ One common technique is to slice up an image and put it back together in an invisible table. This was done here to place animations and interactive buttons on the page.

➤ Image Maps and Image Tables

Another navigational feature of HTML is image maps. These are images in which certain areas have been designated as *hot spots,* or hyperlinks. Hot spots can be any shape, from rectangular to elliptical to polygonal, and you can knock out areas of a shape that's a hot spot. ImageReady and GoLive both support image maps (to create an image map in ImageReady, use the **Image Map** tools in the **Tool** palette), but I recommend that you use GoLive unless you need to be able to work with high precision.

Image maps are great, but they don't support rollovers. Since rollovers are so popular these days, Web designers often use image tables instead. The basic idea is to slice up an image into pieces and to drop each piece into the appropriate cell of an invisible table so that the image appears to be one large image in the browser. Besides being able to make each slice a link, you can optimize every slice in the table separately. Finally, if you want to animate part of a larger image, you can slice it and put it back together in an image table.

▲ There are several ways to create an image table, one of which is to use the Slice tool, which lets you draw rectangular areas in your image. Then ImageReady or Photoshop will automatically slice the remaining areas of the image. Another great benefit of the slices is that you can optimize each one differently. Just open the Optimize palette (Window > Show Optimize) in ImageReady and select a slice with the Slice Select tool. Change the settings in the Optimize palette, and when the slice is exported, ImageReady saves it with its those particular settings.

THE WEB GALLERY

All Web sites are copyrighted by their owners and were printed with permission. To submit your Web site to be published in one of my books, please go to mitomediabooks.com.

Being a Web designer has one advantage: the source of inspiration is right there—accessible 24/7. And becoming a great Web designer involves studying and learning from others. This little Web gallery shows some of the Web sites that I find remarkable for one reason or another.

52MM.COM

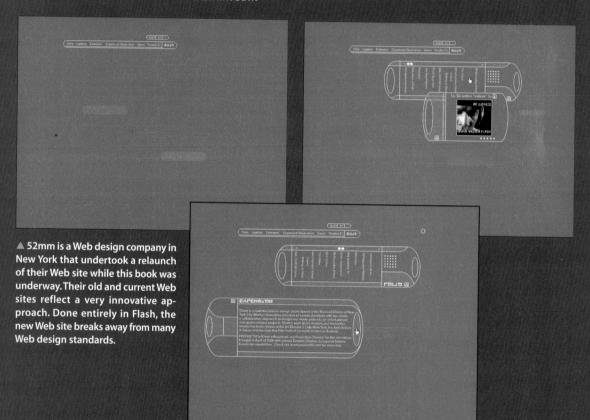

▲ 52mm is a Web design company in New York that undertook a relaunch of their Web site while this book was underway. Their old and current Web sites reflect a very innovative approach. Done entirely in Flash, the new Web site breaks away from many Web design standards.

ARKARTS.COM

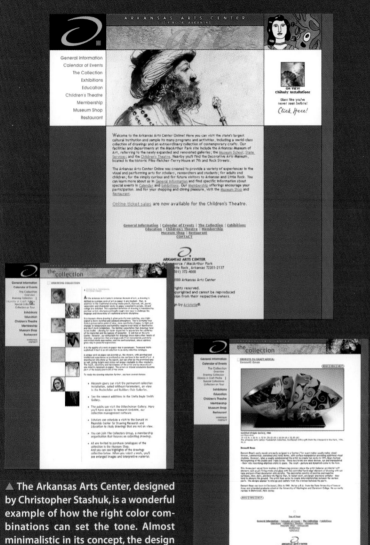

▲ The Arkansas Arts Center, designed by Christopher Stashuk, is a wonderful example of how the right color combinations can set the tone. Almost minimalistic in its concept, the design doesn't try to compete with the exhibits, still the Web site comes across as very rich. Above is the main page for one of the exhibitions; each of the miniatures on the page above leads to one of the exhibits (see right). On the very right, you see the online museum store.

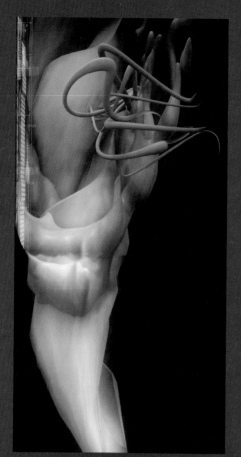

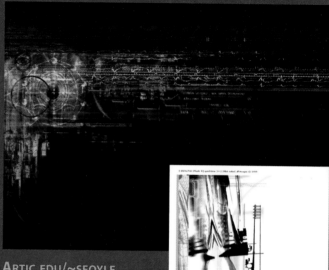

Artic.edu/~sfoyle

The work of Sean Patrick Foyle is nothing less then remarkable. His pieces of online artwork done with Flash and 3D software are a mustsee! Several antimated layers create an animated texture that draws the viewer in. While the site lacks a clear concept and navigation (it takes a while to explore it), it is worth the effort just to marvel at it.

www.cia.com.au/dfm/tintin

Up for more inspiring artwork? Justin Fox worked in Web design for many years and uses a subdirectory of his Web site to host some of his work and writing. His views and his approach to design are a great break from the mainstream.

CONTEMPT.NET

"Advertising may be described as the science of arresting the human intelligence long enough to get money from it", says a quote on the Web site of the Contempt Web Design Company. It is apparent that this motto reflects the program on their own Web site: every reload of the main page shows a different image and the quotes change constantly to keep the viewer's attention.

DIGITALWHIPLASH.COM

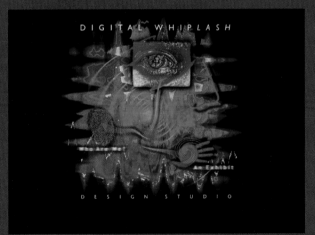

▲ Another design studio, but with a unique style (in particular when it comes to their own homepage). The coloring is unusal: bright, almost neon-like colors over black.

esign Concepts

E3DIREKTIV.COM

imes doesn't take much to
impression: the Web site of
gn company E3 Direktiv fea-
mple but very elegant intro.
phere rolls from the back to
, opens up, and four "baby"
fall out. Then one splits in
reate the four dots of the
vigational elements. Done
this animation captures the
attention every time.

ELVIS.COM

Creating a Web site for Elvis Presley would
have to be one of the toughest things to do.
For one thing, there is an abundance of material that needs to be viewed and orga-
nized, and at the same time, expectations
are high and everyone involved has their
own opinion. Long awaited by his fans, the
Elvis Presley Web site starts off with a Flash
animation as splash screen of a hip-swing-
ing Elvis. Defying convention, the main pages have the navigation on the right side (in the shape of the body of a gui-
tar). Pages further down in the hierarchy, however, switch
the navigation to the left side, which is not the best solution
in terms of information architecture.

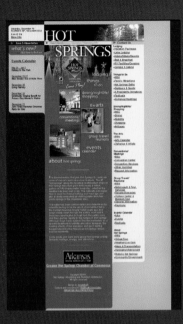

HOTSPRINGS.ORG

This site stands out because of its tasteful color combination and the use of rounded corners in the tables. HTML doesn't allow for rounded table cells, so these rounded corners are all images that were placed inside the cells to create that rounded appearance.

WWW.HYPER-ACTIVE.CO.ZA

You just have to love the funky design of this Web design agency in Cape Town, South Africa. The site features Flash and HTML versions, both nice to look at and with bold coloring. The HTML version proves once again that great design doesn't require you to pull any HTML stunts: the complexity of the HTML page comes from a large background image that uses a dimmed version of the logo. The navigational buttons are made of one transparent GIF image that uses an image map.

WWW.IDEO.COM

"It is impossible to get out of a problem by using the same kind of thinking that it took to get into the problem" says a quote from Albert Einstein on the IDEO Web site. One look at the home page and it's apparent how committed the designers at IDEO are to coming up with new ideas and solutions.

▲ The main page shows how great Web design can look despite its limitations: using just images in tables, the design makes great use of the space.

▲ The top and right screen shots show how the designer used the center space for the local navigation. The portfolio (bottom) extends the design to the right.

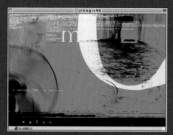

Jiong.com

Instead of just creating a portfolio, the designer Jiong Li made his art part of the Web site. If you click on the splash screen, another browser window that contains a simple horizontal frameset pops up. The icons on the bottom lead the viewer through five sections of the Web site; the background color of the frame that is hosting them always blends with the artwork in the frame above.

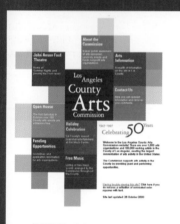

Lacountyarts.org

Color and simplicity are the keys with this Web site. Designer Linda Chiavaroli hand-coded the HTML instead of using an HTML authoring tool. To convert the text and headlines into images, she used Photoshop.

▲ If the artist Mondrian had created a Web site, it might have looked much like this. The main page consists of one large table with many cells, some of which are merged to create larger squares.

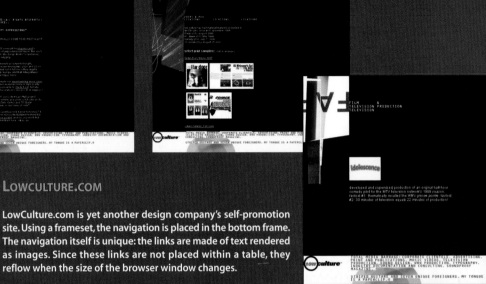

LOWCULTURE.COM

LowCulture.com is yet another design company's self-promotion site. Using a frameset, the navigation is placed in the bottom frame. The navigation itself is unique: the links are made of text rendered as images. Since these links are not placed within a table, they reflow when the size of the browser window changes.

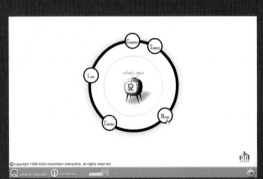

WWW.NEOSTREAM.COM

Neostream is an interactive media design agency based in Sydney, Australia. Using a combination of HTML and Flash, the site has received a couple of awards.

NETDIVER.NET

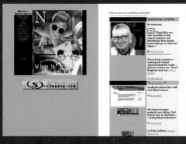

◀ Netdiver (http://netdiver.net) is a Web resource for the new media community. The most remarkable part of the site—in terms of design— is the illustration for each section.

P2OUTPUT.COM

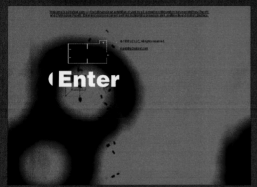

▲ This Web site looks very edgy and artsy, mostly because of the background images. These are mostly blurred and give the design some depth, but unfortunately, if you get to the level of the portfolio examples, the site loses its edge.

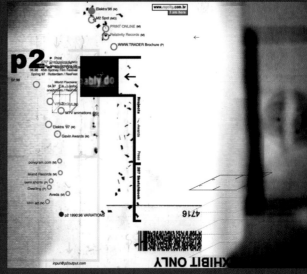

RONCHAN.COM

Chances are that you have seen this fabulous illustrator's work somewhere, either in a magazine or on a book cover. The design of his site reflects his style. The Flash intro in particular is worth watching (the animation is like the opening of a movie from the 1960s).

WWW.ANTIDOT.DE/EYESAW

The German designer Dirk Uhlenbrock is not only very talented, but also very generous. Every three months, he publishes a new issue of Eyesaw in which he gives away his font creations for free (a must-have for any designer who loves funky type). The Web site is also stunning and comes with an unusal design concept: the navigation bar is in the middle of the page (in a frameset). Clicking on one of the buttons (which represent the issues) changes the page in the top frame; the links in the top frame then control the page at the bottom. As in a children's book, this creates a great number of possible combinations. It should come as no surprise that the Art Directors Club awarded this site the Silver Medal in the Interactive Category in 1999.

▲ Stepping backward in time: each issue of Eyesaw is accessible via the navigation bar in the middle of the page. The issues are displayed in the top frame, and the bottom frame displays the content.

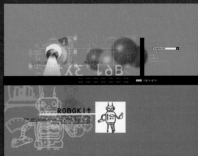

▲ Still available on the site are the old issues (with the old design). Though not as innovative in their design as the current one, they are still very inspiring.

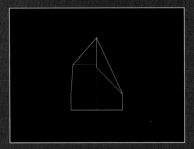

THEVOID.CO.UK

Done almost entirely in Flash, the Web site of "The Void New Media" company in the UK has received a lot of recognition for its design (Cool Site of the Year Winner, Shocked Site of the Day, Cool Homepage Site of the week). The design builds on a pill package as a metaphor and it is prescription free.

UMBRA.COM

This online store for designer stuff has two interesting features: the navigation on the left uses a little square to indicate which section the visitor is in currently. At the same time, rolling the cursor over one of the sections will reveal a submenu. When visitors choose an item, a small pop-up menu allows them to change colors (which are then displayed simultaneously).

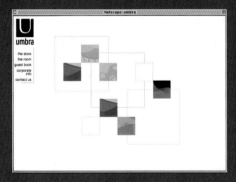

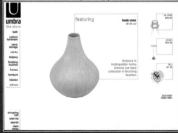

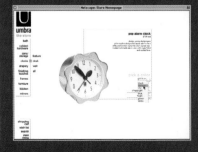

WIDESHOT.COM

Nomen est omen: wideshot.com expects users to have at least a 21-inch monitor to view the displayed artwork.

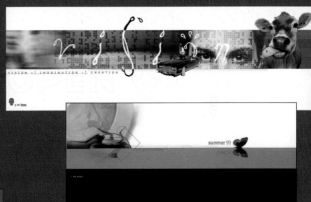

XONETIK.COM

This site is a work-in-progress, because more than half the content is still missing. Another drawback is that the navigation is not very intuitive (to fully understand it, you have to read the instructions). But these things aside, the site has many interesting ideas.

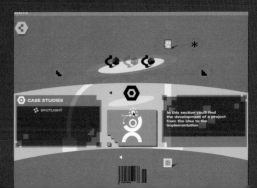

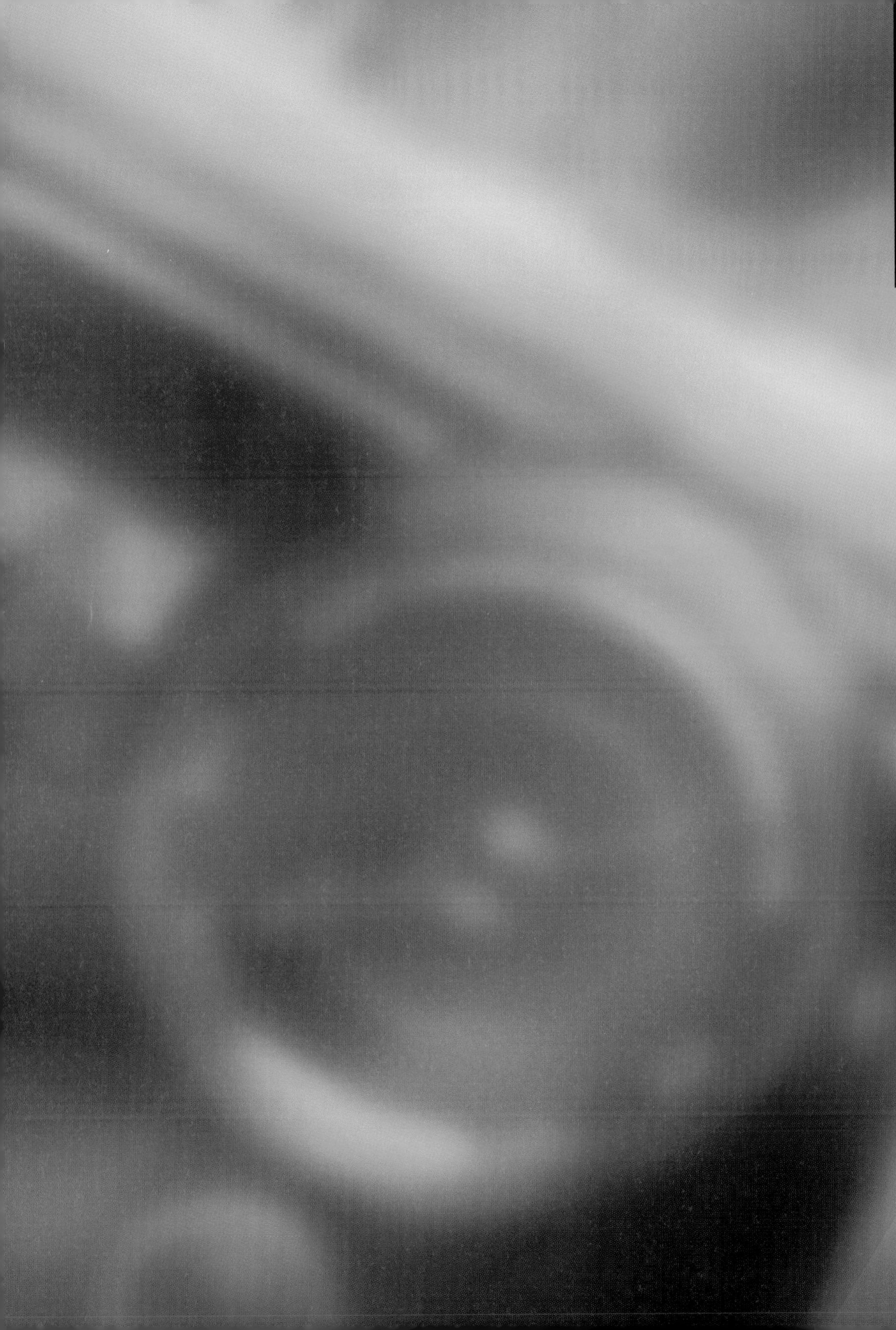

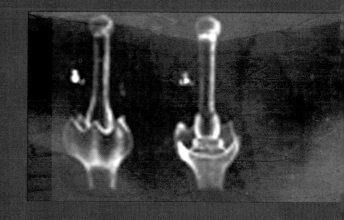

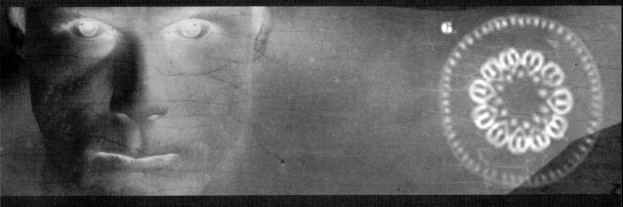

OPTIMIZING PHOTOSHOP

Optimizing Adobe Photoshop

Photoshop was originally developed for the print medium, but over the years it has become the primary tool for multimedia and Web designers as well. Because of its "print" history, not all the default settings in Photoshop are optimal for Web designers, but it takes only a couple of minutes to change this.

OPTIMIZING THE COLOR PICKER

You are probably familiar with Photoshop's Color Picker, which you can access by clicking on the colors in the tool palette. This Color Picker shows you color values of several color models at once, but choosing colors from the Web–safe Color palette used to be tedious because you had to enter the numerical RGB values. In 5.5 Adobe introduced a little enhancement that makes it easier to select only Web–safe colors: the option **Only Web Colors** will limit

▲ If you want to work with a different color picker, you can switch to Apple (or Windows) in the Preferences dialog box.

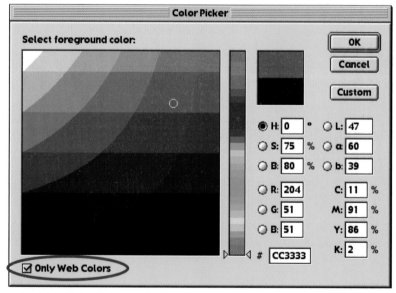

▲ The Adobe Color Picker now features an option that makes the selection of Web-safe color much easier.

the color spectrum to the 216 colors of the Web palette. Still, if you want to work with an alternative color picker, you can select **Apple** or **Windows** (depending on which platform you work in) in the **Preferences** (**File > Preferences > General**).

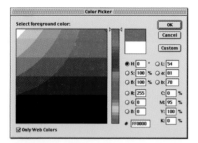
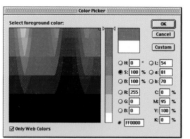
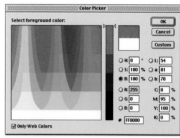
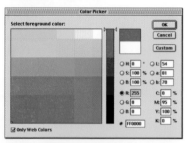
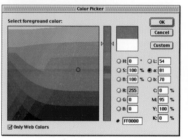
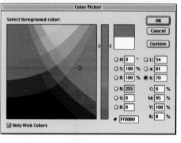
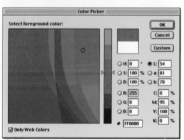
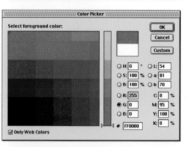
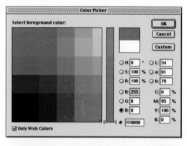

▲ The Adobe Color Picker lets you look at the colors in the spectrum from different perspectives. In the examples above, you always see the color Red, but each time with a different option: in the top row (upper left corner) the Color Picker shows Red with respect to Hue. But it can also show the color Red to Saturation (upper middle) and Brightness (upper right). In the middle row you see the color as slices of the color cube. The slider next to the Color Picker field represents the edge of the color cube. Last but not least, the bottom row shows Red in the LAB color model. The ability to change the angle on the color spectrum is very helpful when you are trying to pick color combinations.

It's very useful to know that you can change the perspective from which you look at the color spectrum—just click on one of the radio buttons next to the value fields and the spectrum in the Color Picker will change accordingly. And if you ever need to match a color on your Web site with the spot color of a company logo on printed material, for example, click on the Custom button in the Color Picker.

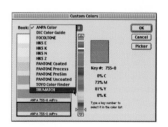

▲ You can select Pantone Colors via the Custom Color Picker.

PHOTOSHOP'S INTERPOLATION METHODS

The original 2-x-2 pixel image (left) was enlarged by 1000% using Photoshop's three interpolation methods. The effect can be seen in these three images: with Bicubic and Bilinear scaling, Photoshop introduces additional colors to smooth out the appearance of your image. Only with Nearest Neighbor does the enlarged result look like the original. ▼

Bicubic

Bilinear

Nearest Neighbor

In general, Bicubic gives you the best results—but not necessarily in every case. The top two images here compare Bilinear (on the left) and Bicubic (on the right). You can clearly see that the blurring effect is much stronger in the image scaled with Bicubic, but Bicubic also produces halo effects in images with sharp contrasts. And while Bilinear (bottom left) creates a blend between only two colors, the Bicubic method (bottom right) generates even more colors. My advice: If you are scaling up an image by a fairly large percentage, you are better off using Bilinear for all images where two solid colors are adjacent, as in this example. If you are scaling up by a smaller percentage, you probably won't even notice the difference between the two methods.

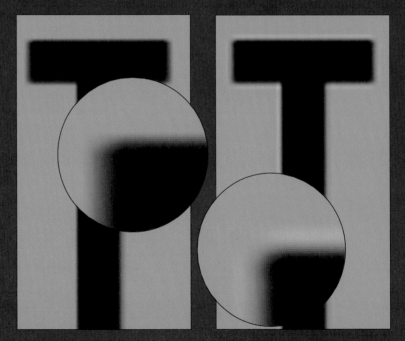

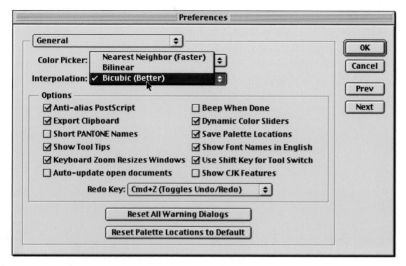

◀ There are several interpolation methods in Photoshop. Although Bicubic is the default setting, it is better to use Nearest Neighbor when creating GIF images.

▲ Avoid saving GIF or JPEGs with the regular Save As command; use the Save for Web command instead, because it automatically strips away the preview that Photoshop saves by default. Even though this preview gets stripped away automatically when you upload a GIF to the server, all your JPEGs will stay inflated. In case you do need to use the Save As command, make sure that you set the Image Preview option in File > Preferences > Save File to Never Save.

Using the Right Interpolation Method

When you scale images in Photoshop, the pixels and their colors are adjusted using one of three methods: **Bicubic**, **Bilinear** or **Nearest Neighbor**.

Photoshop defaults to the Bicubic method because it usually gives you the best result when resizing an image. In this method, Photoshop analyzes the values of adjacent pixels and calculates the middle value between them (when sampling down) or creates additional intermediate colors (when sampling up).

However, the Bicubic creation of colors may create a problem if you want to work with GIFs or colors from the Web-safe color palette. Imagine, for example, that you have created an illustration using only colors from the Web palette, but when you resize you get a lot of non-Web-safe colors at the edges that will ultimately dither on monitors with 256 colors. Moreover, these additional colors may have a dire impact on how well the image compresses. Therefore, use Bicubic only for photos that are to be saved as JPEG images. Any illustration that you plan to publish as a GIF is better resized using the Nearest Neighbor color adjustment. If you resize using the Resize command, you can select the method in the dialog box, but if you use the Layer Scale command Photoshop automatically uses the default method set in **Preferences**.

The Bilinear method works similarly to the Bicubic method, but according to the Photoshop manual it uses a simpler algorithm, and is therefore less accurate. Even though this is true, my experience has been that the Bilinear method is better for images with strong contrasts. The side effect of

▲ Photoshop automatically adds the correct file extension if Append File Extension is set to Always in Preferences. This is helpful if you plan to use the Save As command to export your images, but it is not necessary if you only plan to use the Save for Web command.

the Bicubic method is a blurrier picture, as you can see in the example with the character "T," where it creates something of an aura, while the Bilinear method creates a blend. The bottom line is that if you resize a graphic that you later want to save as GIF, use the Nearest Neighbor interpolation method so that you end up with fewer additional colors in your image. While this may seem like a minor point, it is much better to do it right in the beginning than to try to fix it later when you index the image.

RULERS IN PIXELS

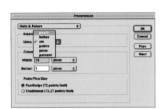

▲ **Set the ruler unit to pixel in the Preferences.**

The most important unit in Web and multimedia design is the pixel, so it makes sense to set the preference unit for **Units & Rulers** to pixels. If the ruler is not visible in your document, select **View > Show Ruler** to make it appear.

GUIDES AND GRIDS

Using guides and grids makes it much easier to slice up an image. Slicing is a common technique for exporting pieces of an image and putting them back together in a table using an HTML authoring tool. Depending on the color of your image, you might want to adjust the color of the guides and grids to make them more visible. You can do this in **File > Preferences > Guides & Grid**.

LOADING THE WEB-SAFE COLOR PALETTE

It is very important to use as many Web-safe colors as possible in your illustration, because you don't want colors to dither on monitors that display only 256 colors. Instead of typing in the color values by hand, it is easier to work with color swatches.

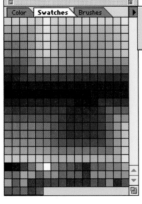

▲ Using Web–safe colors is much easier if you load them into the Swatches palette using the Load Swatches command. You can append or replace the current color swatches with several versions of the Web-safe Color palette. One is called Spectrum (see here to the left). Since the colors in the Swatches palette always adjust to the width of the palette, you may have to experiment with the width of the palette. For example, in order to see the Spectrum palette as you can see it here, the width is adjusted to 16 swatches.

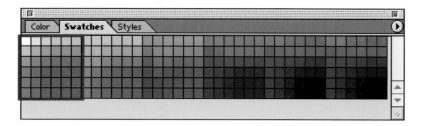

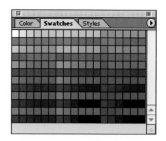

You can open the Web-safe color swatches via **Window > Color Swatches**, and then use the palette menu to replace the standard swatches (**Replace Swatches**). In the file dialog box that appears, navigate to the Presets folder in the Color Swatches folder (most of the available color swatches are already listed in this menu and you can select them directly).

To select a color from the swatches palette, simply click on it. Saving a color is as simple as clicking on an empty field; the tool switches momentarily to the paint bucket and fills the swatch with the current foreground color that is selected in the tools palette.

▲ In this example, you can see what a difference it makes to adjust the width of the Swatches palette. On the left the Web-safe Colors Swatches palette is set to a width of 36 swatches; on the right it is set to 18 swatches. While both widths give you an idea of how the colors relate to each other, the left example is clearly more intuitive. Every 6x6 pixel block represent a slice of the Web-safe color cube.

GAMMA

As you probably know, the brightness of a monitor is measured on a Gamma scale. If you have worked in desktop publishing before, this was of little concern to you. After all, the end product is paper, and all that matters is the right calibration of the monitor with respect to that. With Web design this is different; the medium is the monitor and Macs and PCs use different Gammas, which means the image you optimized for one platform may look too bright or too dark on the other. The differences in Gamma between the two platforms is roughly 10 percent (the Macintosh Gamma is 1.8 and the Windows Gamma is 2.2). As a rule of thumb, if you work on a Macintosh make your images a little brighter with **Image > Adjust > Brightness/Contrast** than you normally would; on a PC make them a little darker.

If you want to have more precise control, you can simulate how your images will look under a different Gamma. Both ImageReady and Photoshop can emulate the Gamma of Macintosh and Windows systems. In Photoshop switch in **View > Proof Setup** between Windows and Macintosh RGB. In ImageReady use **View > Preview** and choose between **Standard Macintosh Color** and **Standard Windows Color**. An alternative is to set the Gamma to 2.0 so that your images look okay on both platforms; then you won't have to flip between the Macintosh and Windows preview when adjusting the colors and the brightness of your image. To set the Gamma on a Windows computer or on a Macintosh, use the Adobe Gamma Control Panel and enter 2.0 as your

▲ If you set the Preview in ImageReady to Windows, the software dims the image's Gamma by a little more then 10% in order to simulate the appearance of the image on a Windows computer.

Photo: Paul Ehrenreich

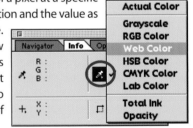

▲ Photoshop 5.x Adobe has included its own Gamma Control Panel that guides you step by step through the calibration process. If you want to optimize your images for the Web, you need to preview them with a Macintosh and a Windows Gamma, but instead of switching the Gamma in the control panel, I suggest that you use a custom Gamma value (2.0) or Photoshop's and ImageReady's Preview Option.

▲ If you work on a Macintosh, make your images a little bit brighter (around 10%) to make them look good in Windows too.

custom desired Gamma value. You can always set the value back by selecting Macintosh Default or Windows Default.

THE INFO PALETTE

The Info palette shows the color value of a pixel at a specific position of the cursor, updating the position and the value as you move the cursor with the mouse. Open the Info palette from the Window menu, then click and hold on the cross icon in the bottom-left corner, and select Pixel from the pop-up menu. The two eyedropper icons in the upper part of the palette allow you to display two different color modes (RGB and CMYK, for example). You can select the settings for these the same way as you did the units—click on the icon to display the pop-up menu with your choices. Make sure that you select the Web color mode for at least one of the displays; this shows the hexadecimal values (HTML) of a color and also—if the image is indexed—its position within the color look-up table (CLUT).

▲ In the Info palette you can switch to the Web Color model by clicking on the eye dropper icon. All colors are then displayed with the hexadecimal value.

THE ACTIONS PALETTE

The Actions palette is a kind of macro processor, and one of Photoshop's most useful tools for Web design. It allows you to record, and automatically repeat, several commands in sequence. You can even assign an action to a key, allowing you to trigger it with a single keystroke. I use this feature extensively; it makes working with Photoshop much more efficient.

ImageReady has an Actions palette that is similar to Photoshop's, but there are a couple of differences that you should know about. The most important is that ImageReady has its Droplet and Batch commands in the Actions palette's menu, while Photoshop has them in the File menu (**File > Automate**).

So what are droplets, you may ask? Droplets are little programs that can be placed on the desktop that will automatically process any images that you drag onto them. Classifying them as programs is technically incorrect, because they still require that the original program be installed; they will start ImageReady or Photoshop automatically if the application is not already open. But other than that, they are self-running and don't require a knowledge of the software. This is great if you have repetitive tasks to do; droplets are a nice alternative to the Batch Processing command. For example, if you have images that need to be resized on a Mac but they are spread out in different folders, all you need to do is to open the folders in List View, select the images that you want to process, and drag them onto the droplet icon. (Unfortunately this procedure doesn't work in Windows.) The images are opened automatically and saved in their original folders. This is a little different than the Batch Processing command, which will only process all images within a folder. Using droplets, you can perform some standard tasks directly from the

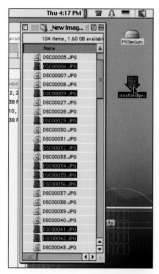

▲ Here you can see how different images in one folder are dragged onto the droplet on the desktop. Droplets have certain advantages over the Batch Processing command.

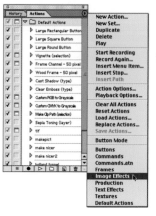

▲ ImageReady's Actions palette (above) and Photoshop's Actions palette (left) are almost identical in their functionality. However, Photoshop has its Droplet and Batch command in the File menu, while ImageReady has them in the menu of the Actions palette.

▲ When the Actions palette is in Button Mode, the actions are represented by buttons instead of folders. Here's the main difference: in Button Mode, one click is enough to start the action. You can also see the key combination that triggers the action in the Actions Options.

▲ Create your own set by clicking on the folder icon.

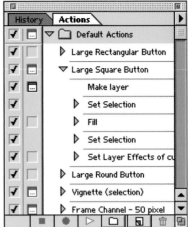

▲ You can record tasks that you need to perform over and over in the action palette; if you do this, you can even batch process an entire folder of images.

desktop without having to open up files in ImageReady or Photoshop.

Photoshop's Actions palette has a feature that ImageReady lacks: the **Button Mode**. Open the **Actions** palette from the **Window** menu in Photoshop. To switch to the **Button Mode**, click on the Palette menu (the triangle in the upper–right corner) and select this command from the options in the menu. If you would like to trigger an action with a keystroke, go back one step (deactivate the **Button Mode**) and then double-click on an action to open up the **Actions Options** dialog. Here you can set the color and the key combination for the action, which is particularly helpful when you use the Actions palette in Button Mode.

To record an action, work with the palette as if it were a tape deck using the buttons at the bottom of the palette. The red circle is for recording, the square stops the current recording, and the triangle plays back the macro. Before you start recording, click on the icon that looks like a sheet of paper to create a new action; otherwise you will record over an existing action.

➤ Toggle Dialog On/Off

When you record an action, you also record the settings in dialog boxes. To use an action flexibly for different images, it is important to be able to adjust the settings in a dialog box.

For example, if the filter Gaussian Blur is used in an action, it will probably be necessary to adjust the value for each image individually. To do this, open the action by clicking on the little arrow in the **Actions** palette and then toggle the dialog on (in the second column, next to the check switch marks). Another good example is if you copy a selection to the clipboard and then you want to paste it into a new document. Photoshop usually uses the exact dimensions of the image in the clipboard when creating the new document (which is good). But if this procedure is part of a recorded action, it will use the same dimensions that the document used when the action was recorded (which is not so good). You can avoid this by locating the New command in the action and toggling the dialog on. If you run the action again, Photoshop will open the New File dialog box, fill in the current dimensions, and wait for you to confirm them. By the way, you can also activate the modal control for all dialog boxes at once within an action. Just click next to the **Toggle dialog on/off** icon next to the action entry in the palette.

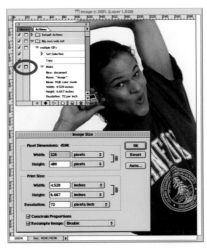

▶ Inserting Stops

If you want to create an action that allows you to make some manual changes with one of the tools, such as creating a selection with the lasso, you must insert a stop in the action. You can select this command from the **Actions** palette menu. Select the step after which you want to insert a stop, and choose **Insert Stop**. In the dialog box that appears, you can enter a comment to remind you what you are supposed to do. You will probably want to write something like "Select the part of the image that you want to copy." Later on, the action will display the dialog box with a stop button, so you can confirm the stop. Once you are done, a click on the play button in the palette to pick up where the action stopped.

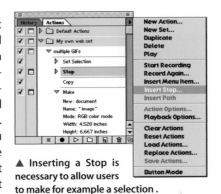

▲ Inserting a Stop is necessary to allow users to make for example a selection .

Because it might not always be necessary to make changes, you can select the **Allow Continue** option in the **Stop** dialog box. Then, in addition to the Stop button you will get a Continue button, which will save you the hassle of clicking the play button in the Actions palette.

▲ The recording button indicates that every step is recorded into the action.

◀ Sometimes when dialog boxes are recorded in an action, you may need to use the "Toggle dialog on/off" switch so that you're able to change some settings. For example, whenever this action plays, it will stop at the New command and display the dialog box to allow the user to set the image size manually. If the dialog weren't toggled on, Photoshop would always use the same image dimensions that were used originally to create this action. So using Toggle lets you use this action flexibly for images in different sizes.

▲ After you are done with the action, just click on the Stop button.

▲ Sometimes you have to include a Stop in an action, for example, to make a selection with the Lasso tool. You can type in some instructions as a reminder when you are inserting the Stop command.

➤ Recording Paths in Your Action

An alternative to alpha channels, paths are a way of creating selections. They can also be used as layer clipping paths or even when making a fill. If you create an action that requires a certain path to work with different documents, make sure that you have copied this path to the clipboard before you start recording the action. Suppose you want to create an action that builds a rounded button in a document. Start recording your action, select the path in the **Path** palette, and use the **Insert Path** command from the **Actions** palette menu (in the upper right corner of the palette). Now, when you apply the action in another document, the path will be pasted into the document.

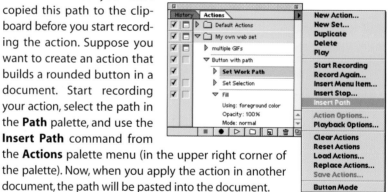

➤ Batch Processing

One of the best features of the Actions palette is the ability to apply an action to several images automatically. This is called batch processing, and it is particularly useful for Web designers, as they often have to convert several images with the same settings. To activate batch processing, first create the action that you want to apply, then choose **File > Automate > Batch**. The **Batch** dialog box displays all the sets and actions listed in the **Actions** palette. Pick the right set and action, then click on **Choose** to select the folder (for Source) containing the images you want to be processed.

The Override Action "Open" Commands option is only important if your action actually has an open command. (Note: It is usually better to open an image before you start recording an action.) If you have no embedded Open command, this option must be deactivated! I emphasize this because people often overlook it and become frustrated when batch processing displays an error alert. By the way, the same is true for the option Override Action Save In Commands in the Destination section. If you have no Save command embedded in the action, don't activate the Override option!

If batch processing doesn't work as expected, use the Log Errors to File command. This simple text file contains all the events and errors that Photoshop encounters while running the batch script, which will usually give you enough information to fix the problem.

Photoshop also comes with a set of ready-made batch-processing scripts that are all listed in **File > Automate.** One that might be particularly helpful to you is Web Photo Gallery. Just select an image folder and this script will generate a main page with all the images as thumbnails. Click on one of the images to bring you to an HTML page with an enlarged version of the image. Best of all, these pages include all the navigational elements to move parallel between the pages.

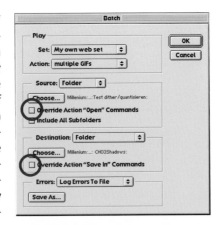

▲You might think that you're being safe by choosing the Override options regardless of whether the action contains any Open or Save commands, but this will confuse the Batch command and you'll get an error message. Only use the Override option when there is an Open or Save command. For any other errors, check the Error Log to find out where the problem lies.

▲ Web Photo Gallery is a special batch processing command that makes it easy to display a couple of images on the Internet: just choose the image folder and all the required HTML pages will be created along with the images and thumbnails.

▲ This is the result of the Web Photo Gallery command: in the bottom image you see the main page with the thumbnail images (a set of screenshots). On the top is an enlarged version of one of the images along with the navigational elements.

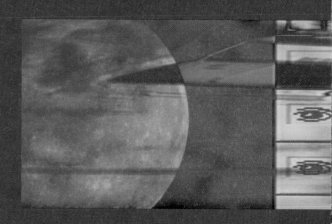

WORKING WITH WEB-SAFE COLORS

The Color Cube

Color is an essential element of most designs. While using color in print media is relatively easy and uncomplicated, this unfortunately doesn't hold true for Web design. There are numerous pitfalls in using color online: for instance, you have to be prepared to compensate for different color depths on different monitors, and color shifts between different browsers and different platforms. Problems like these make it a real challenge to get your Web site to look as fantastic as you intended. Knowing why color doesn't always equal color and how you can fix the most common problems is essential to achieving consistently great-looking designs.

COLOR DEPTH

As I've mentioned elsewhere, the most common color problems occur because different monitors offer different color depths. But what does "color depth" actually mean? To answer this question, it helps to look at how a computer stores images in memory.

Binary Code	Hexadecimal Code
0000	0
0001	1
0010	2
0011	3
0100	4
0101	5
0110	6
0111	7
1000	8
1001	9
1010	A
1011	B
1100	C
1101	D
1110	E
1111	F

➤ How Computers Store Information

All computers save information as bits. A bit is the smallest unit of data that a computer recognizes; it means either On or Off (or the mathematical equivalent: 1 or 0) All the information on your computer, from software to photographic images, is saved on the hard drive or stored in memory (RAM) in the form of bits. Because you can't do much with just one instance of on or off, a number of bits are combined to form a byte. Eight bits equal one byte, which is able to represent—in different combinations of 1 and 0—up to 16 numbers. This hexadecimal system is represented by the numbers 0 through 9 and the letters A through F.

➤ Color Depth of an Image

In order to save an image, you have to store the vertical and horizontal position of the pixels as well as their color value. Most image formats use a color depth of 24 bits (or hexadecimal FFFFFF), which allows you to represent 16,777,216 color values (256 levels for each color channel).

Not every monitor or graphics card can display so many colors, so color values may be rounded up or down (when necessary) to the closest equivalent. This causes the color displayed on the monitor to shift. Many graphics software packages try to compensate for this error by using a technique called "dithering" (see the "GIF" chapter). But dithering can't change the fact that an image that looked great on your monitor may look terrible on someone else's. The monitor dithering has no permanent effect on the image; the information in the file is still stored with 24 bits of color information, and as soon as you view the image with a graphics card that is capable of displaying all those colors, you'll see the photo in its original quality.

WEB-SAFE COLOR PALETTE

The Web-safe color palette is a collection of colors that look the same on any monitor that's capable of displaying 256 colors—basically on every computer monitor. There was a time when 16-color monitors were considered the latest in technology, but don't worry, most of those machines are safely tucked away in museums. Even so, while the latest surveys show that most home-computer users now have monitors and video boards capable of displaying at least 16-bit color (which equals 65,536 colors), quite a few monitors in the corporate world are still limited to 256 colors. If you expect most of

MONITOR COLOR DEPTH

Technically, a computer monitor can display far more than 16 million colors; it's simply a question of how much VRAM (Video RAM) is installed in the graphics card—it also depends on the video card's ability to handle more than 24-bit display. Since the human eye can't distinguish this kind of subtlety anyway, 32-bit video cards use the additional 8 bits to address a transparency channel, also known as alpha channel.

Bits	Colors
1 Bit	2
2 Bit	4
4 Bit	16
8 Bit	256
16 Bit	65,536
24 Bit	16,777,216
32 Bit	4,294,967,296

your Web site visitors to be home users, you can build images using thousands of colors, but if you expect some users to access your site from work, you should use as many colors as possible from the Web-safe color palette.

The Web-safe color palette actually consists of only 216 colors; the remaining 40 are reserved for the operating system (Windows or Mac OS). Those 216 colors are evenly divided and assigned to different shades and intensities of red, green, and blue. In addition, the palette uses a linear system in which every color value is increased or decreased by 20 percent; this was

THE UNWRAPPED COLOR CUBE
My preferred Web color chart, beginning on page 120, "un-wraps" the traditional Web color cube. On the first spread I show the shell, or outer mantle, of the cube, and the next two spreads show the inner, deeper levels of the cube. To find related colors, simply identify the colors in corresponding positions in each chart. Each color field is identified by the hexadecimal and RGB values, as well as by a Web color number (0 to 215). Since these charts were printed in CMYK, they will unfortunately differ from what you see onscreen.

done largely for convenience, since the resulting hexadecimal values (00, 33, 66, 99, CC and FF) are easy for programmers to remember. So if you want to create an element in GoLive using a Web-safe color, just use these hexadecimal values (in any combination) and you are sure to get a Web-safe color that won't dither on 256-color monitors.

The linear division of the color space means that the Web-safe color palette doesn't give you much choice if you want to create, for example, shades of brown or pink skin tones. The palette would have been much more useful if it had been modeled after the color perception of the human eye; there's no reason not to include different color values, but unfortunately this wasn't considered important enough at the time the palette was devised.

THE WEB-SAFE COLOR PALETTE SEEN AS A CUBE

You often see the Web-safe color palette presented as a cube in which red, green, and blue are placed at three opposite corners; cyan, magenta, and yellow are dropped in between those colors; and white and black take up the remaining two corners. Most books show the cube in six slices, which, in my opinion, isn't very helpful, because it's very difficult to see the relation of the colors. If you pick a color and want to find a related color, you have to locate it in another slice. Even though this isn't very difficult, it isn't natural either, and it takes up a lot of time.

I wanted to find a way of showing the relationship that each color has to its neighbor, as well as making it easy to find colors with the same quality (light, dark, pastel, and so on). While searching for this new color organization (which I did back in 1997; I published the first edition of this book in 1998), I realized that the best solution was basically to dismantle the color cube rather than slice it. This approach has many advantages: first, it shows the whole spectrum with all the colors and their relationships. Second, it is sorted by brightness and luminance, which makes it a breeze to pick, for instance, two pastel colors with the same quality. I call my analysis the Unwrapped Color Cube chart, and it begins on page 120.

▲ The Web-safe color table, shown as a cube. The eight corners of the cube are occupied as follows: Three corners show the basic colors red, green, and blue. Their complementary colors cyan, magenta and yellow are placed on opposite corners. Black and white occupy the remaining two corners.

00 FF 00	33 FF 00	66 FF 00	99 FF 00	CC FF 00	FF FF 00
00 CC 00	33 CC 00	66 CC 00	99 CC 00	CC CC 00	FF CC 00
00 99 00	33 99 00	66 99 00	99 99 00	CC 99 00	FF 99 00
00 66 00	33 66 00	66 66 00	99 66 00	CC 66 00	FF 66 00
00 33 00	33 33 00	66 33 00	99 33 00	CC 33 00	FF 33 00
00 00 00	33 00 00	66 00 00	99 00 00	CC 00 00	FF 00 00
00 FF 33	33 FF 33	66 FF 33	99 FF 33	CC FF 33	FF FF 33
00 CC 33	33 CC 33	66 CC 33	99 CC 33	CC CC 33	FF CC 33
00 99 33	33 99 33	66 99 33	99 99 33	CC 99 33	FF 99 33
00 66 33	33 66 33	66 66 33	99 66 33	CC 66 33	FF 66 33
00 33 33	33 33 33	66 33 33	99 33 33	CC 33 33	FF 33 33
00 00 33	33 00 33	66 00 33	99 00 33	CC 00 33	FF 00 33

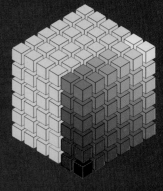

THE WEB-SAFE COLOR CUBE SHOWN IN SLICES

Choose the colors for your design from this table and enter the color values into the program. In Photoshop, you can select the Web-Safe Colors Only option in the Color Picker. You can also use the following table:

Hexadecimal	in %	in RGB
00 =	0%	0
33 =	20%	51
66 =	40%	102
99 =	60%	153
CC =	80%	204
FF =	100%	255

The hexadecimal color value "CC FF 33" translates to red = 80 percent, green = 100 percent and blue = 20 percent. In an RGB color picker, values are divided into 256 steps, so accordingly, you would need to enter red = 204, green = 255 and blue = 51.

The color fields with white outlines represent shades of gray.

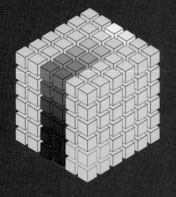

00 FF 66	33 FF 66	66 FF 66	99 FF 66	CC FF 66	FF FF 66
00 CC 66	33 CC 66	66 CC 66	99 CC 66	CC CC 66	FF CC 66
00 99 66	33 99 66	66 99 66	99 99 66	CC 99 66	FF 99 66
00 66 66	33 66 66	66 66 66	99 66 66	CC 66 66	FF 66 66
00 33 66	33 33 66	66 33 66	99 33 66	CC 33 66	FF 33 66
00 00 66	33 00 66	66 00 66	99 00 66	CC 00 66	FF 00 66
00 FF 99	33 FF 99	66 FF 99	99 FF 99	CC FF 99	FF FF 99
00 CC 99	33 CC 99	66 CC 99	99 CC 99	CC CC 99	FF CC 99
00 99 99	33 99 99	66 99 99	99 99 99	CC 99 99	FF 99 99
00 66 99	33 66 99	66 66 99	99 66 99	CC 66 99	FF 66 99
00 33 99	33 33 99	66 33 99	99 33 99	CC 33 99	FF 33 99
00 00 99	33 00 99	66 00 99	99 00 99	CC 00 99	FF 00 99

00 FF CC	33 FF CC	66 FF CC	99 FF CC	CC FF CC	FF FF CC
00 CC CC	33 CC CC	66 CC CC	99 CC CC	CC CC CC	FF CC CC
00 99 CC	33 99 CC	66 99 CC	99 99 CC	CC 99 CC	FF 99 CC
00 66 CC	33 66 CC	66 66 CC	99 66 CC	CC 66 CC	FF 66 CC
00 33 CC	33 33 CC	66 33 CC	99 33 CC	CC 33 CC	FF 33 CC
00 00 CC	33 00 CC	66 00 CC	99 00 CC	CC 00 CC	FF 00 CC
00 FF FF	33 FF FF	66 FF FF	99 FF FF	CC FF FF	FF FF FF
00 CC FF	33 CC FF	66 CC FF	99 CC FF	CC CC FF	FF CC FF
00 99 FF	33 99 FF	66 99 FF	99 99 FF	CC 99 FF	FF 99 FF
00 66 FF	33 66 FF	66 66 FF	99 66 FF	CC 66 FF	FF 66 FF
00 33 FF	33 33 FF	66 33 FF	99 33 FF	CC 33 FF	FF 33 FF
00 00 FF	33 00 FF	66 00 FF	99 00 FF	CC 00 FF	FF 00 FF

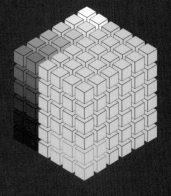

The Unwrapped Color Cube©

Here is the traditional Web-safe color cube "unwrapped." This is the first mantle of the cube, and inner mantles are on the following pages.

Hex	Value
FF FF FF	0
FF 00 33	215
00 00 00	0
FF CC CC	7
FF FF CC	1
CC FF CC	37
FF 99 99	14
FF CC 99	8
FF FF 99	2
CC FF 99	38
99 FF 99	74
99 FF CC	73
FF 66 66	21
FF 99 66	15
FF CC 66	9
FF FF 66	3
CC FF 66	39
99 FF 66	75
66 FF 66	111
66 FF 99	110
66 FF CC	109
FF 33 33	28
FF 66 33	22
FF 99 33	16
FF CC 33	10
FF FF 33	4
CC FF 33	40
99 FF 33	76
66 FF 33	112
33 FF 33	148
33 FF 66	147
33 FF 99	146
33 FF CC	145
FF 00 00	35
FF 33 00	29
FF 66 00	23
FF 99 00	17
FF CC 00	11
FF FF 00	5
CC FF 00	41
99 FF 00	77
66 FF 00	113
33 FF 00	149
00 FF 00	185
00 FF 33	184
00 FF 66	183
00 FF 99	182
00 FF CC	181
CC 00 00	71
CC 33 00	65
CC 66 00	59
FF0033	53
CC CC 00	47
99 CC 00	83
66 CC 00	119
33 CC 00	155
00 CC 00	191
00 CC 33	190
00 CC 66	189
00 CC 99	188
99 00 00	107
99 33 00	101
FF0033	95
99 99 00	89
66 99 00	125
33 99 00	161
00 99 00	197
00 99 33	196
00 99 66	195
66 00 00	143
66 33 00	137
66 66 00	131
33 66 00	167
00 66 00	203
00 66 33	202
33 00 00	179
33 33 00	173
00 33 00	209
00 00 00	215

Conversion Table

Hex	in %	R/G/B	R=MY	G=CY	B=CM
FF	100	255	100%	100%	100%
CC	80	204	80%	80%	80%
99	60	153	60%	60%	60%
66	40	102	40%	40%	40%
33	20	51	20%	20%	20%
00	00	0	00%	00%	00%

000000					00 00 00					00 00 00				
0					0					0				
CC FF FF					00 00 33					FF CC FF				
36					42					6				
99 FF FF	99 CC FF				00 00 66			CC 99 FF	FF 99 FF	FF 99 CC				
72	78				84			48	12	13				
66 FF FF	66 CC FF	66 99 FF			00 00 99		99 66 FF	CC 66 FF	FF 66 FF	FF 66 CC	FF 66 99			
108	114	120			126		114	54	18	19	20			
33 FF FF	33 CC FF	33 99 FF	33 66 FF		00 00 CC	66 33 FF	99 33 FF	CC 33 FF	FF 33 FF	FF 33 66	FF 33 99	FF 33 66		
144	150	156	162		168	144	108	60	24	25	26	27		
00 FF FF	00 CC FF	00 99 FF	00 66 FF	00 33 FF	00 00 FF	33 00 FF	66 00 FF	99 00 FF	CC 00 FF	FF 00 FF	FF 00 CC	FF 00 99	FF 00 66	FF 00 33
180	186	192	198	204	210	174	138	102	66	30	31	32	33	34
00 CC CC	00 99 CC	00 66 CC	00 33 CC		00 00 CC	33 00 CC	66 00 CC	99 00 CC	CC 00 CC	CC 00 99	CC 00 66	CC 00 33		
187	193	199	205		211	175	139	103	67	68	69	70		
00 99 99	00 66 99	00 33 99			00 00 99	33 00 99	66 00 99	99 00 99	99 00 66	99 00 33				
194	200	206			212	176	140	104	105	106				
00 66 66	00 33 66				00 00 66	33 00 66	66 00 66	66 00 33						
201	207				213	177	141	142						
00 33 33					00 00 33	33 00 33								
208					214	178								
00 00 00					00 00 00	00 00 00								
215					215	215								

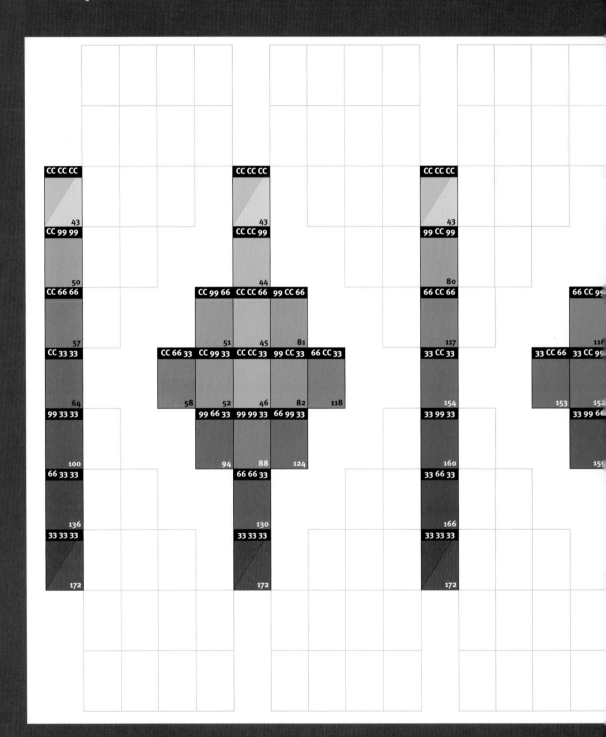

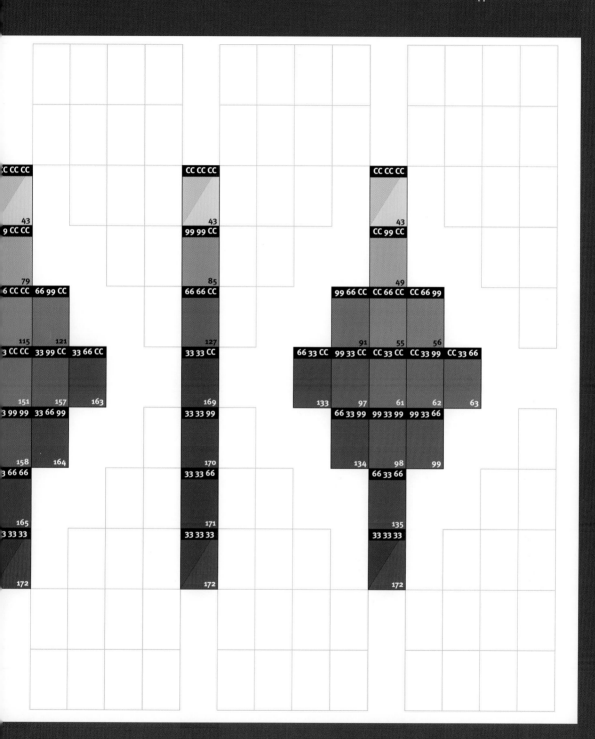

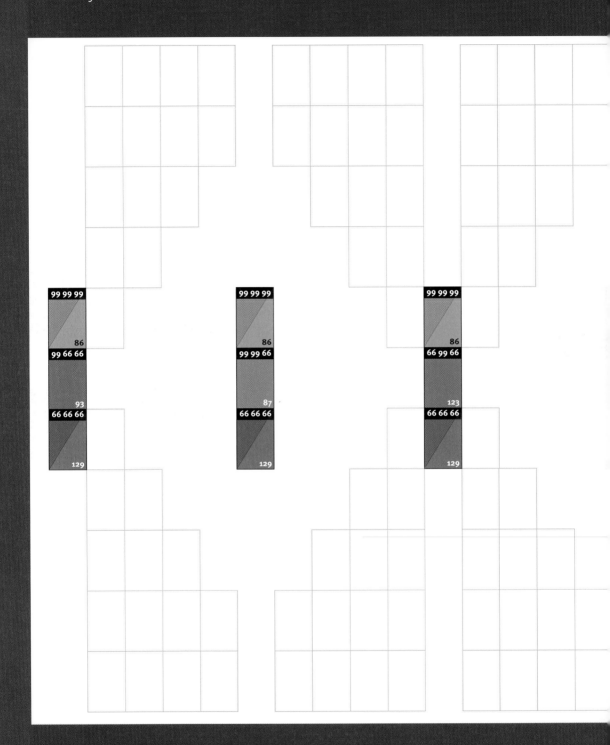

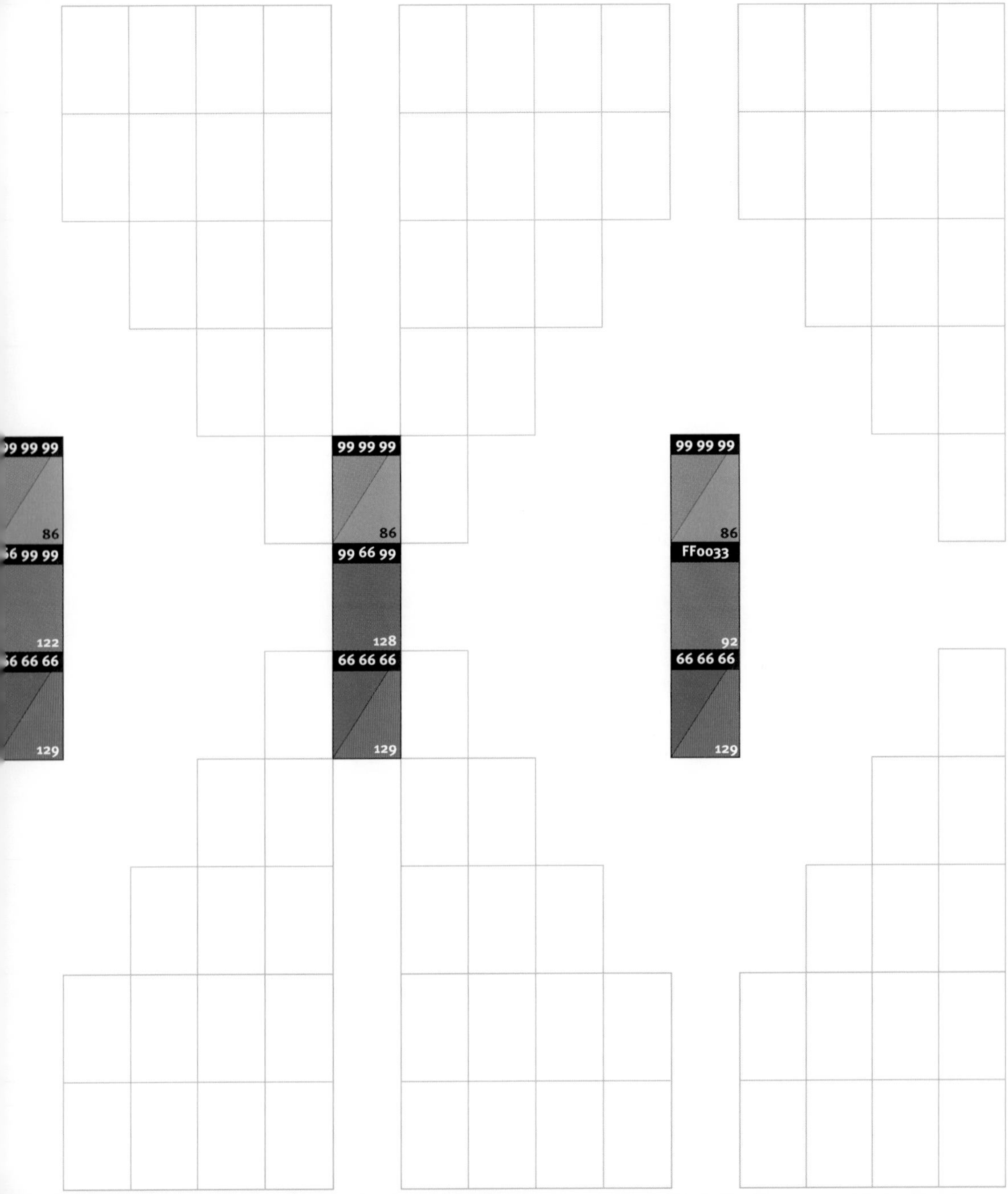

99 99 99

86

6 99 99

122

6 66 66

129

99 99 99

86

99 66 99

128

66 66 66

129

99 99 99

86

FF0033

92

66 66 66

129

WORKING WITH WEB-SAFE COLORS

When designing a Web site, it's important to work with as many Web-safe colors as possible; this will help you avoid any problems later. This is rather simple when you're designing and coloring elements, because all you need to do is use the **Web-Safe Colors Only** option in Photoshop's **Color Picker**. And if you forget to do this, you can always apply the color into the Web-safe palette when you optimize and export GIF images in the **Save for Web** dialog box. If, for some reason, you need to use a non-Web-safe color and you want to make sure that it looks good on 256-color monitors, here are a few ways to do so:

➤ Changing to a Web-Safe Color Before Exporting

If you have a solid-colored area that you want to change into a Web-safe color, use the **Paint Bucket** tool. Set the foreground color in the **Tool** palette and then click on the area you would like to fill—that's it! Well, it would be if you wanted to fill a rectangle, or any other shape that has vertical and horizontal edges. More likely, however, you'll want to fill an area with anti-aliased edges, which means that there will be intermediate colors at the edges to blend the element with the background. You can adjust those pixels, too, by checking the **Anti-Aliased** box in the **Paint Bucket Options** bar. In addition, consider whether the shape that you are filling is on its own layer (with **Transparency** at the edges) or if it is part of a layer with adjacent pixels. If it shares the layer with other pixels, set the **Tolerance** to 0 and check the **Anti-Aliased**

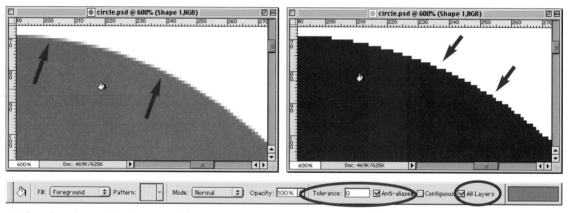

▲ When changing a solid-color area of an image with the Paint Bucket, Photoshop fills all pixels with the chosen foreground color. To fill this red circle with another color without resulting in jagged edges, you must check the appropriate boxes in the Paint Bucket Options bar. In this example, where the circle is on its own layer, you would set Tolerance to 0 and check the Anti-Aliased and All Layers boxes.

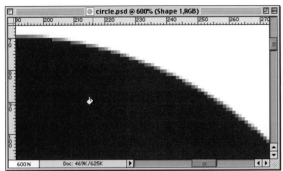 

▲ When using the Paint Bucket tool to change a solid-color area that's not on its own layer, you must also check the Anti-Aliased option (right). Otherwise, the anti-aliased pixels won't be filled, creating a jagged edge (left).

option. If the element is on its own layer, check the **All Layers** option, or Photoshop will fill the anti-aliased pixels at the edge regardless of whether or not you've selected the **Anti-Aliased** option.

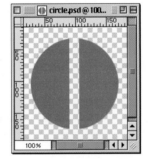

By now, you've probably noticed the **Contiguous** option and wondered what it does. The **Contiguous** option is important if the area you'd like to fill consists of elements that aren't necessarily adjacent. By selecting the **Contiguous** option, you can instruct the **Paint Bucket** tool to affect only the pixels that are adjacent, or contiguous. If the **Contiguous** option is off, the **Paint Bucket** replaces all occurrences of the target color with the foreground color, whether or not adjacent to the spot where you clicked.

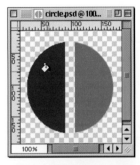

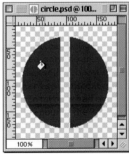

It is not always possible to use the **Paint Bucket** to change the color; sometimes there are too many areas to be changed—for example, text is rendered and every letter has to be changed individually. In that case, use the **Color Range** command from the **Select** menu. **Color Range** allows you to pick a color with the **Eyedropper** and specify a **Fuzziness** value to include colors within a certain range of the selected color. **Color Range** is a powerful command; read more about it the next chapter, "Photoshop Techniques."

Once you've made a selection with **Color Range**, use the **Edit > Fill command** and choose the foreground or background color from the **Use** pop-up menu.

▲ If you use the Paint Bucket tool with the Contiguous option checked, only the area on which you click will fill, because the two halves are discontiguous (top). To fill both half circles with a single pour of the Paint Bucket (bottom), deselect the Contiguous check box.

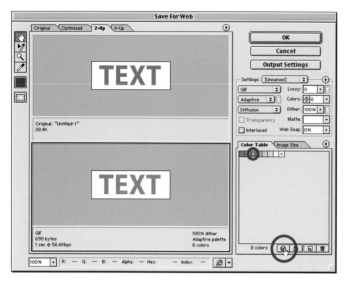

▲ Clicking on the Snap button at the bottom of the Color Table palette converts a selected color to the nearest Web-safe equivalent.

➤ Changing to a Web-Safe Color When Exporting

It's not always necessary to make a color Web-safe before you optimize it as GIF in the **Save for Web** dialog box. Since GIF works with a color look-up table, all the colors in the image are listed and you can easily convert them to Web-safe hues by selecting them and then clicking on the **Snap** button (with the cube icon) at the bottom of the **Color Table** palette. Keep in mind, however, that this is method is specifically to convert colors to the Web-safe palette. If you would like to change a color to a shade that's outside of this palette, you better use the **Paint Bucket** tool or the **Fill** command.

➤ Creating Non-Web-Safe Colors with Patterns

Wouldn't it be great if you could use a non-Web-safe color and still be sure of how it will render in different browsers? As a matter of fact, you can—thanks to a nifty little trick that involves using patterns. It's simple: by making a pattern from two or more Web-safe colors you can create the illusion of a color that's outside of the Web-safe palette. This works so well and has become such a popular trick that Photoshop and ImageReady include a filter called **DitherBox** that does this for you automatically. To understand the effect better, try the following:

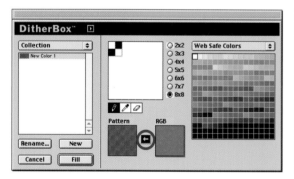

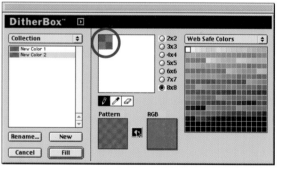

▲ Click on the RGB color field in Photoshop's DitherBox filter to open the Color Picker, where you can choose any non-Web-safe color. Then click on the arrow button to convert it to a pattern consisting of two Web-safe colors.

1. Create a new image in Photoshop with **File > New command.**

2. Choose Filter > Other > DitherBox. In the **DitherBox** dialog box, click on the RGB color field to open the **Color Picker.** Uncheck the **Only Web Colors** option, and choose the color you want to use in your image. Click **OK.**

3. Click on the left arrow next to the RGB color field, and **DitherBox** automatically generates a pattern, comprising two Web-safe colors, that simulates your non-Web-safe color. Pretty cool. You can preview it in the **Pattern** color field, and see the two individual pixels in the dither pattern grid.

4. To edit patterns, use the **Pencil** tool to choose Web-safe colors from the swatches on the right side of the dialog box; click in the pattern grid to apply it to a pixel. You can adjust the grid from 2x2 to 8x8 pixels, applying as many Web-safe colors as you want. Experiment with checkerboard patterns and stripes, and with contrasting and complimentary colors. In most cases, a 2x2 pattern is enough; patterns shouldn't be overly complicated.

5. To name a pattern, double-click on its default name (such as New Color 1) or click the **Rename** button. If you create multiple patterns, they're saved as a "collection." To delete a pattern, select its name and press **Delete** on your keyboard; if you choose **Delete** from the **Collections** pop-up menu, you will delete all of the patterns you've created.

After applying the pattern fill to the image, you can zoom in to see it clearly. Keep in mind that if you intend to use the image as a tiled background for an HTML page, the dimensions of the image must be even multiples of the fill pattern; otherwise you'll end up with noticeable edges when the image is repeated in the browser. Also, you can apply a **DitherBox** pattern to a particular area in your image by selecting it with a marquee tool or the **Color Range** command, and then choosing **DitherBox.**

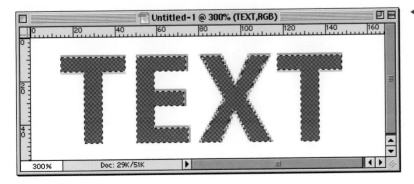

◀ This text was selected with the Color Range command and filled with a DitherBox pattern.

Photoshop Techniques

Photoshop Techniques

Many designers these days start out by designing their Web sites in Photoshop to present their ideas. Only after the client has approved the plan does the designer actually build the site with an HTML authoring tool such as Go-Live. This process makes a lot of sense, since it is much easier to create and change a design in Photoshop than in HTML. Also, thanks to their low 72-dpi resolution, those Photoshop files stay relatively small and manageable even if you use plenty of layers.

In this chapter you will learn all the basic techniques you'll need to create a Web site quickly and efficiently in Photoshop. For example, I'll cover how to work with the Layers palette and how to use guides to split up an image into smaller pieces. The next chapter will focus on creating some of the fancier design elements.

HOW LARGE SHOULD YOUR CANVAS BE?

When you design a site, you should have a clear idea of who your target audience is going to be and what kind of equipment they will be using. For instance, since not everyone has a 21-inch monitor, it doesn't make much sense to create a design that requires that kind of viewing space. Many Web design

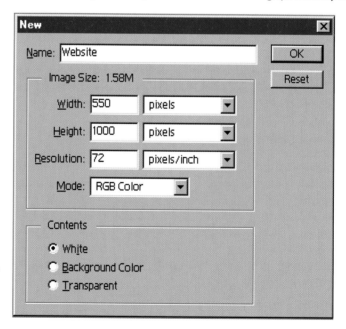

When creating a new document via File > New, it is important to consider the monitor size of low–end computers. ▶

books recommend designing for 14-inch monitors running at 640 x 480 resolution, but this can be very limiting. Recent surveys show that most computer users these days have fifteen- or seventeen-inch monitors running at
800 x 600 resolution; however, there is a growing user base for WebTV, which
uses fairly low resolution. You'll have to decide if you want to play it safe and
go for 640 x 480 or take a chance on using a higher resolution. You can always
split the difference and base your design on 640 x 600. This way, the width of
your design won't force users with smaller screen to scroll left and right to
view the entire page.

Select **File > New** (Command-N/Ctrl-N) to create a new Photoshop document. Designate 72 dpi as the resolution, and anything between 640 and 800
pixels for width. Since it's easy for people to scroll down in a browser, you are,
of course, free to use any length that you like, but it's a good idea to keep the
main visual elements within 340 vertical pixels. That's the area that everyone
will be able to see, even on the tiniest screen with all the browser's navigational toolbars displayed.

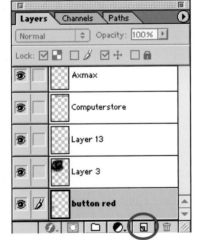

▲ As a reminder of how much of
the Web site can be seen on
smaller monitors, a horizontal
guide is placed at approximately
350 pixels. When designing the
site, you should place the main
and key elements in the top part.

Working with the Layers Palette

The Layers palette is one of the most
important tools in Photoshop; if you're
not already familiar with it, you should
start by reading the Photoshop manual. Working with layers is essential for
Web design. To get you started, here
are some basics:

► The Layers Palette Quick
Guide: Opening the Palette

You can open the Layers palette via
Window > Show Layers. When you
start a new document, you will usually
see only one layer (the background layer), but as soon as you paste something

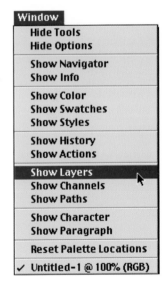

▲ Open the Layers palette from
the Window menu. Just click on
the Create New Layer button to
create a new layer.

from the Clipboard into your new document, it becomes an additional layer.
You can easily see this, as each layer usually has its own icon, which helps you to
find various elements. You can also use the **Layers** pop-up menu, accessed from
the triangle in the upper-right corner of the palette, to create new layers. A third
way to create a layer is by clicking on the **Create New Layer** button at the bottom of the palette. Regardless of how you create layers, they all work the same.

▲ You can group several layers by clicking in the second column in the Layers palette. The Chain icon shows which layers are linked together. When selecting a layer and moving it, the grouped layers will behave like the one in the right-hand picture.

➤ Making Layers Visible/Invisible

You can hide a layer or make it visible by clicking on the **Eye** icon next to the layer listing.

➤ Moving Layers

You can arrange your layers using the Move tool in the upper-right corner of the Tools palette. First activate the layer in the **Layers** palette, then select the **Move** tool, click on the image, and drag the layer to the desired position in the palette. It's just as easy to move several layers at once so they keep their relative position. Click in the second column of the **Layers** palette (next to the **Eye** icon), and a **Chain** icon should appear. Now the layer is linked to the currently selected layer and you can treat the two layers as a group.

By the way, if a new layer is larger than your background layer (the material you've pasted into the document has larger pixel-by-pixel dimensions than the document you're pasting into) it won't get truncated if you move it outside the working area. Even if you flatten multiple layers to one layer, they will keep the measurements of the largest one. You may want to crop some of your layers to save on memory and disk space. Use the **Crop** tool to select the entire image, then double-click inside the rectangle and all your layers

THE LAYERS PALETTE: OPACITY AND BLENDING MODES

A layer's opacity defines how well you can see through it. You can enter a value directly, or click and hold on the arrow to use a slider. ▶

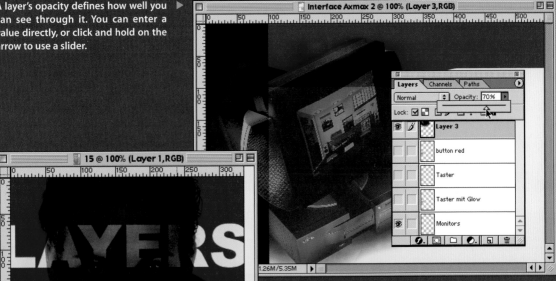

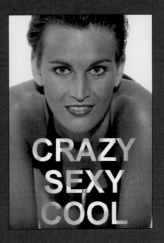

◀ Select from a variety of blending modes: Dissolve, Multiply, Screen, Overlay, Soft Light, Hard Light, Color Dodge, Color Burn, Darken, Lighten, Difference, Exclusion, Hue, Saturation, Color and Luminosity. Multiply is useful for combining the color values of one layer with the layers beneath, as you can see in the example on the left. Difference (see below) is great for photo compositions, while Screen is helpful for getting black text on white to take on the colors of the background. For instance, if you have a black and white layer and use Screen, the black areas will reveal the underlying layers while the white parts will cover them. Photoshop's online help has excellent definitions of the different modes, but only experimentation and trial-and-error will help you understand how they work on real images.

will be cropped. Be careful, however, because you don't want to accidentally truncate a layer that you want to keep intact. In this case use the **Rectangular Marquee** tool instead—activate the layer you want to crop, then select the portion of it you want to keep. Invert the selection via **Select > Inverse**, and press **Delete** to remove the unwanted area. Since you can't go outside the image area with the **Select** tool, you may have to move a layer with the **Move** tool to delete parts that are hidden.

➤ Blending Modes and Opacity

Layers can have an opacity level of anywhere from 1 to 100 percent. You can use the **Opacity** slider in the **Layers** palette to select how much you can see lower layers through the current layer. In addition, you can combine layers using one of several mathematical algorithms, such as Multiply, Overlay or Soft Light.

➤ Layer Masks

Sometimes you only want to make part of a layer transparent—this is where you can use layer masks. To add a layer mask to a layer, select the layer and either choose **Layer > Add Layer Mask > Reveal All,** or click on the **Add Layer Mask** button in the **Layers** palette (the second from left). A new (white) area should appear next to the layer thumbnail in the palette. You will see a chain symbol between the icons, which works just the same as it does with layers. Click on the symbol to group or ungroup the layer mask and the layer.

After you've added a layer mask, ▶
a white or black area (depending
on whether you chose Reveal all
or Hide all) is visible next to the
layer preview. You can then use
the Airbrush tool to change the
transparency of the layer mask.

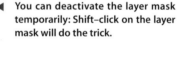

▲ The black areas in the layer mask reveal the background. To make sure that you paint with the Airbrush inside the layer mask, click on the Layer Mask Preview.

◄ You can deactivate the layer mask temporarily: Shift–click on the layer mask will do the trick.

◄ If you want to see just the layer mask, press Alt/Option and click on the Layer Mask icon in the Layers palette.

To make part of your layer transparent, select the **Airbrush** tool (or any other appropriate tool), click on the layer mask icon in the palette (it should acquire a heavier border and the color fields in the **Tool** palette should switch to black and white) and start painting onto the layer mask. To see any effect, you have to use the right color: Black represents 100 percent transparency; if

Photo: Paul Ehrenreich

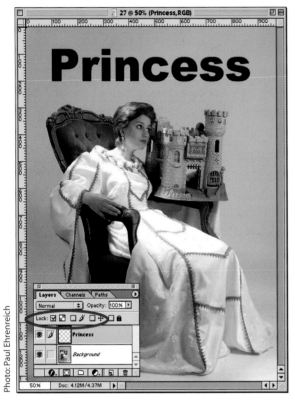

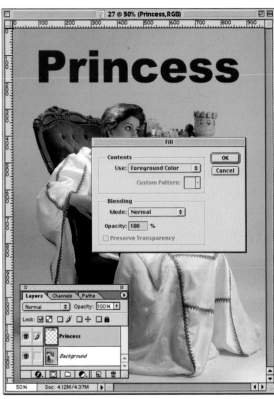

▲ You can fill a layer (in this example a converted text layer) using Layer > Fill. It's important to have the Lock Transparent Pixel option checked in the Layers palette; otherwise the entire layer would be filled.

If you forgot to check the Lock Transparent Pixel box, the whole layer will be filled. In that case, just use Undo and try again. ▶

you want to make parts of your image transparent, be sure you select black when painting. The inverse is also true: if some parts of the layer are too transparent, you can use white to make them more visible. By the way, you can view the layer mask by clicking on the icon in the palette while pressing the **Option** key. This can come in handy when placing text in the layer mask.

➤ Transparency

For many design tasks that involve layers, you may want to leave the transparent parts out. To make sure the transparent area is not affected by any filter or command, select the **Lock Transparent Pixel** option in the palette and everything that is completely transparent will be protected. Take, for instance, the common task of changing the color of an area with the **Fill** command: if the **Preserve Transparency** option is not selected, the **Fill** command will fill the whole layer, but if it is selected, it will fill the whole layer including any anti-aliased edges.

➤ Adjustment Layers

Photoshop has a great feature that can help you adjust and manipulate images and layers without permanently affecting the image. This feature, called adjustment layers, lets you apply color adjustments such as a Brightness/Contrast change to one or more layers, but you can turn it on and off at any time. This form of "undo" gives you great power and flexibility; you can even apply a layer mask effect via an adjustment layer. To give you an idea of how to use adjustment layers, try the following:

◀ There are two ways to create an adjustment layer: one is through the Layer menu, the other is by clicking on the Create New Adjustment Layer button at the bottom of the Layers palette (left image), which pops up a list of blending modes. Clicking on the Eye icon in the Layer palette will deactivate the Adjustment Layer (right image).

▲ This dialog box is only visible if you've selected New Adjustment Layer from the menu.

◀ The adjustment layer also has a layer mask that can be manipulated using a tool such as the Airbrush tool. This gives you precise control over where and how much adjustment you get. In this example, the background of the photo is blacked out so the Brightness/Contrast Adjustment Layer is only affecting the person in the photo.

1. In the Layers palette, select a layer in an image file; the adjustment layer will be inserted above the currently selected layer and will affect all layers beneath.

2. Choose Layer > New Adjustment Layer, and choose from the submenu of available commands, or click the **Create New Adjustment Layer** button at the bottom of the **Layers** palette. If you go through the menu, you'll first be able to name the layer and choose a blending mode and opacity, and then you can make your color adjustment.

3. You can modify the opacity level and the blending mode of an adjustment layer at any time in the **Layers** palette, or paint into a layer mask to apply an adjustment to a selected area.

➤ **Selecting Layers**

If you work with the Layers palette frequently, sooner or later you will find it tedious to have to select a layer in the palette before you can move and drag it. This process is not very intuitive, especially if you have used a graphics program like Adobe Illustrator where you can simply click on an object to make it active.

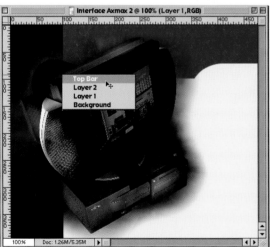

▲ With the Move tool activated, clicking inside the document window while holding the Control key (Mac) or the right mouse button (Window) displays a pop-up menu from which you can select one of the layers directly.

Well, you won't find the same convenience in Photoshop, but you will find something that comes close: select the **Move** tool, hold down the **Command** button (**Control** on PCs), and click on the object you want to move. (Or, check **Auto Select Layer** in the **Move Tool** options bar and you won't have to hold down a key to do this.) Photoshop will automatically select the layer of the object and the currently activated layer will be displayed at the top of the document window.

Sometimes there are just too many layers on top of one another, which makes it hard for you (and for Photoshop) to be clear about which layer you want. In this case select the **Move** tool, right-click (Windows) or Control-click (Mac OS) in the image, and choose the layer you want from the floating context-sensitive menu that appears; in this case, it's a list that identifies all of the layers that contain pixels under the current pointer location. Contextsensitive menus are available for almost all Photoshop tools. If you're using the Pencil or Paintbrush tool, for example, you can Control- or right-click to select a different brush shape and size, as well as select a blending mode.

➤ **Layer Thumbnail**

There are different thumbnails available in the Layers palette; to switch between them, select **Layers Palette Options** from the palette's pop-up menu. You can select one of three thumbnail sizes or you can turn off the thumbnail altogether.

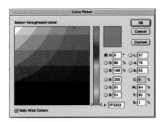

▲ **Layer Palette Options lets you choose the size of the layer thumbnail.**

CHANGING COLORS

One of the most common tasks you'll have to perform when designing Web pages is changing the color of an object. The easiest way to do this for a solid-colored area on a layer is to use the **Lock Transparent Pixels** box in the **Layers** palette. A typical scenario would be when you realize that a button is not using a Web-safe color and that it dithers too much on low-end monitors. So now you want to change its color to the closest color in the Web-safe color palette—here's what you do:

1. **Activate the layer** that contains the object you want to color. Make sure the **Lock Transparent Pixels** option is selected.

2. **Pick up the color** of the object that you want to change by clicking on it with the **Eyedropper** tool (it now becomes the foreground color in the **Tool** palette). Double-click on the color field in the **Tool** palette to open the Color

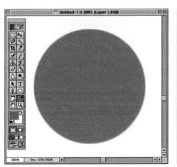

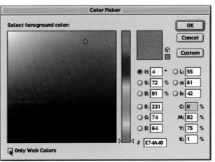

▲ **After activating the Only Web Colors option, the current color will be shifted.**

The Paint Bucket tool was used to fill the area. It's important to activate the Anti-Alias option in the options bar. ▶

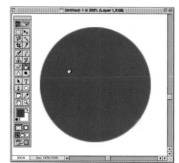

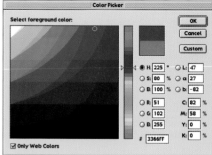

In the mock–up of the Axmax Web site, several paper clips were used as navigational elements. The basis for all these paper clips was a single photo of a blue paper clip that was modified using the Replace Color command.

Using Hue and Saturation, the former blue color can be changed to any other color in the spectrum. ▼

Picker and change the color to the closest Web-safe color by checking the **Only Web-Safe Colors** box.

3. Choose the **Paint Bucket** tool. If the options bar is not showing, open it and you will see a parameter for **Tolerance, Contiguous** and **Anti-Alias.** If the **Tolerance** is set to zero, only the pixels with the same color will be filled. Checking **Contiguous** restricts the fill to areas connected to the chosen pixel clicked.

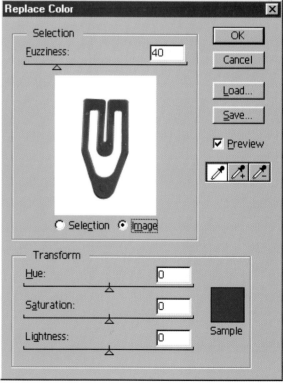

The most important option for this example (changing the color of a button) is **Anti-Alias**: checking it ensures that intermediate colors at the edges will be filled, and this is the default setting. When you've specified your options, click inside the object whose color you want to change.

➤ Changing the Color of an Object

If you come from the world of desktop publishing, this technique may be completely new to you since you seldom need to change colors in a photo intended for print. But if you do Web design, this trick can save you the cost of an entire photo shoot since it lets you reuse one element of a photo over and over again. For example, imagine that you want to use paper clips in different colors as navigational elements. One way to do this would be to get these paper clips and do a photo shoot, but it is also possible (and more affordable) to use one paper clip from a stock art photo CD and change its color. Here how you would do this:

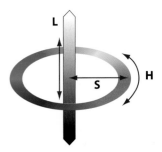

▲ This graph shows how the Replace Color command works: the Hue slider rotates the colors within the spectrum, the Saturation slider represents the movement toward the center, and the Lightness slider changes the colors along the vertical axis.

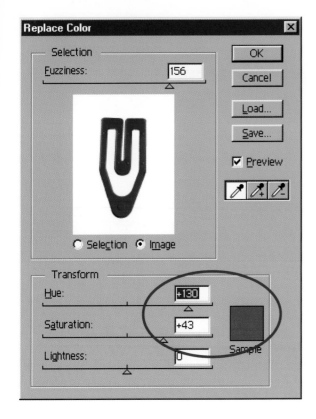

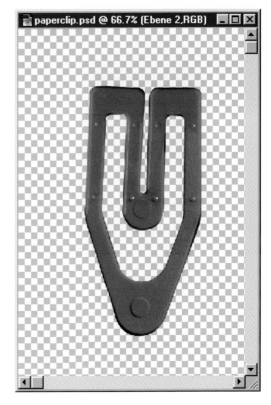

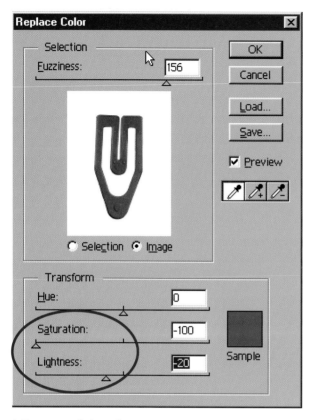

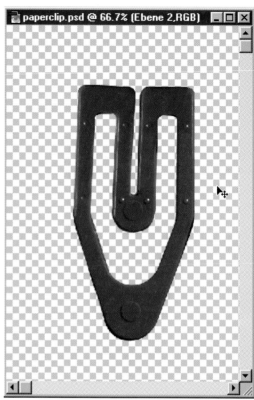

▲ To create variations of gray, reduce the Saturation to zero and
then use the Lightness slider for
various shades of gray.

1. To change the color of an object such as the paper clip, choose **Image >
Adjust > Replace Color**. Select the **Preview** option on the **Replace Color**
dialog box.

2. Using the Eyedropper tool, select a hue that is between the darkest and
lightest color value of the object. Then use the **Fuzziness** slider to adjust the
tolerance (in this case it was changed to 160). You can select additional colors by
using the **Eyedropper** tool with the plus sign until the entire object is selected.

3. Once all the colors in the paper clip are selected, use the **Hue** slider to
shift through the color spectrum. If the preview is activated, you can see how
the changes affect your original image. To get white and black including various levels of gray, use the **Saturation** slider and set it to -100. You can then
set the level of gray with the **Lightness** slider.

Photo: Paul Ehrenreich

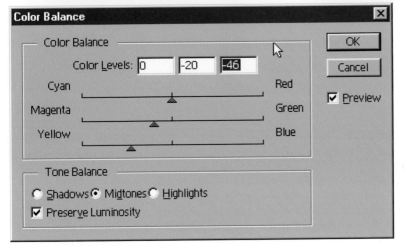

Color Balance

Color Balance

Color Levels: 0   -20   -46

Cyan ——————————————— Red

Magenta ——————————————— Green

Yellow ——————————————— Blue

OK

Cancel

☑ Preview

Tone Balance

○ Shadows ◉ Midtones ○ Highlights

☑ Preserve Luminosity

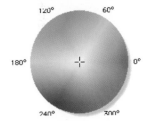

▲ This color wheel shows how color balance works. Cyan and red are on opposite sides of the spectrum, as are magenta and green, and yellow and blue. Use the sliders to move between the poles. For example, to correct an image containing too much blue, you would move the bottom slider to the left.

CORRECTING COLORS

One of the standard tasks in Photoshop is color-correcting photos. This is particularly important if the photo wasn't shot in a professional studio. Often, those images suffer from a shift in colors due to variations in lighting conditions. Daylight, for instance, brings out different color frequencies than neon light, and you have to correct those color differences in Photoshop.

Photoshop offers two commands aimed at color correction: Color Balance and Variations. Both do exactly the same thing, but their approaches and interfaces are different. The Color Balance command (**Image > Adjust > Color Balance**) allows you to change the color via three sliders, while in the

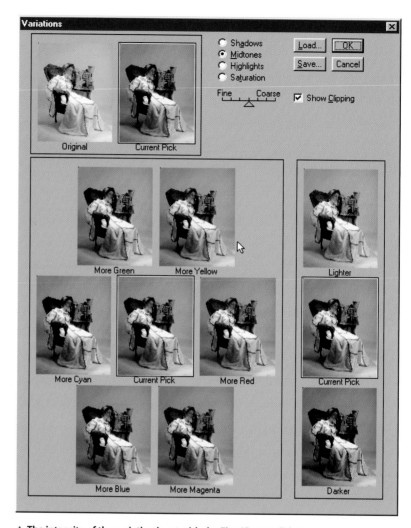

▲ The intensity of the variation is set with the Fine/Coarse slider.

Variations command (**Image > Adjust > Variations**), you work with a pre-view in which you see several variations of the same image and select the one you like the best. Both functions shift the image color toward the value on the opposite side of the color wheel, so to correct a red tone in your image you would add more cyan, to compensate for too much green you would shift toward magenta, and to correct for blue you would add yellow.

Even though the Variations command seems more intuitive, you can actu-ally get a more precise result by using Color Balance, because it lets you set the value for each color between 0 and 100. The Variations dialog box, however, forces you to choose one of only six possible alternatives. The only tricky part of using Color Balance is deciding which color needs to be shifted, but once you have determined that, making the actual correction is simple: just move the appropriate color slider in the correct direction. (For instance, if the image has too much yellow, the move the Yellow/Blue slider toward blue.)

If you are using the **Variations** command to correct colors, adjust the **Fine/Coarse** slider until one of the previews is the right color; click on it, and it becomes the new **Current Pick**, with new variations around it.

The Hue/Saturation dialog box offers you direct visual control of the Hue slider. In the bottom image you can see how much the spectrum has shifted. ▼

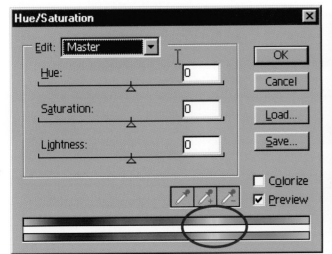

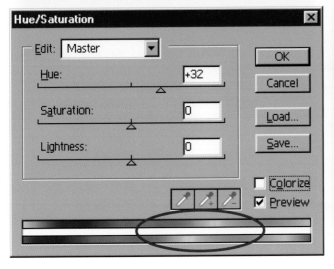

With Hue/Saturation, you can also shift and correct only certain parts of the spectrum. In this example, all the red tones were shifted.

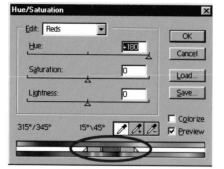

▲ The original image (top) was modified twice with the Hue/Saturation command.

Another great tool for color correction is the **Hue/Saturation** command (**Image > Adjust > Hue/Saturation**). The two color bars at the bottom of the dialog box help you to understand what you are doing because they show the color spectrum and how it is changed (which you can see in the color bar below). Using the **Hue** slider, you can rotate the color wheel so that the **Saturation** slider that controls the movement towards the center of the color wheel while the **Lightness** slider controls the L-Axis.

Consider using **Selective Color** as an additional tool for making color corrections. Although it's generally used for correcting colors for printing, you can use it for RGB images, too. The main advantage is that it allows you to correct

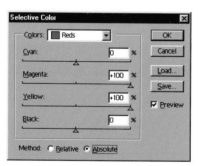

◀ Desktop publishers might find it easier to do color corrections in CMYK. You can do this with the Selective Color command.

The red color of the chair was changed and made brighter using the Selective Color command. ▼

the image by using the process colors cyan, magenta, yellow, and black. Most designers who come from desktop publishing are more familiar with defining colors this way, so using this command can make life a little bit easier.

AVOIDING HALOS

In order to create lines and edges that are not perfectly vertical or horizontal, Photoshop employs an approximation based on the available resolution. To get the best result, many programs—including Photoshop—use a technique called anti-aliasing, in which pixels at the edges of an object are smoothed to blend with the background.

The intermediate colors that anti-aliasing creates are only a problem if you are planning to use transparency with a GIF. If the image is viewed on a browser in front of the same color as the transparency color, you won't have a problem. But if you change the background in the browser at some point, your image may show a halo at the edges. Fortunately, Photoshop offers you a great way of dealing with this problem. Here's an example that you are very likely to run into: rendering a headline as an image.

▲ If you select Anti-Alias in the options bar, the edges will be smoothed. When the image is later exported as a GIF with transparency, this can become a problem, since the extra colors at the edge become visible.

To make sure the text image displays correctly in the browser and blends perfectly into the background, it is important that before you render the text, you use a background color that's as close as possible to the one on your Web page. To accomplish this, follow this procedure:

1. Create a new document and choose **White** or the **Background Color** as its contents. Select a foreground color (which is going to be the font color), and click on the working area with the **Text** tool. Photoshop will automatically create a new layer. Choose a font and size in the **Text** options bar and choose one of the anti-aliasing options.

2. Since you want the background to be transparent, hide the background layer by toggling off its visibility in the **Layers** palette. A checkerboard pattern signals that the background is now transparent. Choose **Save for Web** from the **File** menu and click on the **Optimized** tab in the **Save for Web** dialog box. Set the format to GIF, and make sure that the **Transparency** option is selected (it is automatically preselected). Select a color in the **Matte** pop-up menu: choose between **Eyedropper Color** (the color in the upper-left corner of the dialog box), **Black**, **White**, and **Other**. If you select **Other**, the Photoshop **Color Picker** will appear, you can select your color, and Photoshop will anti-alias the edges with this color.

▲ The red of the background was selected as a transparency color, which will make the anti-aliased edge visible.

After the text is placed with the Anti-Alias option activated, hide the background layer by clicking on the Eye icon in the Layers palette.

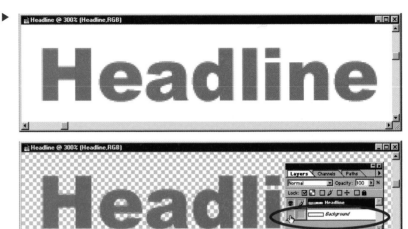

▲ Select Transparency and choose the background color from the Matte pop-up menu: the text will then be anti-aliased towards that color.

3. Click OK. The **File Selector** dialog box appears, giving you the option of saving your image along with an HTML file (click on **Options** and choose the appropriate settings). You can use this file to check the result in a browser. Save in HTML, then open the file in Netscape Navigator or Microsoft Internet Explorer to see how your text looks in front of the background color you selected.

Vector Graphics: Using Illustrator with Photoshop

▲ An invisible frame the same size as the target image will allow you to preserve the absolute position of elements when you paste them into Photoshop.

With the release of version 6.0, Photoshop's ability to work with vectors has greatly improved: with the introduction of layer clipping paths it is now possible to place vector graphics on their own layer. Now that it has the new vector tools, Photoshop is well-equipped to handle most of your needs. For more complex vector graphics or some special effects (such as creating text along a path), you still have to use Illustrator, but Adobe has done a remarkable job of making both programs work together.

◄ Photoshop can't draw text along a path, but you can easily do this in Illustrator, then copy and paste it into Photoshop.

➤ Importing Vector Graphics

There are basically three choices when importing vector graphics from Illustrator: they can be imported as pixels, paths, or shape layers. However, these choices are only available if you use the Clipboard to copy and paste the element, which requires that you have Illustrator installed on your computer. If you don't, you can only convert the Illustrator file by opening it in Photoshop. Photoshop can open native Illustrator files (they don't need to be in any special format); just use the **Open** command and look for the file on your hard drive. The **Rasterize** dialog box will appear, letting you enter the resolution and dimensions (the values that are already filled in are the current values of the document, but you can scale an illustration simply by entering new dimensions). Rasterizing an Illustrator graphic in Photoshop—rather then rasterizing and exporting it from Illustrator—has the advantage that transparent areas stay that way (when converting them in Illustrator they are rendered to white).

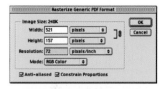

▲ When opening an Illustrator file, Photoshop rasterizes it. Changing the Resolution has no effect on the size at which the illustration is later displayed. To scale an illustration during import, change its dimensions.

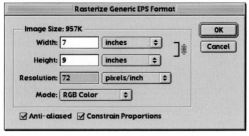

▲ You can even use elements and designs created in a layout program like QuarkXPress or Adobe InDesign and import them into Photoshop. Just save the page as an EPS and open the file in Photoshop.

Rasterizing an EPS: Most graphics programs let you save image files in an editable EPS format, thus making it possible to have illustrations generated in one graphics program easily transferable to another. In most cases you will find this option listed in the Save dialog box or as an Export command. Photoshop can even interpret an EPS file that was created in QuarkXPress, although it doesn't always work and you may end up with unexpected results, especially if the layout includes both images and text.

➤ The Right Size

Enlarging an image in Photoshop compromises its quality, so you should design your graphics to work in 1:1 scale. Because one point is equal to one pixel in Photoshop, it's a good idea to choose points as the general units in

▲Use points as your unit in Illustrator—every point will translate to one pixel when you're importing an element into Photoshop.

▲ In Illustrator, hold down Alt/Option and click in the work area to bring up a dialog box in which you can enter the dimensions of an element.

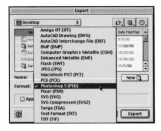

▲ To open an Illustrator file in Photoshop with its original layers intact, export it from Illustrator as a Photoshop file format, and be sure to choose Write Layers in the Opotions bar.

Illustrator. You'll find these settings in Illustrator in **Edit > Preferences > Units & Undo.** If you'd rather specify something in points, you can always enter "pt" when you create an object using a dialog box. (Press **Alt/Option** and click with the tool inside the work area. Illustrator will display a dialog box for numerical entry.) This way, an object created in points in Illustrator will have the same size in pixels when brought into Photoshop.

➤ **Preserving the Layers**

It is possible to export an Illustrator file as a Photoshop file with its layers intact using the Export command, although you'll lose all of your blending modes and have to reconstruct them in Photoshop. (Before Illustrator 8.0, getting multiple layers into Photoshop was a hassle and it either had to be done layer by layer or you had to have MetaCreations Painter 5.) In the **Export** dialog box, select the Photoshop format from the pop-up menu and name the file. In the Photoshop **Options** dialog box that appears, set the resolution to 72 dpi and check the **Write Layers** box.

▲ The original image was shot inside a store with no flash; it is therefore underexposed and contains a lot of digital grain.

FIXING DIGITAL PHOTOGRAPHS

While pictures captured by digital cameras usually don't suit the high-resolution requirements of print publishing, they are more than sufficient for Web design—and for Web designers who don't have the budget for photo shoots, digital cameras are essential. They also free designers from copyright issues involved with stock photo CDs, which are not always royalty-free and sometimes have restrictions for online publishing. So it's no wonder that the digital camera industry is booming and that mid-range cameras have become quite affordable.

The biggest problem with digital cameras is that the CCDs (which capture the image) create a digital grain when the shot is not well lit. If you downscale the image and save it as JPEG, this might not be much of an issue, and using the Hue/Saturation and Levels commands may be enough to fix the image. But if the image is used as a background, you have to salvage the picture with a regimen of blurring, sharpening, and blending (this trick was developed by Deke McClelland, author of *The Macworld Photoshop Bible 2.5*), as follows:

1. Adjusting the Levels: Almost every picture taken with a digital camera needs some adjusting, and balancing the brightness and contrast of an image is best done with the **Levels** command. The **Levels** dialog box displays a histogram of the image1s highlights and shadows. Click on the **Auto** button to automatically redistribute the black and white values proportionally between the extremes, or use the black-and-white triangle to do this manually. The most important option is the middle slider, which lets you change the gamma value by moving it to the left to bring out the midtones.

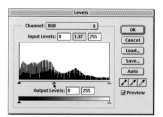

2. Saturating the colors: Digital camera CCDs take pictures with an 8-bit blue channel, an 8-bit green channel, and an 8-bit red channel, which are combined to form a 24-bit full color image. Every picture made with a digital camera can use some adjustment with the **Hue/Saturation** command, and now that the colors are washed out through the application of the **Levels** command, it is time to do some magic. But because we are also trying to fix the graininess, we will do a little more then just increase the **Saturation.** First make a copy of the layer by dragging the layer onto the **Page** icon at the bottom of the **Layers** palette. (Alternatively, select everything with **Select > Select All**, copy it with **Edit > Copy** and paste it with **Edit > Paste**.) Now use **Image > Adjust > Hue/Saturation** and increase the Saturation up to the point where the grain looks really extreme (which happens when the slider is moved to 60-80 percent).

▲ After using Levels, copy the layer for all further steps.

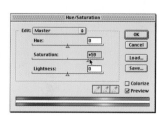

 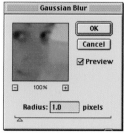 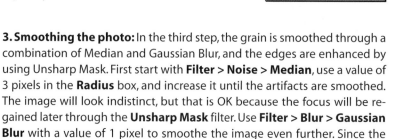

▲ These are the filters (and values) that were used on the copied layer.

▲ Before all the filters are applied to the copied layer, increase the Saturation to around 70.

3. Smoothing the photo: In the third step, the grain is smoothed through a combination of Median and Gaussian Blur, and the edges are enhanced by using Unsharp Mask. First start with **Filter > Noise > Median**, use a value of 3 pixels in the **Radius** box, and increase it until the artifacts are smoothed. The image will look indistinct, but that is OK because the focus will be regained later through the **Unsharp Mask** filter. Use **Filter > Blur > Gaussian Blur** with a value of 1 pixel to smoothe the image even further. Since the edges are now completely softened, it is time to regain some of the edges by

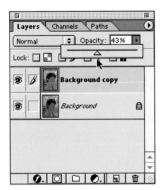

using **Filter > Sharpen > Unsharp Mask** and a value of 500 percent. This exaggerated value is necessary to compensate for the extensive blurring (the **Radius** needs to be set to the same value that was used in the **Gaussian Blur** filter.) The result will undoubtedly look different from what you had expected, but that will change when you blend the two layers.

4. Blending layers and finishing touches: Now lower the **Opacity** level of the **Background Copy** to blend the two layers. The actual opacity can be

▲ The last step is to blend the copied layer with the background layer. This smoothes out the digital grain, and after merging both layers, the image is ready for further editing. To get the result seen on the right, the image was run through the Levels command again and partially smoothed with the Mask Filter.

as low as 5 percent (or even less) if the original photo was already in a pretty good shape. Problem-prone images require higher **Opacity** levels, but should not exceed 50 percent. It is easy to get carried away and end up with an image that looks artifical, but the goal is to get a natural looking image that doesn't show its digital origin. Flatten the layers at the end and apply color and focus adjustments as you would if this image came from a film source.

As usual, there is more then just one solution to any problem. My way of getting rid of the digital grain works a bit differently (and works on some images with really bad color shifts): I use three copies of the layer, increase the **Saturation** for them and rotate the **Hue** by +120°/-120°. Together with the

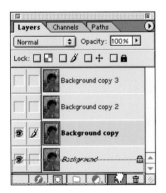

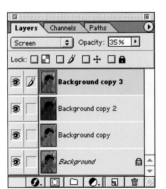

layer mode **Screen,** I use the **Opacity** slider to adjust the colors. This has the side-effect that the image will also get lighter, which makes this procedure ideal for all images that are underexposed. Here's how this works:

1. Make three copies of the **Background** layer by dragging the layer onto the **Page** icon. Hide all but the first copied layer by clicking on the **Eye** icons.

▲ A different technique to get rid of digital grain uses three copies of the background layer. For two of the layers, the Hue is shifted by 120° and then blended with the background.

2. Use Image > Adjust > Hue/Saturation for the first **Layer** copy. Use the value 120° for the **Hue,** which will shift all the colors towards green. Then boost the colors by entering a **Saturation** value of 20–40, depending how strong the artifacts are in the picture, and confirm with OK. (The lower the value, the better your ability to make subtle corrections, which is what we are aiming for here. In this tutorial I used a value of 20). Use **Screen** as a **Layer Mode** and gradually decrease the value with the Opacity slider until the green artifacts in the image have disappeared. Repeat the same procedure for the second copy of the layer, but this time set the **Hue** value to -120, which shifts the colors towards blue. (Again, increase the **Saturation** and then use **Screen** as your **Layer Mode**.) For the third copy of the **Layer**, leave the **Hue** value as is and only increase the **Saturation**: with this layer you can control the brightness of your image.

3. Use a Hue/Satuaration Adjustment layer to regain some of the **Saturation** that the image might have lost. By now, the image by now should have improved substantially enough that you can flatten it. Another little tip: If you want to smoothe the image even further (like the skin tones in this example), make a copy of this flattened layer and use the **Median** filter and then the **Unsharp Mask** filter (with 500 percent **Sharpening** and the same **Radius** that you used on the **Median** filter). Now create a **Layer Mask** for this layer and paint a black foreground color in it with the **Airbrush** tool to mask all the important parts (like the edges of the body or the details in the back of this picture).

This technique comes close to the result that you could get if you used the Curves command. Curves has the big advantage that it can be applied as an adjustment layer, meaning that you can easily disable the effect later or change the settings, all without having to deal with three copied layers. If you want to give this a try, open the image and select **Curves** from the **Create Adjustment Layer** button at the bottom of the **Layers** palette. Switch from RGB to the individual channels and adjust the curve by adding new points and dragging them to new positions. It takes some experimenting to find the best settings, but since you will probably have images from the same digital camera, you may find a

◀ It is important that the two layers are shifted by 120° in opposite directions

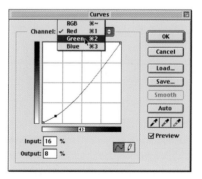

▲ The before/after image shows how effective this method is: the skin looks natural again.

◀ The simplest technique for compensating for some of the digital grain is to use the Curves command and set the curves individually for each channel.

setting that works for most of the images. Record this in an **Action** so that you can fix your images in the future with one mouse click.

OPTIMIZING IMAGES

Except for navigational elements such as buttons, most images on the Web are photos. Preparing photos for the Web requires different skills from those required to prepare them for printing. Compression, which is not an issue in desktop publishing, becomes a main focus in designing for the Web—along with differences in gamma and brightness on various computer monitors. Simply saving a photo in JPEG format is not enough to make it Web ready.

➤ Eliminating Noise and Scratches

One of the first steps in preparing a photo for the Web, regardless of whether it will be saved as a GIF or a JPEG, is to get rid of noise and scratches. Print is much more forgiving of small imperfections than a monitor is—plus these flaws can actually have an impact on compression. For big scratches, you will probably have to make corrections manually with the Rubber Stamp tool, but smaller problems can be corrected with some of Photoshop's filters.

➤ Removing Noise

Noise in a photo can come from imperfections in the film itself, or from a bad scanner. It can have an impact when you save a GIF (depending on your settings) or a JPEG. The rule of thumb is the less noise you have, the better compression you will achieve.

Photoshop provides not one but three filters designed to reduce noise. Each one employs a slightly different approach; you shouldn't select one arbitrarily.

The **Despeckle** filter reduces noise by blurring the image subtly while preserving areas with strong contrasts. In other words, Despeckle blurs only those pixels with minor differences in color, so contours don't become fuzzy. Unlike the standard **Blur** filter, which affects everything in the photo (making it look out of focus), when you use **Despeckle,** the photo doesn't lose too much quality. It's great for small amounts of noise, but if the contrast of the noise is very high (for example, if there was dust on the photo you scanned) you may not get the result you want. For smoothing gradations or blended color areas in an image with strong contrasts, the **Despeckle** filter is the way to go. You can apply it more than once until you get the desired blurring effect.

REMOVING DUST AND SCRATCHES

Here are a couple examples ▶ of how a photo with dust and scratches can be repaired. In the original photo (on the left) there are very heavy scratches that were treated with the Despeckle filter. Even though they have almost vanished, you still can see parts of the scratches (right). In cases like this try using the other filters that are mentioned here.

Photo: Paul Ehrenreich

With the Median filter you ▶ can achieve quite impressive results. As you can see in this example all scratches were eliminated with almost no traces.

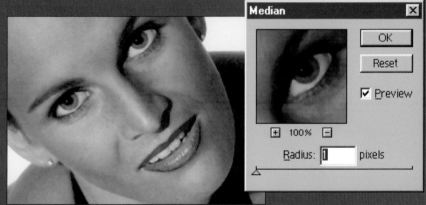

The Dust & Scratches filter ▶ lets you use the Radius slider to define what will be treated as dust. The Threshold slider adjusts the filter's sensitivity to contrast and Saturation changes. One side effect of this filter is that it blurs the image; to avoid a serious loss of quality, use this filter on selected parts of the image.

▲ With Unsharp Mask you can bring even very blurry photos back into focus.

The **Median** filter adjusts the brightness of adjacent pixels by interpolating their color values while disregarding all the values beyond a certain threshold. It works a lot like the **Despeckle** filter, except that **Median** interpolates while **Despeckle** blurs. You use a slider to select the range of pixels that you want Photoshop to interpolate; it's best to stay between one and three pixels. Since a GIF compresses more efficiently if several pixels on a horizontal row have the same color value, this filter can be particularly handy if you are preparing GIFs.

The **Dust & Scratches** filter lets you designate the size of the dust and scratches that you want to eliminate by using the **Radius** slider. If you set the slider to 1 pixel, only 1-pixel scratches will be corrected; all larger scratches will be ignored. Use the **Threshold** slider to define the degree of contrast that Photoshop should use to distinguish a scratch.

Sometimes the situation is the other way around: noise isn't a problem, but the images lack pep and contrast. Most Photoshop beginners make the mistake of using the **Brightness/Contrast** function found on the **Image > Adjust** menu, but this is only one of the many options you can use to enhance your image—and it's usually not the best one. Here's a list of tools and functions you can use to enhance dull images.

➤ Brightness/Contrast

The **Brightness/Contrast** command allows you to adjust these two parameters. Because everyone is familiar with these effects from their TV, there isn't much to add, except that before you go for Brightness/Contrast, you ought to try the **Levels** command. It often yields better results.

➤ Levels

When you select the **Levels** command (**Image > Adjust > Levels**), Photoshop creates a histogram of the image. That means it looks at each pixel's brightness value and presents this information in a graph. This makes it easy for you to see the kinds of visual information in your image, but more importantly, Levels lets you extend the tonal range of the image. If the majority of your image's tonal values are in the range of 20 percent to 80 percent, you can expand those values to the full range of zero to 100 percent, which will instantly give your image much more contrast and detail. To stretch the histogram of an image to the maximum amount, simply adjust the black and white **Input Levels** triangles to the left and right of the histogram. Click **OK,** and the shadows and highlights will be adjusted. The slider triangle in the

CORRECTING IMAGES WITH LEVELS

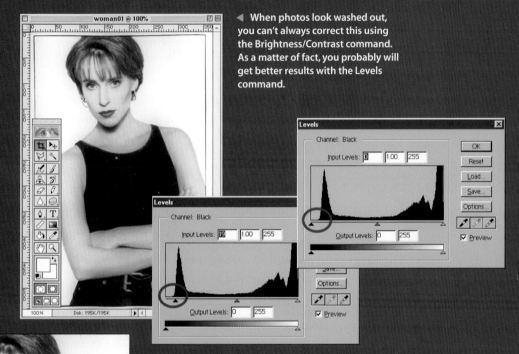

◀ When photos look washed out, you can't always correct this using the Brightness/Contrast command. As a matter of fact, you probably will get better results with the Levels command.

▲ To adjust the tonal range of your image, move the black point and white point sliders to the edges of the histogram (in this example only the black point slider needed to be adjusted). You can also move the grey slider for a non-linear adjustment.

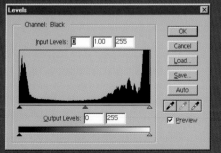

◀ Click OK, then reopen the Levels dialog box to see the results of the adjustment. Now the colors use the full range of 256 levels.

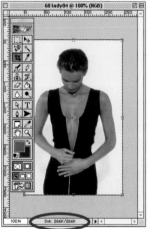

▲ Sometimes the most effective compression tool is the Crop tool. Select the important parts of the photo with the Crop tool and then double–click inside the frame.

middle sets the value for 50 percent, meaning it will indicate the middle of the tonal range. Checking the **Preview** box lets you see the effect of the sliders interactively. Once you click **OK**, call up **Levels** again to see how the tonal range has been stretched.

➤ Unsharp Mask

A soft focus is a common problem with photographic images. Photoshop provides a set of filters to enhance sharpness; they are all gathered in the **Filters** menu under **Sharpen**. The most useful filter in this collection is **Unsharp Mask,** which lets you set the precise amount, radius, and threshold for sharpness enhancement. As with **Levels**, you can watch the effect of adjusting these parameters if you check the **Preview box.** If you plan to save the image as a JPEG, you should use this effect sparingly because JPEG's compression algorithm actually works best on slightly blurry images.

CHANGING THE IMAGE SIZE

One of the tasks that you will need to perform frequently is to scaling or cropping images (or entire designs). The command for changing the image size is **Image > Image Size, and** it is pretty straightforward: the dialog box displays the width and height of your work area, and you can change its dimensions simply by entering new values (make sure the units are set to pixels). To the right, you'll see a chain icon that indicates which parameters are linked, depending on whether you have selected **Constrain Proportions** and/or **Resample Image** at the bottom of the dialog box.

Constrain Proportions ensures that if the width is changed, the height changes accordingly (and vice versa). Unless you plan on intentionally distorting the image, perhaps as a special effect, this option should always be checked. The **Resample Image** option ensures that Photoshop resamples the image if you make any changes in its resolution. You can choose **Nearest Neighbor**, **Bilinear**, or **Bicubic**. For photos, you'll probably want **Bicubic**.

The **Image Size** dialog box also displays a value for resolution. Ideally, this value should be set to the screen resolution of 72 dpi, but this is more or less a cosmetic task. To a browser or HTML-authoring program it makes no difference whether the resolution of an image is set to 72, 85, or 255 dpi. To the browser, a pixel is a pixel—it will always display the real size of the image. I mention this because it is different from desktop publishing, and a lot of designers who come from that field ask this question.

Most often you will want to resize an image by a certain percentage. Instead of doing this by calculating pixels or inches, use the **Units** pop-up menu to change units to percent. Now enter the percent reduction you want. For best results, use values like 25 percent, 50 percent, 200 percent, etc.

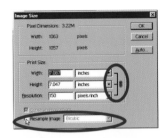

➤ Changing the Size of a Layer

If all you want to do is to change the size of one layer, use **Edit > Free Transform**, which you not only scale the layer but also rotate and skew it. To scale a layer, move one of the corners or side handles (for proportional scaling, hold the **Shift** key). You can rotate the layer by bringing the mouse close to the frame (not the handles), and when the mouse cursor becomes a bent arrow, click and rotate the layer. Skew a layer by pressing **Command** (**Ctrl** in Windows) and dragging one of the corners. To finish the task, double-click inside the frame.

▲ If the Resample Image option is deactivated, all three image parameters—width, height, and resolution—are interdependent.

➤ Changing the Canvas Size

Changing the canvas size is another important function of Photoshop; this allows you to add or remove space around an image. To enlarge the canvas size, simply enter the new width or height in the **Canvas Size** dialog box (**Image > Canvas Size**) and choose where you want that space to be added by clicking on the squares. The selected square indicates where on the enlarged canvas the original image will be placed. For example, if you change the width of the canvas and select the leftmost square, the original image will go on the left and the additional pixels will be added to the right of the image.

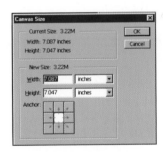

You can use the same technique to crop your canvas size: simply reduce the number of pixels listed under width or height and click **OK**. Alternatively, you can use the **Crop** tool in the **Tool** palette, but the **Canvas Size** command has the advantage of letting you crop the image to a specific dimension by entering a numerical value. You can also enter a specific dimension with the **Crop** tool, but personally I find that a cumbersome—you have to enter the dimension in the options bar and then select the area in your document. Using the **Crop** tool is helpful if the cropped area is asymmetrical, but most of the time all you need is to crop a little space on one side or the other. In my opinion, the **Canvas Size** command is the easiest way to do that.

▲ You can easily add pixels or subtract pixels from the canvas with the Canvas Size command.

You can download the files for this tutorial (and the others in this book) at www.mitomediabooks.com.

If you're interested in seeing the final result, check out www.basilio.org.

The photos were taken by Tom Behrens.

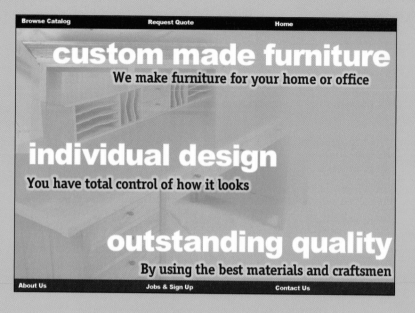

TUTORIAL: CREATING A PHOTO COMPOSITION

Many Web site designs are a combination of one or more photos and graphical elements. In this tutorial I'll show you some of the basic techniques for working with layers and layer masks to create such photo compositions.

If you paste the images into the new document, they will be placed on a new layer automatically. If you use the Free Transformation command, the layers are scaled and arranged.

1. Create a new document that is 630x440 pixels. The design is compact, almost like a CD-ROM interface, because the Web site doesn't have much content to display, and what content there is will later appear in a frame.

The photo composition consists of four images.

2. The background is composed of four images. You can import the images for the photo composition simply by opening the images, selecting everything (**Select > Select All**), and copying to the Clipboard. When it's pasted into a new document, the image will automatically be placed on a new layer. Since all the images are too big, they need to be scaled and placed with **Edit > Free Transform**.

3. You'll need to use layer masks to blend the four layers into each other. To create a layer mask for an activated layer, use the **Layer > Add Layer Mask > Reveal All** command. Then use the **Airbrush** and a black foreground color to paint the areas of the layer mask that should blend with the layer below.

▲ Blend the layers using layer masks.

4. Using blending modes, you'll blend the four layers with the background layer, but first you need to fill the background layer with a color—#FF9933, a bright orange—by clicking on the foreground color in the **Tool** palette and selecting it in the **Color Picker**. Select the background layer and fill it with the **Paint Bucket** tool. Then select all the other layers and change the blending mode to **Overlay** (only the layer with the desk is set to **Darken**). Now, all the layers blend together with the orange background. You can adjust their overall opacity using the **Opacity** slider in the **Layers** palette. It might be necessary to do some more work on other layer masks, because now areas that were covered by the layer above might be visible. The background is basically finished. To organize the layers, create a new layer set by clicking on the folder icon at the bottom of the **Layers** palette. Drag all the layers into this folder.

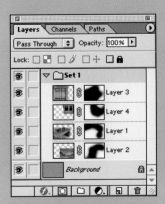

▲ After all the layer masks are in place, change the blending mode to Overlay (and Darken for the layer with the desk).

5. Lastly, you'll create the text layers and buttons. For the text layers, use the **Text** tool and click on the document. Some of the text layers use the **Outer Glow** effect so that they'll stand out more. Create the navigation buttons at the top and the bottom by drawing the shapes on their own layer with the **Rectangle** tool (the blue color is #333366, the brown #660000).

In the final Web site, the text was animated with GoLive's **Timeline Editor**. If you want to experiment with this feature, you can take advantage of a new command that GoLive offers: **Import Photoshop as Layers**. To do this, save a copy of the file, delete all the unnecessary layers (the buttons, for example), and flatten the images with the background color. GoLive will place each of the text layers in a new layer automatically, so that they're ready to be animated.

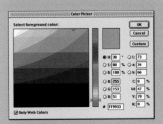

▲ The background layer is filled with orange.

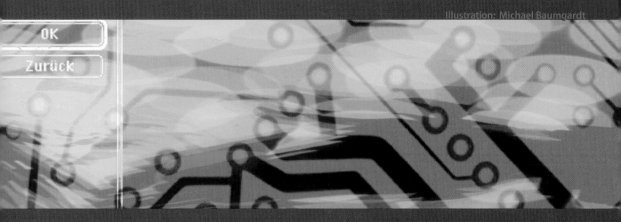

Illustration: Michael Baumgardt

DESIGNING WEB ELEMENTS

Most of the Web sites these days come in four flavors:

- minimalist and text-based, such as search engines like Yahoo or Excite

- underground design with an edgy, experimental look, www.jiong.com

- extremely graphical, where pages are based on colored tables, such as www.cgdesign.com

- rich and opulent, with a lot of depth, such as www.carnegiehall.org

Designing Web Elements

Jean-Paul Sartre once said history could be viewed as if one were looking out the back of a moving car: all the nearby scenery is a blur that starts to come into focus somewhere down the road. Learning to design a Web page is similar: at the beginning you may have only a vague idea of what is possible and how to realize it in this medium. But the more you explore the Web and look at what other designers have done (and study how they did it), the more your own vision will manifest itself.

This chapter explains some common Web design techniques, such as creating backgrounds and navigational elements. While it may be tempting to use some of the techniques or effects here just for the sake of it, that can backfire. If you look at well-designed Web sites (a great starting point for that is www.coolhomepages.com), you will see that very few use such gimmicks as 3D buttons. So use the techniques here sparingly and don't get carried away.

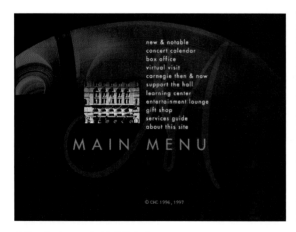

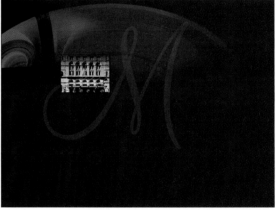

▲ For the Carnegie Hall Web site, Andreas Lindström used a background image (right) and placed text and images on top of it.

CREATING BACKGROUNDS

One very popular HTML function involves filling the background of a Web page with a pattern or image. A lot of Web sites use this trick in one form or other, and it is part of the standard repertoire for any Web designer.

➤ Background Images

Andreas Lindström, who created the Web site for Carnegie Hall, has his own special way of using backgrounds in his designs. He likes to use dimmed

MONITOR SIZES AND THEIR RESOLUTIONS (WIDTH X HEIGHT)				
14"	**15"**	**16"/17"**	**19"**	**21"**
640x480	800x600 (SuperVGA)	832x624 (Mac) 1024x768 (Win)	1152x870 (Mac) 1152x864 (Win)	1280x1024

Since the 4.x browsers interpret cascading style sheets (which let you repeat a background only once), it is safe to use this technique. However, it is not a bad idea to check how your Web site looks without the background because you never know how your site is going to be accessed (WebTV, for example, is limited in what it can display.)

images that blend with the background color, combining them with smaller images in the foreground. This creates an interesting dynamic and lends depth to the site.

There is a catch to using the background function, however. Since the background image is repeated in the browser by default, the same image will display again when the viewer scrolls down or to the right. From the chart, you can see that you may need to make your background image 1280 pixels wide and at least 1024 pixels high to ensure that users with larger monitors don't see the repetition. However, because this creates a lot of unnecessary overhead, many designers limit their background images to 800 pixels in width or, even better, they use cascading style sheets. Since cascading style sheets can limit the number of repetitions for a background image, the image doesn't have to be very large. If you wanted to have just a small image in the upper left corner that fades into the background color of the browser, you could use cascading style sheets to reformat the BODY tag and have the background image be repeated only once. Instead of creating a 800 x 800 pixel image, you would only need a 200 x 200 pixel image, a savings of over 93 percent (see "Image Inflation," page 288).

▲ The Jazz Central Station Web site (www.jazzcentralstation.com) uses a sidebar background as the main design element. A dimmed logo in the main area creates a certain richness and depth when it is later combined with the content.

If you intend to use a large image as background, you most likely have to dim the image somewhat, otherwise any text that is placed over it will not be legible. To dim an image, use the **Opacity** slider in the **Layers** palette in Photoshop. This requires that the image be on its own layer. If that is not the case, select the background layer with **Select > Select All**, then cut it with **Edit > Cut** (the background layer will be filled automatically with the background color of the **Tools** palette), and paste it with **Edit > Paste**. Photoshop will insert the **Clipboard** on its own layer, and then using the **Opacity** slider, you can dim the image.

Dimming alone will not guarantee that the background color and the image will blend together enough to make the text on top of it legible. If you are looking for alternative methods or something that you can use in addition, try applying a blending mode to the layer: **Multiply, Soft Light,**

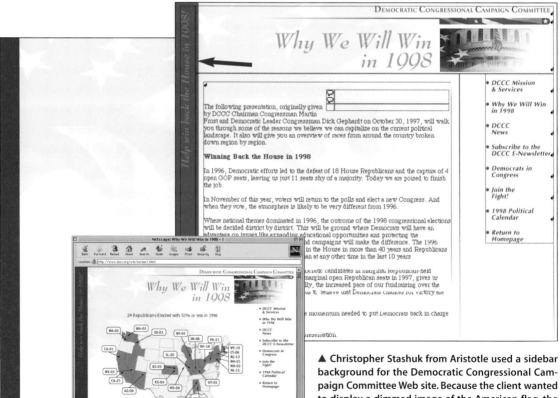

▲ Christopher Stashuk from Aristotle used a sidebar background for the Democratic Congressional Campaign Committee Web site. Because the client wanted to display a dimmed image of the American flag, the background had to be wide enough to avoid repeating the image. The blue sidebar uses a table to display the current topic (see top).

Hard Light or **Luminosity** work well, but you have to experiment to see which is best for specific images. Another nice technique is to apply a **Gaussian blur** to the image (**Filter > Blur > Gaussian Blur**); done to the extreme, this can create a great background texture, but even a little blur-ring helps improve the legibility of text.

The last technique that is used for large background images is blending the edges to create a gradual fade. You can do this by applying a layer mask (**Layer > Add Layer Mask > Reveal All**) and using the **Airbrush** tool and painting with black into the layer mask. All the dark areas of the layer mask will be transparent. Use a large brush size with soft edges, and make sure that the layer mask is activated when you paint into the image, otherwise you will paint over the image.

Photoshop 6.0 lets you use the Shape tool to create a sidebar. This has some advantages, such as the ease with which you can resize and apply textures.

▲ The Rocktropolis Web site (www.rocktropolis.com) is another good example of a side-bar background. One problem, however, is the browser offset, which causes all elements (including this navigation bar) to shift by a couple of pixels. The designer compensated for this by making the turquoise background in the navigation bar smaller by 15 pixels. But if you don't need to be backward-compatible to 3.0 browsers, you can simply solve the browser offset by setting it to zero, as explained in the "GoLive Basics" chapter.

➤ Sidebars as Background

You have certainly come across Web sites that use a sidebar with text or nav-igational elements. This is a popular design concept, since it doesn't require frames and can be done simply by using a pattern as background. All you have to do is color one side of the background. Since the background image is repeated, it can be as small as one pixel tall.

Using a one-pixel image is a bit extreme, of course, and doing this does have a drawback: it requires a lot of processing power on the part of your site visitor, since the browser has to render the background every time the win-dow is resized or the page is scrolled quickly. With a background image that is 1 pixel high (and, for example, 800 pixels wide), the browser has to repeat the background more often—and while this may not be noticeable on today's high-speed computers, on an older, low-end machine, that extra demand can slow down the browser. Using a pattern with a height of 40 to 80 pixels is less

The first versions of HTML contained only simple background features. The background image was merely repeated horizontally and vertically. Recent browsers are more flexible and allow you to repeat a pattern horizontally or vertically. You can even define the number of repetitions. This is perfect when you want to display the background only once. Unfortunately, older browsers (or some exotic browsers) don't understand these tags, which are part of cascading style sheets. If you need to be compatible with those, use the old technique.

demanding. If you use textures, save the image as a JPEG. In that case, use a dimension that is divisible by eight, because the JPEG's compression algorithm works with 8 x 8 blocks (read more on this in the "JPEG" chapter).

● Designing a Simple Sidebar

To create a simple sidebar, create a new document via **File > New** and enter something like 40 pixels for the height and 800 pixels for the width. Use the **Rectangular Marquee** tool to select a rectangle in the left-hand part of the image; the **Information** palette will display the width of the selection. Next choose a foreground color by double-clicking on the swatch to access the color picker, and use the **Paint Bucket** tool to fill the selected area with color. Then choose **File > Save for Web**. Images like this are ideally saved as GIF and use as few colors as possible.

● Designing a Sidebar with Texture

Although the sidebars in the example above are easy to create, they look rather technical. A sidebar with texture, however, can contribute significantly to the design. To avoid unwanted visible breaks at the edges, the upper and lower edges of the image should fit seamlessly. Follow the steps below:

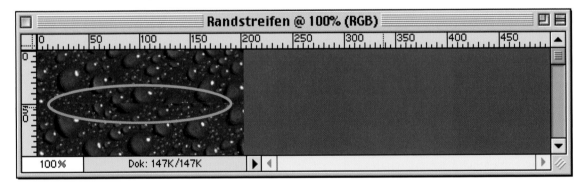

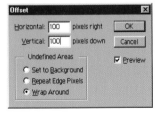

▲ A break in the image is visible after using the Offset filter. You can remove this break with the Rubber Stamp tool.

1. Create a new file and place a background or texture on the left side of the image. Choose the **Offset** filter (**Filter > Other > Offset**).

2. Enter half the height of the sidebar for **Vertical: Pixels Down**, and activate the **Wrap Around** option. This assures that image elements that disappear at the bottom will reappear at the top. Check **Preview** to see the effect prior to clicking **OK**.

3. Now you need to remove the break in the image. Depending on the image itself, either the **Smudge** tool or the **Rubber Stamp** tool will be most appropriate. Generally, the **Rubber Stamp** tool is more suitable for retouching. With Option/Alt pressed, click on the image region you want to use as a source. Release the key and click in the image where you want to fill in the information you've just picked up. As you move the tool around, you will see a cross following your movement; it marks the spot that you clicked on the first time while holding Option/Alt. To get the best results, you will have to change this point frequently; otherwise you will still see an edge.

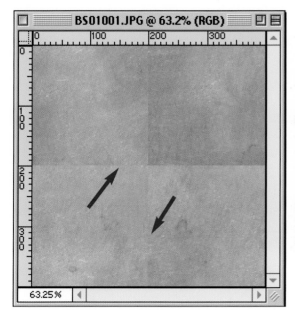
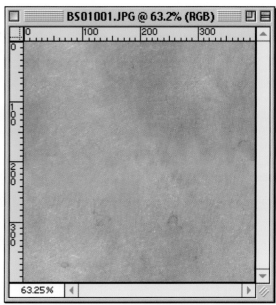

4. After the image has been smoothed out to create a seamless transition, use the **Offset** filter to convert the image file back to normal. (Enter a negative value and use the **Wrap Around** option.) The exported image will appear in Navigator or Explorer as one big background.

▲ After the Offset filter has been applied, you can see the edges of the pattern quite clearly (left picture). To make the pattern seamless, you need to fix the edges with the Rubber Stamp tool.

● **Texture Backgrounds (wallpaper)**
When the background feature was first implemented in HTML, many Web sites used textures or patterns to fill the entire page (amateur Web designers, in particular, found this appealing). This is not to say that pattern backgrounds can't be used tastefully. There are good examples of Web sites where designers used patterns with subtle coloring to avoid interference with text. Using a pattern that's large enough will make the continuous repetition less obvious. Here's how to prepare a pattern background:

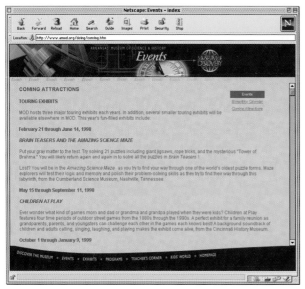

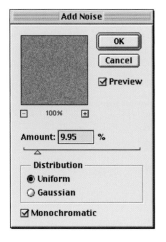

▲ This Web site by Christopher Stashuk is a good example of a subtle background pattern that complements the design.

1. Load a file with a texture and use the **Crop** tool to select the region that you'd like to use (crop by double-clicking inside the selection). Open the **Offset** filter and enter approximately half the pixel size of the image in the vertical and horizontal boxes. Activate the **Wrap Around** option to make sure that moved image elements reappear on the opposite end.

2. In the center of the picture, you will now see the image break in the shape of a cross. It needs to be removed with the **Rubber Stamp** tool (or in some cases with the **Smudge** tool). Press Option/Alt and click on the image spot you want to use as a source. Release Option/Alt and paint over the image break (a copy of the source area will be used). You might have to constantly change the source for the **Rubber Stamp** tool in order to get the result you want, but in the end you should have an area that shows no more edges. You can use the **Offset** filter one more time to double-check that there are really no more visible edges, or you can just move the pattern into its original position by entering a negative offset with the same values that you used before.

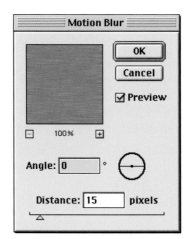

▲ After applying the Add Noise filter to the gray filling, you can use the Motion Blur filter to create the fiber. Finally, you'll need to sharpen the texture with the Sharpen filter to bring out the texture.

Finding a texture that doesn't interfere with text and actually enhances the design is not easy. Sometimes it is easier to create a texture directly in Photoshop. One of the more popular tricks is to create a brushed steel texture, which I will show you here:

1. Create a new file that measures 100x100 pixels. Fill the document with a neutral gray.

2. Add noise with the **Add Noise** filter (**Filter>Noise**). Use the **Monochromatic** option and use an amount around 10 percent.

3. With Motion Blur (Filter > Blur > Motion Blur), the noise will turn into "fibers" if you're using a blur of 5 to 20 pixels (any angle is okay; 0 to 20 degrees seems to look most realistic). Use **Filter > Sharpen > Sharpen** to make the fibers more distinct (applying this filter one time is usually enough). Then use the **Offset** filter, as explained before, to create the texture.

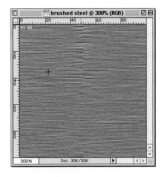

▲ You'll then need to fix the edges of the brushed-steel texture like any other texture.

Another important use for a pattern background is to create colors that are outside the Web-safe color spectrum. You do this by using the **DitherBox** filter to combine two Web-safe colors in a very tight pattern—essentially, you're controlling the dithering rather than allowing the browser or monitor to do it. The advantage is clear: your background will look the same in all environments.

1. Create a new image in Photoshop with **File > New**. Make sure that the dimensions are a multiple of the fill pattern. These fill patterns in the **DitherBox** can be 2x2 pixels, 3x3 pixels, 4x4 pixels, and so on up to 8x8. In most cases the standard fill pattern of 2x2 is enough, so for this example, I'll use a dimension of 500x50 pixels for the background image. If the dimensions don't match up correctly, you will end up with visible edges every time the image is repeated in the browser (see picture on next page).

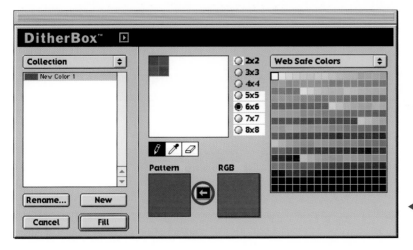

▲ Double-click on the listings to name the fill pattern.

◀ Clicking on the arrow and the filter will automatically suggest a fill pattern.

2. Choose Filter > Other > DitherBox. In the **DitherBox** dialog box, click on the RGB color field to open the **Color Picker**. Since you don't want the color to come from the Web-safe color palette, deactivate the **Only Web-Safe Colors** option, then choose a color for the pattern and click **OK**.

3. Click on the arrow button and the filter will automatically generate an appropriate fill pattern. In the **Pattern** field (to the left of the arrow button), you can see a preview of the filled area, and you can see how closely the color matches the one in the RGB field.

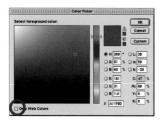

▲ Deactivate the Only Web-Safe Colors option before you pick a color.

▲ If the dimensions of the background image aren't set up correctly, you'll be able to see the repetition of the pattern quite clearly, as in this example (see magnification). To prevent this, make sure that the dimensions of the image are divisible by the size of the fill pattern.

4. To edit the pattern, select the **Pencil** or **Eyedropper** tool, choose a color from the palette on the right side of the dialog box, and apply it to the fill pattern. **Double-click** on the listing or click the **Rename** button to rename the fill pattern. To delete the new colors (called Collections), choose **Delete** from the pop-up menu above the listings. But remember, this will delete all the patterns in the listings.

5. Simply click the Fill button to fill the current document with the pattern.

When you magnify the filled document, you can see the checkerboard pattern clearly. You don't have to stick with that look; you can get a slightly varied result by placing the same-colored pixels in a row. Although the difference is subtle, this pattern might look better on your Web site. You can also experiment with larger fill patterns; just click on the radio buttons in the dialog box and edit the extra pixels with the **Pencil** tool.

CREATING BACKGROUNDS WITH A VECTOR GRAPHICS APPLICATION

Graphics applications like Adobe Illustrator are also great for designing graphical background patterns. These patterns would be difficult to create in Photoshop, even with its new vector tools. The basic procedure for creating a seamless pattern in Illustrator is simple:

1. Draw a rectangle or square and note the value. You will need this information later to move the elements by the same amount as the dimensions. Alternatively, you can press Option/Alt while clicking on the document to bring up a dialog box into which you can enter the dimensions of your object. One point in Illustrator equals one pixel in Photoshop, which is useful later when you're converting the graphic to a bitmap or importing the shapes into Photoshop.

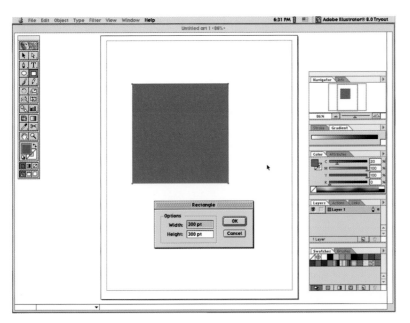

▲ Select the Rectangle tool, press Option/Alt, and click in the work space to access a dialog box for numeric entry of image size.

▲ Illustrator comes with a variety of patterns. Those shown here are in the Pattern Samples folder in the Other Libraries folder within the Illustrator 9 folder. Black-and-white in their original form, you can use the Appearance palette to add color to them.

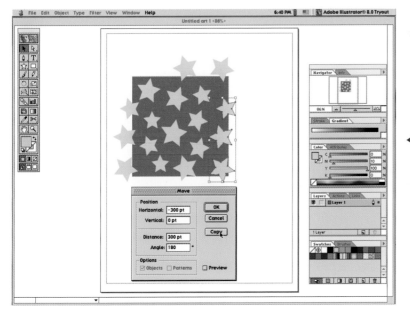

◀ To create a pattern that tiles seamlessly, make sure that your pattern elements cross the boundary of the rectangle only on two sides, such as the top and left. Select the elements that cross the left edge of the rectangle and use the Move command to move copies of them to the opposite side of the rectangle. Then select the elements that overlap the top of the rectangle, and move copies to the bottom edge.

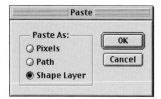

▲ To import a shape from Illustrator, use the Paste command and select Path or Shape Layer.

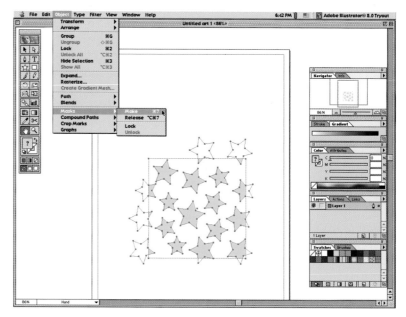

▲ To mask the elements, you need to move the rectangle to the front with Object > Arrange. Then use Object > Clipping Mask > Make to crop all overlapping areas.

2. Create all the objects and elements inside the rectangle. It's important to know that objects that cross the boundaries on the right edge of the rectangle will reappear on the left side. Do this with the **Move** command, which allows you to move an element by a specific amount while simultaneously making a copy. Follow the same procedure for objects that cross the upper and lower edge of the rectangle

3. Make a clipping mask to eliminate the parts of the elements that are outside the rectangle. In Illustrator, the rectangle needs to be the foremost object. Use **Object > Arrange > Bring to Front**, and then select all objects. **Object > Clipping Masks > Make** will mask all extraneous parts.

4. Photoshop can interpret Illustrator files directly—simply save the Illustrator file as EPS and Photoshop will automatically convert it to a bitmap upon opening it. If you would like to import the pattern as a shape, you have to copy the pattern to the clipboard with **Edit > Copy** and then switch to Photoshop and use **Edit > Paste**. Photoshop displays a little dialog box where you can choose to paste the **Clipboard** as **pixels, paths** or **layer shapes** (pick either **paths** or **layer shapes**). By the way: if you have a new

ALIEN SKIN EYECANDY **4000**

EyeCandy 4000 is the new version of the popular Photoshop plug-in. It boasts a huge variety of effects that can come in handy when doing Web design: the Chrome filter (right) would take several steps to do manually—with EyeCandy 4000 it takes only the adjustment of a couple of sliders. Old users of EyeCandy might be dissappointed that the interface doesn't look as hip as the previous one, but the interface is simple and efficient. Check Alien Skin (www.alienskin.com) for more details.

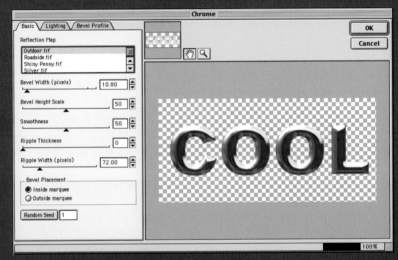

◄ This is just a selection of the filters that ship with EyeCandy.

▲ To fill a text layer with a text-ure, the texture layer must be above the text layer.

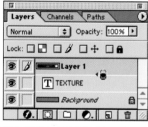

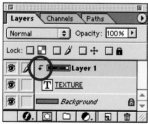

▲ If you press Option/Alt, the cursor switches to the clipping group icon when you bring it over the lines between the two layers. After clicking, an arrow indicates that one layer is masked by another.

Photoshop document in the exact same size as the pattern, you don't need to create the clipping mask in Illustrator.

DESIGNING TEXT

One of the Web design elements that I won't describe in detail is text. Besides using it for button labels, the Text tool is only necessary if you want to render headlines as images or if you need to simulate HTML text for your mockup. Do the latter simply by drawing a text frame with the **Text** tool and setting the anti-aliasing to **None**. Other than that, working with text is straightforward and it is explained well in the Photoshop manual.

There is one Photoshop feature, however, that is helpful for creating type that contains a photographic image or a texture. This feature is called clipping groups. It basically lets you mask the content of one layer with another. This feature is great for using a texture or a photo to fill type, because you don't have to convert your text layer to a bitmap layer, and you can still edit the text.

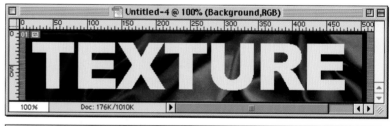

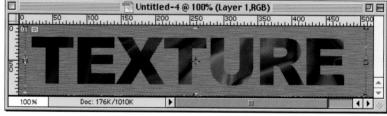

To fill a text layer with the content of a photo layer, the photo layer has to be above the text layer. If that is not the case, then move the layer in the **Layers** palette by dragging it to the right position. To convert the text layer below to a clipping group, bring the mouse cursor over the line between the two layers and press Option/Alt. The cursor will change to two overlapping circles to indicate that you can now create a clipping group by clicking.

You can see the result right away and you are now able to move the two layers independently by using the **Move** tool. To move both layers at the same time, link the two layers by clicking in the second column (next to the **Eye** icon) and a chain icon will appear.

DESIGNING BUTTONS

Photoshop and ImageReady offer layer styles that let you apply drop shadows and bevels to your buttons, and generally make designing buttons a lot easier. One big advantage is that they aren't applied permanently—you can modify or remove them at any time. Here's how to create a button in Photoshop using a layer style comprising several layer effects:

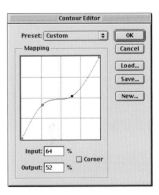

▲ Clicking on any of the Contour buttons opens the Contour Editor.

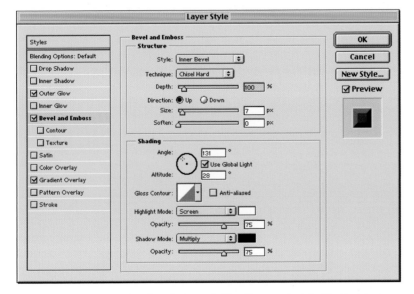

▲ The Layer Style dialog box lists all the available effects on the left side. To activate an effect, you must check it. To edit the effects, select one in the listing.

1. Create a new layer in the **Layers** palette, then draw a shape with the **Rectangle** or another shape tool. Now select **Layer > Layer Style > Bevel and Emboss.** In the **Layer Style** dialog box, you can adjust many parameters of the bevel, including its structure (contour, dimensions, and style) and shading (light angle, and blending modes of the bevel's illumination and shadows).

2. For the Highlight Mode, define how you want to combine the light reflections with the layers. You should already be familiar with these modes—they are the same as the blending modes in the **Layers** palette. To see the light reflections clearly, choose **Normal** or **Screen**. Avoid **Multiply** because it doesn't produce a visible edge.

You can choose a highlight color by clicking on the color field next to the **Highlight Mode** pop-up menu. You can also define custom values for **Opacity**.

3. Use Normal or Multiply mode in the **Shadow** section. As with the highlights, you can choose a shadow color.

4. Depth and Size set the intensity and width of the bevel. If you're using several objects with layer effects, activate **Global Angle**. This way you can change the effect angle for all the layers at once. Perhaps the most important settings are in the **Style** pop-up menu of the **Bevel and Emboss** dialog box: Outer Bevel, Inner Bevel, Emboss, and Pillow Emboss. **Outer Bevel** and **Inner Bevel** produce standard buttons, while **Emboss** processes all the edges, making the button appear to be carved out of the background. This can be attractive if you use it with text. Another great feature is the **Contour** effect, which is part of **Bevel and Emboss**. To understand what this effect does, look at the example below: the contour of the object has its own beveled shape.

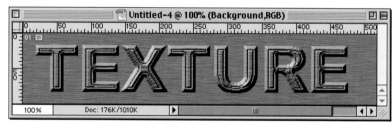

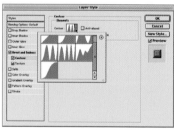

▲ These are some of the new layer effects (from top to bottom): Drop Shadow, Inner Shadow, Outer Glow, and Bevel.

▲ Bevels like this one would not be possible without the Contour effect: it lets you assign a separate bevel shape to the contour.

A layer can use multiple layer effects. To see which are active, select **Layer > Layer Styles** and note which effects are checked on the menu. Choose one of the effects from the menu to open the **Layer Styles** dialog box and click on the listing in the left column to see the settings for each effect. If you know that you will need a specific setting more then once, save it as a **Style** by clicking on **New Style**. All the saved **Styles** are listed in the **Styles** palette.

To deactivate an effect without going into the dialog box, just drag it to the **Trash** (in the **Layers** palette) or hide it by clicking on the **Eye** icon.

ALIEN SKIN XENOFEX

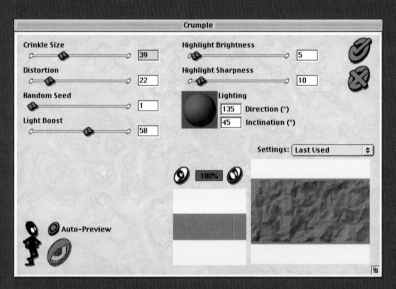

Alien Skin Xenofex is a collection of 16 Photoshop filters, all in the Alien Skin Interface design. The effects include Crumple, which creates the look of crumpled paper, and Television, which gives an image the appearance of being viewed through a TV screen. Filters like Television can create interesting background images or logos. Other effects, such as Electrify, may make for some nice animations. One filter even simulates the stain from coffee cups.

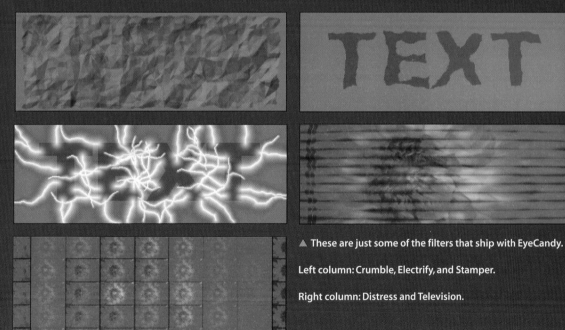

▲ These are just some of the filters that ship with EyeCandy.

Left column: Crumble, Electrify, and Stamper.

Right column: Distress and Television.

TUTORIAL: DEVELOPING A WEB SITE IN PHOTOSHOP

The best way to learn is to read about it and then do it. For this reason, I created this simple mock-up for a (fictitious) consulting company that uses many of the elements that you find in real-world Web sites. I will walk you through every step of the development from the design—showing you some of the new features of Photoshop 6—through the optimization of the images, up to the point of creating an HTML page in GoLive.

1. Creating a sidebar: after creating a new 640x600 file (**File > New**; **Contents: Background Color**), create a second (temporary) document for the fill pattern; make it four pixels wide by one tall. The first pixel is a light gray (RGB: 204, 204, 204), the second

▲ This mock-up of a Web site shows you some of Photoshop's new features.

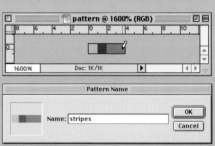

pixel is a dark gray (RGB: 102, 102, 102), and the third and fourth pixels are a medium gray (RGB: 153, 153, 153). Use the maximum magnification to paint the pixels with the **Pencil** tool. To define a color, click on the **Foreground Color** field in the **Tools** palette and make sure that the **Only Web-Safe Colors** option is selected in the **Color Picker**.

Edit > Define Pattern will store this small document as a pattern. You won't need this document anymore, but you can save it for later in case you want to edit it. Switch back to your first document and display the rulers (**View > Show Rulers**). To create the actual sidebar, use the **Rectangle** tool, but before you start, make sure to select the **Create New Shape Layer** option and check that **No Style** is selected from the **Layer Style** pop-up menu. You are now ready to create a layer with a layer clipping path: usually this would require that you first create a new layer, but since this is a new document and we are working on the background layer, Photoshop will create a new layer for you automatically.

▲ Use the Only Web-Safe Colors option when creating the pattern.

Draw a 150-pixel-wide rectangle for the sidebar; it will fill with the foreground color. To fill it with the pattern, create a pattern overlay layer effect: choose **Layer > Layer Style > Pattern Overlay**, and select the pattern that you saved previously from the pop-up menu. Voila. Your sidebar is done.

2. Creating the arch: when designing a Web site in Photoshop, you should decide early on whether you intend to use frames or just tables when you prepare the HTML. This decision affects what you can and can't do when designing in Photoshop. While this particular design could also be re-created with tables, it is much more suitable for frames and we want to design the arch that is later going to be in the top frame.

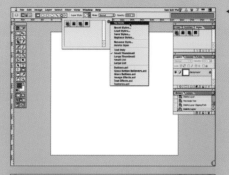

▲ The shape is filled with the pattern. In the Layers palette, you can see the new layer with its clipping path.

Create a new layer in the **Layers** palette (by clicking on the **Create New Layer** button) and use the **Rectangle** tool to draw a shape that's 95 pixels tall and offset from the top by 20 pixels; you will have to zoom in to do this precisely. If you need to adjust the shape later, you can do so with the **Path Component Selection** tool, with the option **Show Bounding Box** checked in the options bar. With this bounding box you can reshape the rectangle as you would in Adobe Illustrator; the only difference is that you have to double-click in the rectangle when you are finished resizing. Another tip: if you adjust the shape while the bounding box is visible, the **Free Transform** tool becomes active and its options bar will display the position of the bounding box.

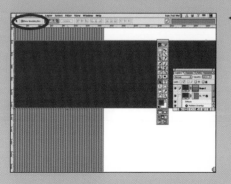

◀ Before drawing with the Rectangle tool, make sure that No Style is selected in the options bar.

▲ In the Layer Effects dialog box, select Pattern Overlay and pick the previously saved pattern.

◀ In the Path Component Selection tool's options bar, check the Show Bounding Box and then drag a handle of the shape to resize the rectangle.

To change the rectangle into an arch, click on the lower right corner of the rectangle with the **Direct Selection** tool (the white mouse arrow), and drag the anchor point up while pressing Shift (to restrict the movement to the vertical axis). Use the **Add Anchor Point** tool to add an anchor point to the middle of the path, and move this anchor with the **Direct Selection** tool until you get a nice arch.

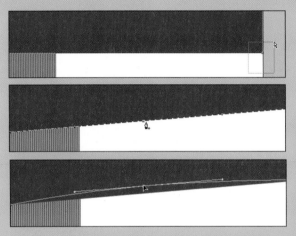

▲ After the lower right anchor was moved up, an anchor point was added to the path and then moved to create the arch.

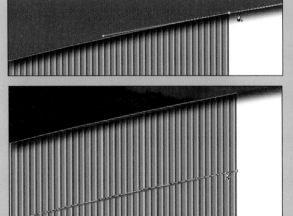

▲ A copy of the arch was created, an anchor added, and the rest deleted. Then the remaining path was copied.

Fill this path with a pattern as you did with the sidebar: open a texture, define it as pattern, and select **Pattern Overlay** in the **Layer Effects** dialog box. Also select **Drop Shadow**.

3. Creating the sidebar navigation buttons: if you are familiar with Adobe Illustrator and working with the **Path** tool, this should be no problem. Duplicate the layer with the arch (using the **Duplicate Layer** button in the **Layers** palette pop-up menu), then choose **Layer > Layer Style > Clear Layer Style** to get rid of the layer effects in this copy. Now cut out the part of the arch that lies over the sidebar and use this as the basis for the buttons (to ensure both arches will match). Select all anchor points with the **Direct Selection** tool—except the anchor point at the lower left-hand corner of the arch, and the newly-added anchor point directly to its right. Then drag the path parallel by pressing **Shift** and then **Option/Alt** before releasing the mouse button to create a copy automatically. Connect the ends of the paths with the **Pen** tool and use the **Convert Point** tool to adjust the handles of the anchor points. Change the color of the shape to black in **Layer > Change Layer Content > Solid Color**. Finally, adjust the **Opacity** of each button, making the lower buttons more transparent. The other two buttons are simply created by duplicating this layer, then moving and adjusting the paths and transparency.

With the **Text** tool, click where you want to place the labels for the buttons and then type the text. Make sure that the foreground color is set to white before you do this, otherwise you have to change the color later by highlighting the text with the **Text** tool and

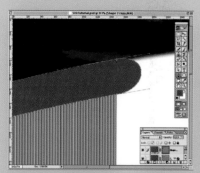
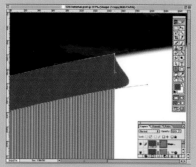
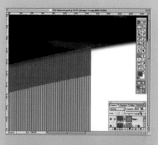

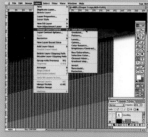

changing the color in the **Color Picker**. To rotate the text layer, use **Edit > Free Transform** (if this command is grayed out, select the **Move** tool first). You will see a bounding box that you can use to scale and rotate the text (consult the Photoshop manual for instructions on how to use the Free Transform command). Once the text is in position, duplicate the layer twice and change the text.

4. Creating the top and bottom navigation bars: for the background of the buttons, create the shape again with the **Rectangle** tool. Instead of using beveled buttons, use the **Inner Shadow** effect and disable the MouseOver rollover state in ImageReady to give the appearance of the gray background moving up when the mouse is positioned over the button. Once you've placed the text for the buttons (and the black rectangle on the left side), create a new folder (**Layer Set**) in the **Layers** palette and drag all

the elements of the top navigation in it. Being able to organize the content of the **Layers** palette in folders is a true blessing of Photoshop 6.0. Not only does it help you keep an overview, it makes it easy to duplicate several layers at once. Select the top navigation bar layer set in the **Layers** palette and use the **Duplicate Layer Set** command in the **Layers** palette pop-up menu. Drag the new set to the bottom of palette.

▲ The path is reshaped using the Convert Point tool and then the content is changed to Solid Color.

▲ With the Text tool, click where you want to place the text. Rotate and resize the text using the bounding box.

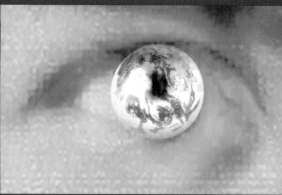

WORKING WITH IMAGEREADY

Working with ImageReady

Some readers criticized the first edition of this book for failing to cover Image-Ready. Of course almost every Photoshop technique I explained then—and those that I explain again in this edition—can be adapted to ImageReady. But ImageReady has some unique, Web-centric features that Photoshop doesn't. This chapter is intended to walk you through these features, from the creation of rollover buttons and image maps to the exporting of content for use in GoLive.

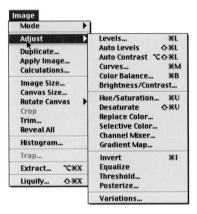

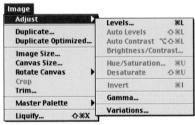

▲ Photoshop (left menu) has more color-manipulation commands than ImageReady (right menu), so it is therefore better suited for photo composition and manipulation.

Photoshop vs. ImageReady

Photoshop's Save for Web dialog box offers virtually all of the same file-optimization capabilities that ImageReady's does, but I would argue that it's a good idea to start out in Photoshop and do as much design and image creation as possible there, then switch to ImageReady only after you've perfected the image. The Photoshop interface is more familiar to most designers, and Photoshop also has many more color-correcting and image-manipulation features then ImageReady does. If you'd like, compare Photoshop's Image > Adjust commands to ImageReady's: Photoshop offers Curves, Color Balance, Replace Color, Selective Color, Channel Mixer, Equalize, and many other important commands for working with images and creating photo compositions that ImageReady lacks.

▲ Switching between Photoshop and ImageReady is simple: click on the Jump To button in the Tool palette, then use the Save command before opening the document in the other application.

Another benefit of designing images and photo illustrations in Photoshop is that it now offers the Pen and Custom Shape vector tools. But that's not all! Photoshop lets you draw multiple paths on one layer, and, like the pathfinder palette in Illustrator, it lets you combine those paths into a more complex shape by adding or subtracting them. ImageReady doesn't have a Pen or Custom Shape tool, and it only allows one shape in a layer. While it is possible to move and transform those shapes in ImageReady, only Photoshop can edit them to add or delete anchor points.

But after you've designed the images for your Web site—adjusted the colors, composed and colorized images, and received client approval—then you can turn to ImageReady to take your content to the next level of Web design. In ImageReady, you can create rollover buttons and image maps, slice images and animate GIFs, and export the final elements to an HMTL authoring program such as GoLive. These are tasks that you just can't perform in Photoshop and that are important in the second phase of Web site design. Plus, the automation features are easier to use in ImageReady. If you don't intend to use any of these features, you might as well finalize your images using Photoshop's Save for Web command, since ImageReady offers no actual advantage over Photoshop for optimizing images. And remember, Adobe makes it easy to switch between Photoshop and ImageReady with the Jump to ImageReady/Photoshop button in each application's Tool palette. Personally, however, I find it cumbersome to deal with two software interfaces, even if the differences between them are only marginal.

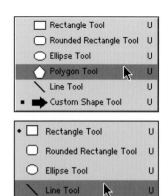

▲ Photoshop has more path and shape tools than ImageReady does, but most importantly, you can edit paths in Photoshop.

THE MOST COMMON MISTAKE

One of the most common misunderstandings about ImageReady is that you can use it as an HTML authoring tool. Here's my advice: don't expect to be able to create slices, click some buttons in ImageReady, and produce an almost-finished Web page that you can use right away in GoLive. Even though ImageReady can generate some HTML code, you should use it only in rare cases. Most of the time it is better to export the images and create the page in GoLive, which reduces mistakes and offers more control over the code.

For example, imagine that you want to design a Web page with a background image, a navigation bar containing rollover buttons, and an animated banner ad. If you attempt to create the rollovers and animation in one document in ImageReady, you will most likely end up with rollovers that act strange or an animation with unnecessary frames, because both design elements are based on image layers. Chances are that you will unwittingly record a layer change for a rollover button or in an animation, or vice versa. Trust me: it is very easy to lose sight of the big picture and wind up having to delete many of the steps that tied your image into a Gordian knot.

So what is the best way to proceed? Ideally you should open your Photoshop design in ImageReady, crop the individual elements, and save them as separate files. This way you'll crop the banner ad and save it as one file before

▲ Creating slices that match the boundaries of a layer is very simple: select the layer and choose Layer > New Layer Based Slice.

If you would like to follow this example, download this file from www.mitomediabooks.com. It is the same file used for the tutorial on page 197.

you start animating it. Then when you're opening and creating the banner ad animation, you can focus on the animation alone and even delete the redundant layers, which makes the Layers palette more manageable.

The last piece of advice that I want to give you is this: don't start working on the rollover buttons if you still need to make some changes in your design. It's far too easy to accidentally record one of the changes in the Layers palette as one state of a rollover button. Creating rollover buttons should be the very last step in the process.

CREATING ROLLOVER BUTTONS

After opening the design in ImageReady, you must use the Slicing tool to create the rollover buttons. Every time you place a new marquee with the Slicing tool, ImageReady optimizes the slices and even creates adjacent slices if necessary (e.g., if you place your first slice in the middle of your document, ImageReady will create five slices in total: the one that you created and one for each side of the marquee). When you export your images together with some HTML code, each slice represents a cell of an HTML table. But ImageReady (and Photoshop) also allow you to export only selected slices. This gives you some flexibility and saves you from having to crop a design when you're designing the rollover buttons.

Use the **Slice** tool to draw a marquee around each button; the buttons should be adjacent unless you plan to use an effect like **Outer Glow**. Name

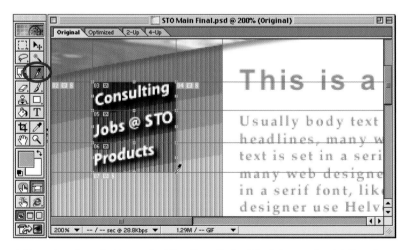

▲ To create rollover buttons, select the slice with the Slice Select tool and define the rollover effect in the Rollover palette.

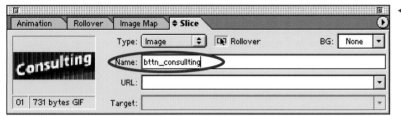

the slices in the **Slice** palette, using an intuitive system: I used "bttn_" in combination with the button's text.

To create a rollover state (an action that occurs when a mouse cursor is rolled over the slice), select a slice with the **Slice Select** tool and then click on the **Create New Rollover** button in the **Rollover** palette. In this example I want to change the color of the button text for my rollover effect. The easiest

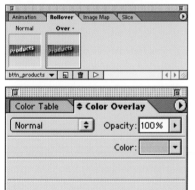

way to do this is to use a color overlay. So I select the text layer in the **Layers** palette, choose **Layer Style > Color Overlay** from the **Layer** menu, and select a different color.

▲ Before applying the color overlay, the right layer needs to be activated. Apply the color overlay to the layer, but only for the second rollover state.

Once you've created your rollovers, optimize each slice individually. Use the **Slice Select** tool to select one slice and then open the **Optimize** palette (**Window > Show Optimize**). In my example, 16 colors are plenty, and I chose an **Adaptive** palette. It is important not to dither here, or else the the background of the buttons will dither, as well. If you wish to place the buttons over the background later on, dithering may cause some visible edges.

▲ Here's a nice little feature: if you click on Rollover Preview, the buttons in your design will behave the same way that they will later in the browser.

After you've created a new site in Go-Live, export the image from Image-Ready by selecting all the slices for the rollover buttons with the **Slice Select** tool and choosing **File > Save Optimized As**. In the **Save Optimized As** dialog box, look for the folder that contains the new site (mirror site). Normally you would save a component directly in the **Components** folder, or data folder (on Macs it's the folder with the extension ".data"), but since we are saving a couple of images that need to be in the mirror site folder, it is easier just to drag the generated HTML document over to the **Components** folder.

▲ These are the Optimize settings used for exporting buttons.

▲ In the Save Optimized As dialog box, click on Output Settings to bring up a dialog box where you can specify the HTML coding and the auto-naming of the slices. It is important that the three slices are activated and that Selected Slices is chosen. This way only the images for the rollover buttons are exported— embedded in an HTML table.

Give the HTML document a name ("navigation.html" for our example), then select **HTML and Images** in the **Format** pop-up menu to save the images along with their HTML code. Since the document is not cropped, choose **Selected Slices** from the pop-up menu near the bottom of the dialog box.

Click on the **Output Settings** button to bring up a dialog box where you can tell ImageReady to write a GoLive-compatible JavaScript for the rollover buttons (choose "Include GoLive Code"); otherwise ImageReady will write its own version. While letting ImageReady generate the code is not a major problem, it will be harder to make changes in GoLive if you decide to add another rollover state to the button. For **Slice Output** choose **Generate Table** (the default setting) and switch to **Saving Files** from the second pop-up menu.

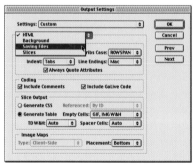

ImageReady has a vast number of options for naming slices automatically. My preference is to use the Slice name combined with the rollover abbreviation ("over" becomes "o") and the image format extension (which you have to use). In this Output Settings (Saving Files) dialog box you also specify a subfolder in which to place the images. Because of this option, I decided to save the navigation bar component in the regular folder rather than directly in the Components folder. The difference is only marginal, but I find it easier to drag just the HTML document over to the Components folder, rather than dragging all the images from the Components folder back into the mirror site, but it's up to you. Before you can drag anything, however, you must make your newly-saved files visible in GoLive. In the **Site Manager** window, select the left side if you saved the files directly to the mirror site or the right side if you saved the files directly into the **Components** folder. Use **Site > Rescan** to have GoLive check the directory for any additional files.

In this case, the Images folder and the navigation.html file appeared in the mirror site and I dragged the HTML document into the Components folder. After confirming the **Move File** dialog box, the component is available in the **Components** panel of the **Site Extras** tab of the **Objects** palette in GoLive.

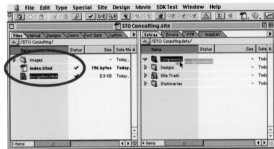
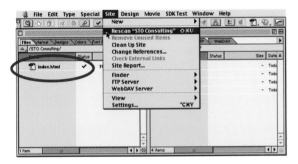

CREATING IMAGE MAPS

For basic image maps—or image maps that use basic geometrical shapes—you can actually use Adobe GoLive: just place an image on an HTML document and click on **Use Map** in the **Inspector**. Then, with the **Region** tools (Rectangle, Circle, and Polygon), create your hot spots and establish their links in the **Link** tab of the **Inspector**.

If you need to create a more precise or more complex image map, GoLive isn't the best choice, however. Let's say that you've created rollover buttons as we just did: in that case, recreating the shapes of the different states on a map can be tedious. GoLive can't zoom in, and working at the edge of an image map is almost impossible. Five pixels from the border, GoLive switches how it displays the mouse pointer because it assumes that you want to move the image.

So ImageReady is your solution. Just use any of the **Image Map** tools to draw your hot spot shapes, then enter the name and URL of that hot spot in the **Image Map** palette. Choose **File > Save Optimized As**, and select **HTML and Images** from the **Format** pop-up menu. In **Output Settings**, choose **Client Side** as the type of image map you're creating, and, last but not least, save the image map into your GoLive site folder. (Alternatively, you can simply define your hot

▲ After clicking on the Use Map option in the Inspector, an image automatically becomes an image map and the toolbar displays the tools to create the hot spots.

▲ In the Site Manager window, select Site > Rescan. GoLive checks for any new files in the site folder and displays them. In this case the Image folder and the HTML file showed up, so the HTML file was then dragged over to the Components folder.

▲ When the HTML document is moved to the Components folder, GoLive needs to update the links to the images, so it displays the Move Files dialog box. Just confirm here and your component will then be accessible in the Objects palette of GoLive.

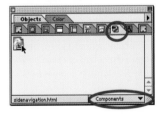

▲ The component will show up in the Objects palette (components must be selected in the lower right corner).

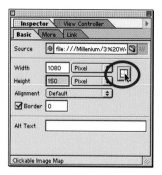

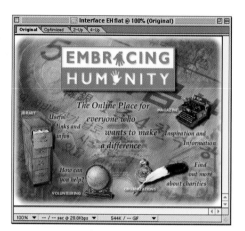

▲ Here is a little trick for the hot spot areas for an image map in GoLive: scale the image to twice the size in the Inspector palette (multiply the values in Width and Height). Now create all your hot spots, then click on the button for original size and GoLive scales everything back, including the areas.

spots in ImageReady, save the file, and then open it in Go-Live, where you can use the point-and-shoot tool to define the URLs in a snap.)

Now start GoLive and choose **Site > Rescan** in the **Site** folder. Two new files will be listed: your image and the HTML document that defines the image map areas. Move the image to your image folder, open the HTML document, and copy and paste the image map into the target HTML document. Finished! Dispose of the redundant image map HTML document by putting it in the **Trash** in the **Site** window.

➤ **Layer-Based Image Maps**

ImageReady offers another particularly helpful feature if you have to create polygon image map areas: you can have ImageReady create an area automatically based on a layer. Just choose **Layer > New Layer Based Image Map Area** to create a rectangular image map area. To change the shape into a polygon, open the **Image Map** palette and select **Polygon** from the **Shape** pop-up menu. With the **Quality** slider you can specify the accuracy with which ImageReady matches the form of the layer. As you can see in the example with the metallic bird, even the layer effects are taken into account. By the way, Adobe Illustrator 9.0 can now also save polygonal image map areas, which is a great help if your image map consists of complex shapes.

▲ When clicking on the image map tool in the Tool palette, ImageReady reveals a list of tools. By clicking on the little arrow at the bottom, the tools will be displayed in their own palette.

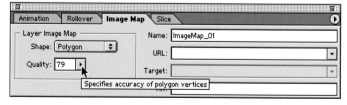

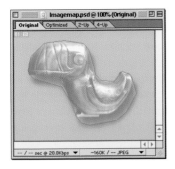

OPTIMIZING IMAGES

The only time you'll have to optimize images in ImageReady is when you're creating rollover buttons, image maps or GIF animations; otherwise, you can use Photoshop's Save for Web command. Since the Save for Web command is now also part of Illustrator 9.0 and GoLive 5.0, it appears that Adobe is going to make this its standard way of optimizing and saving images for the Web. For that reason, the chapters on optimizing GIF, JPEG and PNG are all featuring the Save for Web command. If you do need to optimize in ImageReady, here's a guide to the differences between the ImageReady interface and the Save for Web command.

The tools on the left side of the Save for Web dialog box—Hand, Slice Select, Zoom, and Eyedropper—are in the regular ImageReady Tool palette. The color

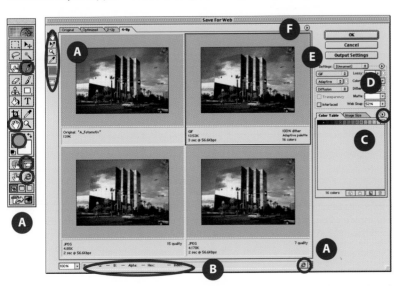

▲ The image map needs to be saved using the Save Optimized As command. In Output Settings, select the type of image map (usually Client Side).

▲ The tools in the upper left corner of the Save for Web command (right image) and the Browser Preview command in the lower right corner, match the Tool palette (image on the left) of ImageReady (A). Integrated in the Save for Web command is the Image-Ready Color Table palette (C) with its menu. Scaling an image for export is done in Image-Ready via Image > Image Size, while the Save for Web command includes this in the Image Size tab (C). The Preview Menu (F) in the Save for Web command combines the View > Preview menu from ImageReady with some of the Download Time selection of the Image Information.

▲ After a rescan in GoLive's site window, the image map—the image and HTML document—is visible. Move the image to your image folder, open the HTML document and copy the image map to the Clipboard, and paste it in your target document. Then put the image map document in the Trash.

▲ The color information displayed at the bottom of the Save for Web dialog box is available in ImageReady's Info palette (B).

▲ The Image Information pop-up menu is at the bottom of the image window in ImageReady. It has some options that have no equivalent in the Save for Web dialog box.

▲ It is possible to save a setting to access it later directly through the pop-up menu.

values displayed at the bottom of the Save for Web dialog box are available in ImageReady's Info palette. The optimization settings and Color Table palette on the right side of the Save for Web dialog box are available in ImageReady as their own respective palettes, but the Image Size palette isn't there. In ImageReady you must choose **Image > Image Size** to glean this information. Finally, the pop-up preview menu in the **Save for Web** dialog box is split in ImageReady: color preview commands are available if you choose **View > Preview**, and the download rates are available in the **Image Information** pop-up menu at the bottom of the image window.

➤ Optimizing for Rollovers

Because ImageReady can create rollover effects, it includes a nice little feature that Photoshop 6.0 doesn't have: **Use Unified Color Table**. This command ensures that the images for all rollover states have the same color table. You're probably asking yourself what difference this makes and what happens if I don't use this option? The answer is simply that this option is your safety belt

for all those visitors who have only 256-color monitors. On those computers, the total number of freely-assignable colors is limited to 216. This means that if you use 10 GIFs and each of them has its own color table of 32 colors (for a total of 320 colors), you have 104 colors that cannot be displayed and therefore will be either snapped and/or dithered. As a result there is a chance that the edges of rollover buttons will become visible.

➤ Droplets

ImageReady's Droplets, which are basically self-executing actions that automate routine tasks, are now available in Photoshop 6.0 as well (choose **File > Automate > Create Droplet**). Droplets in ImageReady are limited to the settings of the Optimize palette, but Photoshop lets you export an action as droplet. This basically means that, given a choice, you are better off using the Droplet command in Photoshop (see the "Optimizing Photoshop" chapter for more details).

TUTORIAL: CREATING SLICES AND ROLLOVERS

Here is the mock-up of the Web site for a consulting company done entirely in Photoshop, created in the previous tutorial. Now we'll slice and export the design and create the rollover buttons in ImageReady.

You can download this tutorial from www.mitomediabooks.com

1. Thinking it through: As you design your Web site in Photoshop, you should be thinking about how you will ultimately recreate it in HTML. It isn't always possible to know this in advance, of course, especially if you want to try something new, but you should ask yourself early on whether your design is better suited to be laid out with frames or just with tables. For this example, we can go either way and create the same slices regardless.

Using Frames: It makes sense to divide this page into three horizontal frames, creating a top that contains the logo, the navigation buttons, and the dark and some of the white background; a middle section that contains the navigation buttons on the left and the body of the page; and a bottom that contains the lower navigation buttons. The middle section needs to be split into two vertical frames to isolate the navigation bar so that it doesn't scroll out of view along with the body of the page. In the top frame, the navigation buttons and the arched background pattern and logo need to be sliced and put back together in a table, as do all the navigational buttons at top, on the left, and at the bottom. Since the upper and lower navigational buttons are identical, we only need to export them once, but the backgrounds in the top and bottom frames do need to be sliced and exported separately.

▲ This page mock-up, created not just as a design concept but also to highlight some of Photoshop 6.0's new features, can be produced in HTML with either frames or tables.

Using Tables: In theory, you could place everything on this page in one large, complex table, but this is not advisable (doing so would be a beginner's mistake). For one, it is very hard to control and fix such a table, but above all, if the content—maybe because of some user preferences in the browser—expands beyond the cell of the container table, your entire design can break apart. A better HTML table for this design would split the page into one large table (shown with red lines in the screen shot on the next page) that contains smaller embedded tables for the navigational buttons and other page

▲ The red lines in the screen shot above delineate a frame layout (blue are the embedded tables). The red and blue lines in the image at right show how the design could be laid out with embedded tables. It's almost the same!

elements (in blue). You probably noticed that the container table has an extra column on the right side. The only purpose of that column is to display the backgrounds for the top and the bottom part of the design. It is possible to set the table up in such a way that this column will automatically adjust to the browser width (see "Tutorial: HTML Authoring," page 304).

▲ This design requires 16 slices. A, B, and C represent the slices for the background image.

2. Creating slices and rollover buttons: Create slices and rollovers as described on page 190, being sure to name each slice before you begin selecting them individually to create the rollover effects. The rollovers for the top navigation buttons were created by deactivating the Inner Shadow effect and activating a Color Overlay for the text instead.

Note that the curved border of the upper background image needs special handling. To avoid an abrupt edge if you're using frames, the background for the top frame needs to continue the gray of the very top buttons and the black of the arch. This can be accomplished by slicing a piece out of the design at the very upper right side and using this as a background image in the HTML document, which will later be loaded into the top frame. The same thing must be done for the sidebar and the bottom navigation buttons: a slice of the texture must be exported for later use as a background image.

▲ After the HTML page is imported into GoLive, it can be broken up into stationery and components (here the navigation component).

3. Optimizing: Once the page is sliced, open the **Optimize** palette (**Window > Show Optimize**), select one slice, and choose the appropriate settings. It helps to view the slice in the Optimized tab of the image window so that you can see the results as you experiment with settings. Note that you can select several slices at once and change their settings at one time. Some slices for this tutorial were best as JPEG, others were better suited to be GIF. Here are the settings I used:

GIF Slice No.	Colors	Palette
1	2	Web
2–7	16	Selective
10, 17, 18, 20, 22	8	Adaptive
12-16	16	Adaptive

JPEG Slice No.	Quality
8	10
9	30

For the GIFs, I did not apply dithering or the Lossy option, but I did use a unified color table for slides 2 through 7, and for slices 12 through 16. The JPEG slices called for different quality settings, but neither needed blurring. Slice 10 was tricky. This slice must be saved as GIF so that it matches the color of the slices beneath, but at the same time it contains part of the arch, which was saved as JPEG how can it be saved as both? do you mean you saved the same slice twice, once as GIF and once as JPEG? If so, add info to table above and clarify sentence. When viewed with 256 colors, it looks okay, but it still needs to be checked in a browser*.

4. Exporting: Use the **Rollover Preview** button in the **Tool** palette, and if everything seems to work as it's supposed to, select slices 1–7 with the **Slice Select** tool and export them via **File > Save Optimized As.** Since this is going to be a component (top_navigation.html), use the **Save Images** and **Save Selected Slices Only** options. Click on the **HTML Options** to display another dialog box that lets you change, for example, the JavaScript Code to GoLive, which you have to do to ensure compatibility with GoLive (see page 192). Then select slices 10 and 12 to 17 and save them as another component (sidebar.html). Finally, select slices 8, 18, and 22 and export them to the image folder in your Web site.

* Browsers might dither the JPEG and the GIF differently when viewed with 256 colors. A few years ago this would have been a bigger concern because 256-color monitors were more common then. Today, however, most people have monitors that support at least thousands of colors. And even if they don't, this difference is probably negligible.

Illustration: Michael Baumgardt

GIF ANIMATION

GIF Animation

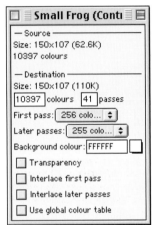

GIF is the most important tool for bringing animation to the Web—and while Flash and Shockwave are steadily increasing in popularity, GIF will hold the top slot for a long time to come. The reason is simple: The files for GIF animations are small, they don't require any special plug-ins, and they are easy to create. Plus, there are many freeware and shareware GIF animation programs available on the Web, such as GifBuilder 1.0 from Yves Piguet. GifBuilder is one of the most popular and well-known GIF animation applications for the Macintosh; it's simple to use, it works well and is quite stable, and it has a couple of features that are very effective for keeping your files small.

There are many other programs too, such as GIFmation, which is distributed by BoxTop (www.boxtopsoft.com), or the GIF Construction Set for Windows. However, if you have Photoshop 6.0 you already own a fabulous GIF animation program: ImageReady. This application is an excellent Web design tool, and provides great support for GIF animation.

BASIC PRINCIPLES

GIF animation works exactly like cel animation: several frames are displayed in rapid succession, which creates the illusion of movement. For each frame in the GIF animation you can define attributes such as position, transparency color, disposal method (whether or not the current frame should be discarded

▲ Theoretically it is possible to use a GIF animation to overcome the 256 –color limitation of GIFs, since each frame can have its own CLUT. There is only one program I know of that utilizes this. It's called "It's a GIF." There is little practical use for it, but if you want to experiment, download it from www.peda.com/iag/.

Click on the Create New Frame ▶ button to create a new frame in the animation. Every change in the Layers palette will now be recorded.

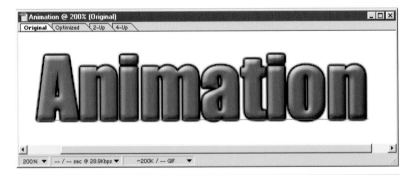

before the next frame is displayed), and how long it will be displayed. As I said, GIF animations are hugely popular effects because they don't need a plug-in, and even exotic browsers (which may not display GIF animation) can still show the first or last picture of the sequence, so you don't have to worry about incompatibility.

To see the **Animation** palette in ImageReady, click **Window > Show Animation**. By default, the Animation palette is grouped with the Rollover, Image Map, and Slice tabs. If one of those is already open, just select the appropriate tab to see **Animation**.

Let's create a tiny animation to get a feel for the process. To do this, create a new image in ImageReady and type a word into it, such as "Animation." In our example, we've used the **Text** tool to do this. Your image is now the first frame in your animation, as you can see in the **Animation** palette. Click on the **Duplicate frame** button at the bottom of the palette, and then use the **Move** tool to reposition the text in the image window. Now when you click on the **Play** button, you can watch your two-frame animation.

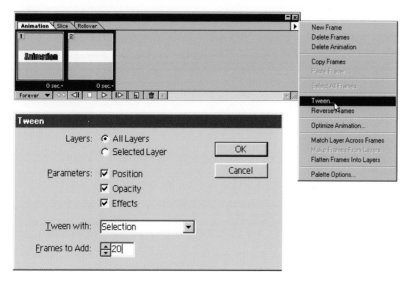

◄ The Tween command is the easiest way to create great animations. Tweening will insert frames after one, or between two, frames that you've selected.

As exciting as this may be, it hardly qualifies as state-of-the-art animation. Of course you could add additional frames and move your text layer around some more, but your animation probably won't be very smooth; it is quite difficult to manually position your text with the accuracy required for professional-looking animation. Fortunately, ImageReady offers a great command called Tween that makes it easy to create and control a sequence of

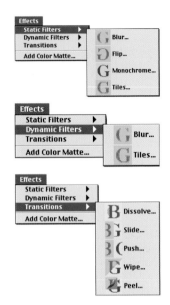

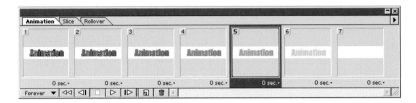

frames based on layers. To see how this works, select the first frame in your animation and add some layer effects, such as an outer glow or a bevel and emboss. Then choose **Tween** from the **Animation** palette pop-up menu. The Tween dialog box lets you decide how to apply your effects to subsequent frames, and it also lets you specify how many frames you want in the final animation. You can choose to apply effects you have created for all layers or just for the selected layer, and whether to vary **Position, Opacity**, and/or **Effects**. Then you can add intermediate frames and specify whether to add them in between the **Next**, **Previous** or a **Selected** frame.

After clicking **OK**, you will see your text slowly fade away, move across the screen, or even gain or lose an effect, depending on what you've specified in the **Tween** dialog box. If you want to preview the animation, click the **Optimized** tab, although viewing it in the browser will give you a far more accurate idea of the animation speed. Use **File > Preview in > Internet Explorer** (or **Netscape Navigator**) to have ImageReady place your GIF animation in a temporary HTML file. In ImageReady, even though frames' delay value might be set to the default of No delay (0.0 seconds), the animation will still play rather slowly, because ImageReady has to process all the layers. Only after all the layers have been flattened and the GIF has been optimized will you get a true sense of the speed of your animation—after which you might want to change the timing on certain frames.

▲ GifBuilder, a free GIF animation program for the Macintosh, offers a variety of effects that can be applied to frames. Like the Tweening command in ImageReady, it will generate all the in-between images automatically. Since GifBuilder is free, you can download it from the Internet if you would like to use these effects.

You can have ImageReady import the animation into a browser to check if everything works. This is particularly important if you work with transparency and disposal methods, since those aren't displayed in ImageReady. In this example you see an animation of a bouncing ball, but the second one (at the bottom) has the disposal method mistakenly set to "Do not dispose."

Changing the speed, or delay, of the animation is very simple. The display time (in seconds) is shown beneath each frame; click on it to reveal some preset options. If you don't see a time value that suits your needs, use Other. You can set the delay time within 1/100th of a second.

LOOPING AN ANIMATION

Do you want your animation to play more than once? No problem. The Loop options are set in the lower left corner of the Animation palette. Choose **Once** to play the animation one time from beginning to end, **Forever** to play it endlessly, and **Other** to specify a particular number of repetitions.

Unfortunately, there is no option for backward and forward—if you need that kind of animation you must create it manually. However, that's very simple; after you have created your animation with the **Tween** command, just Shift-click to select the intermediate frames (not the first and last frame), and then press Option/Alt (which creates a copy of the frames). Now drag the frames to the right side of the last frame and choose **Reverse** Frames from the **Animation palette** pop-up menu.

▲ The standard settings for looping an animation are Once and Forever. To set a specific number of loops, use Other.

SAVING ON BANDWIDTH BY SCALING ANIMATIONS

Since an animation consists of a series of images, its file size is necessarily larger than that of a single image—and as you know, file size is always an issue on the Web. If color reduction and other compression tricks don't shrink the file enough, consider using a little HTML trick that can save as much as 75% on file size. In HTML you set the dimension of an image with the IMG tag's two attributes, WIDTH and HEIGHT. The browser usually uses these attributes

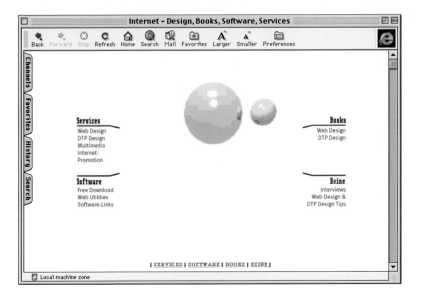

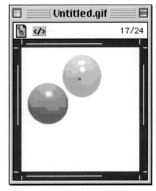

▲ This animation of two rotating balls was scaled to 200% in GoLive, which kept the file size under 10K.

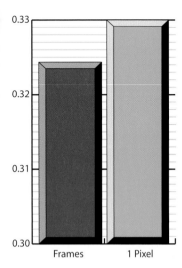

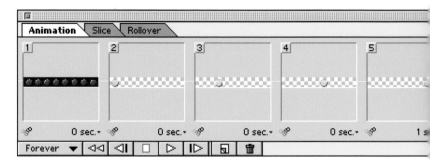

▲ The zero-second trick is a good way to reduce file size. However, even though the frame is reused several times in an animation, the information for Position, Transparency, and Delay still requires some memory—roughly 25 Bytes. I did a test animation by repositioning a frame containing one pixel. The file was larger than that of an animation done with the Tweening command (see chart above). This means that for every 40 frames you are using in your animation, your file size will gain 1 KB just for the Position, Transparency, and Delay information.

to determine the size of the image before it has downloaded, but you can also use them to scale an image. So to gain savings in file size, consider shrinking the animation to 50 percent via **Image > Image Size**, and then doubling its dimensions in the HTML code. Because it's an animation, the decrease in image quality is in most cases not as obvious as with a regular image. (For those of you wondering how we end up with a 75 percent saving when we only reduced the image size by 50 percent, remember that the 50 percent reduction applies to both the width and height of the image, and therefore the final image is only a quarter the size of the original.)

Disposal Methods

Since GIFs support transparency, that means you can create animated GIFs that have transparency. When that's the case, you can select what's called a disposal method to specify what, if anything, is visible through the transparent areas of your frames. Think for a minute about cel animation, where the

◄ Clicking on the Preview in Default Browser button (in the Tool palette) displays the animation along with its HTML code and basic information about the file, such as its size and optimization settings.

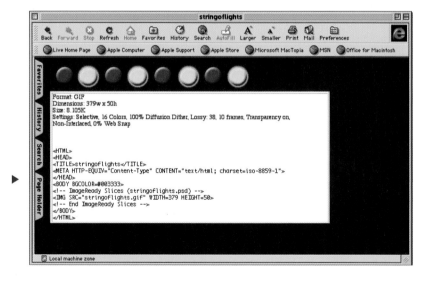

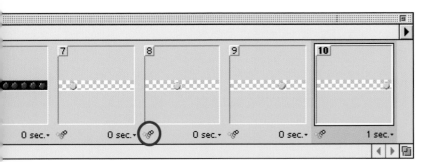

▲ To create an animation of a string of blinking lights, I set the delay to zero and the disposal method to "Do not dispose," as indicated by the circled icon. This way the background string of "darkened" lights will remain visible while individual lights flash.

▲ As you can see in the Layers palette, the entire animation is based on the background layer with all the lights off and one layer with one light on. This layer is moved and the effects settings are changed. It's important that for all the frames with the light on, the background must be hidden.

background of a scene and all the characters are painted on separate sheets of transparent celluloid. This lets the animator reuse the background and animate the characters independently. The same idea lies behind disposal methods. They let you hold a previous frame as a background image, while subsequent frames add the animated character.

You can see the disposal method of a frame by right-clicking (PC) or Control-clicking (Mac) on it. A pop-up menu will appear, offering the options Automatic, Do not dispose and Restore to background. Automatic discards the current frame if the next frame contains layer transparency. According to Adobe this is the best option for most animations, so it is the default setting.

Alternatively, you can choose Do not dispose, which keeps the current frame onscreen while the next frame is displayed. If the second frame contains transparent areas, the first frame will show through. If you start with a full frame (an image that uses the entire frame), define it as Do not dispose, and follow it with several partially transparent frames, all the frames with partial transparency will be combined with the frame that was specified as Do not dispose.

Finally, Restore to background is like Automatic in that it discards the current frame when the next one comes up, but it's different in that you can set a background color or pattern that shows through transparent areas. Use this method if you want to use transparency to have a moving object blend in with the background in the browser.

Important: ImageReady does not simulate the disposal method, so you always have to check your result in the browser by using **File > Preview in > Internet Explorer/Netscape Navigator**.

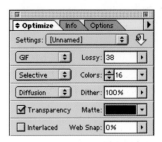

▲ In this particular animation, the glow of the lights needed to fade into the background, so the Matte option was used.

CREATING ANIMATED COMPUTER TUTORIALS

Would you like to create a Web site that features step-by-step tutorials on how to work with computers? Then you should check out Gif·glF·GiF (for Macs). This software allows you to record the contents of your computer screen and save them as a GIF animation (you can download the demo at www.peda. com/ggg/). You can even change the image size to 50 percent or 25 percent (the image in the screenshot was downsampled to 50 percent). Also, you can record just a portion of your screen. Because the program saves the recording as an optimized GIF animation, only the elements that change are recorded, so the overall file size is amazingly small—perfect for the Web. You can also use ImageReady if you have a screen capturing utility (like Snapz Pro from Ambrosia Software; Mac only) that can record and save the screen as a Quicktime movie. Then use ImageReady to convert the movie to a GIF animation (open the movie with **File > Open**) and use the Optimize feature to reduce the amount of data.

ImageReady converts regular ▶
Quicktime movies to a GIF
animation when the movie is
opened.

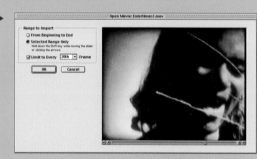

▲ The Gif·glF·GiF
software allows to
capture the screen
and records it as GIF
animation.

OPTIMIZING ANIMATIONS

As you may have realized by now, you don't have to use full frames in your animation, which means you can reduce your final file size by cropping frames to only the parts that are important. ImageReady has a special feature that does exactly this for you. It actually goes through your animation frame by frame and figures out if there are overlapping parts in two sequential frames that are identical. If there are, it crops the frame to only the part that changes. Static areas are eliminated and don't use up precious memory. To activate this feature, select **Optimize Animation** from the **Animation** palette pop-up menu, and then check **Optimize By: Bounding Box.** Since this technique is so effective, you should try to create animations where subsequent frames build on the previous one as often as possible.

This feature can be particularly helpful if you are converting QuickTime movies to GIF animations, something that ImageReady can do easily. Just choose **File > Open** and choose the QuickTime file. An Import dialog box appears and prompts you to specify the number of frames and other parameters. Optimizing the converted file with the Bounding Box option will reduce the file size tremendously. Just make sure that you select Automatic as your disposal method.

▲ Set disposal methods by right-clicking (Windows) or Control-clicking (Mac) on the frame.

Another great feature is the Redundant Pixel Removal option in the Optimize Animation dialog box. It improves the animation by replacing every static pixel with transparency. Since this allows for a better compression (remember, GIF uses a pattern-recognition algorithm that makes same-color areas compress well), the savings can be amazing—particularly in cases where the Bounding Box doesn't work so well. Such a case might be if you create an animation that has changing elements in the upper-right and lower-left corners. Since the Bounding Box can't crop very much, you still end up with large frames even though all the pixels in between might be static. Redundant Pixel Removal fixes the problem!

THE ZERO-SECOND TRICK

Another great way to optimize animations is to use the zero-second trick. Theoretically you can set a delay time of zero seconds (no delay) for each frame in your animation, but in reality, browsers need some time to display each frame. However, this minimal display time is brief enough to make a frame appear almost simultaneously with the previous frame. You can use this to optimize GIF animations by splitting up a frame into two frames, then putting them together by setting the first frame to a zero-second delay.

For example, I created a string of blinking lights effect composed of a background image with all lights off (red) and one single image with a light on (yellow). I placed the image of the yellow light on the background image in several positions and set all the frames to a zero-second delay. Then I selected Do not dispose as my disposal method to keep the background with the darkened lights visible when the yellow lights displayed in sequence, making them appear to blink. (The delay will be more visible on slower computers.)

Obviously, it takes a lot of work to create an animation this way, but you can substantially reduce the amount of data by eliminating redundant pixels.

This technique is also ideal if you have two animations that you want to run asynchronously. For instance, if you want to animate a clock, you need

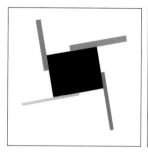

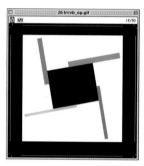

▲ On the top you can see some screen shots of the animation on the Little Rock Web site. On the bottom, the individual frames are displayed and you can see clearly how the Frame Optimization cropped each frame to just the parts that change.

an hour hand and a minute hand that move at different speeds. You'll need 12 positions for the hour hand and let's assume that you'll use 8 positions for the minute hand (to make life easier). With the zero-second trick, your animation requires only 21 individual images (20 images for all the hand positions, plus the background image) instead of 96. So you can see that certain animations benefit tremendously from this technique, but there are limitations on how far you can push it; after all, even a frame that contains a preloaded image requires some memory—and all the information on position, disposal method, and transparency color can add up.

◀ The Little Rock Web site splash screen (www.littlerock.com) uses a cleverly-designed GIF animation in which each frame is cropped to just the areas that change from the previous frame.

TUTORIAL: ROTATING A LOGO

Probably one of the most common animations is the rotating logo. To pre-pare such an animation in ImageReady, you first need to create the 3D logo in an animation application and export the animation as either an image se-quence or a QuickTime movie.

1. Importing frames: To import a QuickTime movie, use the **File > Open** command; to import an image sequence, choose **File > Import > Folder as Frames**, which will import all images in a selected folder. To avoid having to rearrange the order of the frames manually later on, make sure the files are named sequentially.

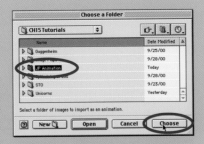

◄ Select File > Import > Folder as Frames and navigate to select the folder that contains the frames of your animation. For this tutorial you can use your own images or download this example from www.mitomedia-books.com.

▲ To change the Delay for all frames simultaneously, select all and then set the time.

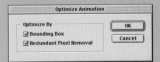

▲ Make sure these two options are selected—they help to keep the file size small.

2. Setting the delay: Since this animation requires that each frame has the same delay, first select the frames with the **Select All Frames** command on the **Animation** palette pop-up menu. Alternatively, you can select the first frame, hold down Shift, and then select the last frame. Click at the bottom of the frame to change the delay time.

3. Optimizing and testing: From the **Animation** palette pop-up menu, choose **Optimize Animation** and check the **Bounding Box** and **Redundant Pixel Removal** options as desired. Also note another trick: the animation on-ly shows a 180-degree rotation, which saves 50% of the file size. Click on the **Preview in Default Browser** button in the **Tool** palette to open the anima-tion in a browser, where you will get a true sense of the animation speed. (The animation preview in ImageReady is much slower.)

▲ Always preview the animation in a browser after you specify the delay time. The preview in ImageReady is not accurate.

4. Scaling the animation: When you import the animation into your HTML authoring tool, try scaling it to twice the size. This makes for an eye-catching splash screen (you can see an example of this at www.plenk-josef.de).

Illustration: Michael Baumgardt

GIF

GIF—Graphical Interchange Format

GIF is the most flexible of all the image formats for the Web. It can display photos with a decent level of quality, does an excellent job of compressing graphics, and even offers animation. So it should come as no surprise that GIF gets such a large chapter. There is a lot to learn—and hopefully I'll be able to answer all your questions.

HOW DOES GIF COMPRESS?

GIF applies two compression techniques to images. One is called CLUT, which stands for Color Look-Up Table. The other is the LZW compression algorithm. Let's take a closer look at each of them to understand why GIF yields much better results with certain images than with others.

➤ CLUT—Color Look-Up Table

To understand why a CLUT is so useful for data compression, it is helpful to understand how image formats work without it. For each pixel that your scanner creates when it digitizes a photo, 24 bits of color information are saved. For an image of 100 x 100 pixels, this requires 240,000 bits of color information. Since very few photos require a full spectrum of 16 million colors (which

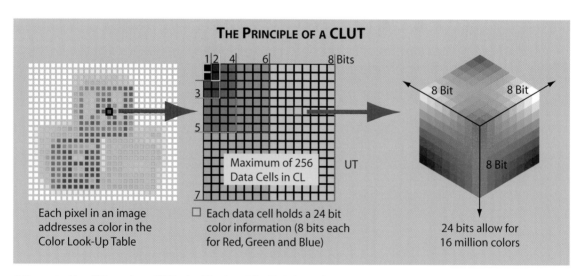

THE PRINCIPLE OF A CLUT

Each pixel in an image addresses a color in the Color Look-Up Table

☐ Each data cell holds a 24 bit color information (8 bits each for Red, Green and Blue)

24 bits allow for 16 million colors

▲ Every pixel in a GIF contains a CLUT value. The size of the CLUT depends upon the number of bits used: one bit can only address two values (0 and 1), two bits can hold four values, and eight bits can store 256 values. Regardless of how many colors a CLUT holds, each color always has 24 bits, which means that GIF has a color range of more than 16 million colors.

is what 24-bit color gives you), someone had the clever idea of limiting the total number of colors to 256 and saving those values (each of them still with
a color depth of 24 bits) in a table. Then, instead of saving a full 24 bits of information for each pixel, you only need a reference to the location in the
table. Eight bits are enough to address 256 locations in the CLUT, a two-thirds
reduction in the amount of data. So instead of 240,000 bits, the same 100-x-
100-pixel image can be stored in 86,144 bits.

All of you math whizzes have probably realized that this is actually a little
less than a two-thirds reduction. The reason is that the CLUT itself requires
some data. In fact, a CLUT with 256 colors needs 256 x 24 bits, which equals
6,144 bits. Our 100-x-100-pixel image will therefore be down to 10,768 bytes.

THE FILE SIZE OF A CLUT				
	Colors	**Bits**	**Bytes**	**KB**
1 bit	2	48	6	0.006
2 bits	4	96	12	0.012
3 bits	8	192	24	0.024
4 bits	16	384	48	0.048
5 bits	32	768	96	0.096
6 bits	64	1536	192	0.192
7 bits	128	3072	384	0.384
8 bits	256	6144	768	0.768

This technique of creating a CLUT and referencing it is called indexing. To
save a GIF in Photoshop 5.0, you first had to switch from RGB mode to indexed color. Thankfully, with the Save for Web command in Photoshop 5.5
and 6.0, you don't need to go through that process any more.

But the more important reason to use Save for Web in Photoshop, and to
take advantage of ImageReady's Optimize palette, is that these features are
intelligent enough to reduce the CLUT to the absolute minimum requirement. For example, if you have only two colors in your image but you choose
to save it in 256 colors, the Save for Web command realizes that the CLUT is
much bigger than it has to be and reduces it accordingly. And the smaller
your CLUT, the less memory your file requires.

So let's have a pop quiz: how large would a 100-x-100-pixel image be if it
had a CLUT with only two colors (black and white)? Since the image has to

refer to only two color values, it only needs one bit per pixel to reference the CLUT. The CLUT itself has two colors, each with 24 bits of color information. The total then is 10,024, bits or 1,253 bytes. If you save the same image with a 256-color CLUT, you'll end up with 16,114 bits instead—an increase of almost 60 percent. Okay, I'll admit that this is an extreme example, but it helps to illustrate the importance of using the Save for Web command. This command makes your life a lot easier, and helps you create the smallest possible image files. In fact, if you save this image with Photoshop's Save for Web command, you will actually get an even smaller file: 266 bytes instead of 1,253 bytes. That additional 80 percent savings comes from GIF's second compression technique: the LZW algorithm.

➤ The LZW Algorithm

CLUT is only part of the reason for GIF's great compression capabilities. The other part is the LZW compression scheme, developed by and named after the researchers Lempel, Ziv, and Welch. The LZW algorithm is based on pattern recognition: basically, it goes through an image file row by row, from top left to bottom right, looking for adjacent pixels of the same color. Let's say, for example, that five pixels in a row are the same shade of red. Here, the LZW algorithm would write down "Five x Red" instead of "Red, Red, Red, Red, Red." Although I've oversimplified a bit, you can see why graphics with large areas of identical colors are well-suited for GIF. For a more detailed explanation of LZW compression, see page 218.

▲ This 100x100-pixel image was indexed with 256 colors and saved as a GIF with a file size of 6,664 bytes, although it should require 10,768 bytes. The difference is due to the LZW compression algorithm.

BALANCING COMPRESSION WITH QUALITY

When you save an image in GIF format, your goal is usually to get the smallest possible file size along with the best quality. To achieve this, you may have to adjust the color depth of the CLUT relative to the LZW compression; the fewer colors the CLUT uses, the better the LZW gets. However, if the image loses too much of its quality and detail, you may want to try dithering to get a better-looking image—even though dithering is counterproductive to the LZW compression.

Luckily, the complex process of adjusting these factors is a breeze with ImageReady and Photoshop. Both programs let you view as many as four versions of your image at once, so you can compare the quality of different settings and optimize an image more easily. To get an idea of how different bit depths, palettes, and dithering settings effect various types of images, check out the GIF comparison chart beginning on page 222. The chart shows the results for a photographic image (Image A), a graphic illustration (Image B),

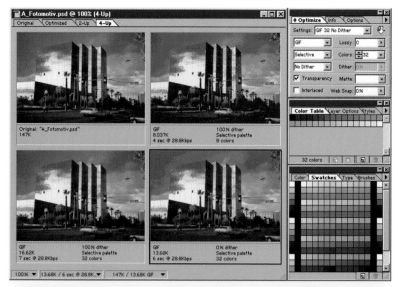

◄ Photoshop has the Save for Web dialog box; the same commands and parameters are available in ImageReady's own palettes and menus. So whenever I explain how to do something in the Save for Web dialog box in this book, remember that you can perform the same tasks in ImageReady.

a photo illustration (Image C), and a color spectrum (Image D), which serves as more of a reference than a real-life example. A spectrum makes a poor GIF since the LZW algorithm can't find many patterns, but it still gives you a good idea how the CLUT effects the image.

LZW PATTERN RECOGNITION

Are you hopelessly curious about why things are the way they are? Then this section is for you: an in-depth look at LZW compression. The fact is, the LZW algorithm works quite a bit like the Color Look-Up Table. The only difference is that LZW stores patterns it finds in the image and indexes them. One funny thing is that once the algorithm builds the look-up table, it then throws it away—it is not stored along with the compressed data. But since there is a logic behind the indexing, the decoder can recreate the look-up table when needed.

Let's look at an example. Say we wanted to compress this chain of characters: ABACABA (imagine that they represent colors). We know that we have four possible values (A, B, C, and D in a 2 bit Color Look-Up Table), so we could start by putting those four values in a table and calling them #0, #1, #2 and #3. As we check to see through the chains of pixels that make up the image, we will always be checking to see if two adjacent pixels match one entry in the index table. If they do, we include the next adjacent pixel and look if this pattern is also already indexed. We keep on checking and including the next pixel until we find one pattern that doesn't match. Then we note the last match in the index, give the new pattern an index number, and go to the next pixel until we're at the end of the image.

In our case the first two characters are AB. Since this pattern is not in our table, we put it down and write 0 for the A that we found. The second character is a B and we check to see if this character and the previous one are already recorded in our table as a pattern. Since they are not, we give this pattern a new index (#4) and write down 1 for the B. The character after that is the A again, so we check if the pattern BA is in the table. That is not the case, so it is indexed as #5 and we note 0 for the third character (A). Since neither the next letter, C, nor the pattern AC is in the table, we put it down as #6 and write 2 for the C. The next character is A and the combination CA gets indexed since it is not in the table, but (!) we realize now that the A and the following character already exist as a pattern, so we write down 4. For the last character, A, we can only write down 0 since there is nothing following, but not before we register the combination ABA as #8.

This example hasn't produced much of a saving—instead of seven characters we have now six numbers, but you can imagine that with larger images the LZW algorithm finds more and more patterns it has already indexed. Once the image is saved, the LZW doesn't require the index table any more (it also helps saving data). To decompress the image, the browser regenerates the index table for each GIF, which takes some time and processor power.

ENCODING EXAMPLE

ABACABA	010240
A =	0
B =	1
C =	2
D =	3
AB =	4
BA =	5
AC =	6
CA =	7
ABA =	8

▲ This is an example of how the LZW-algorithm would index seven pixels (each letter in ABACABA represents a pixel with a color; same letter equals same color.) Each line in this table represents a position in the index table: in the first four position of the index are the basic colors (ABCD), followed by the various patterns that the algorithm finds. At the end the result is 010240, which is only a saving of one (instead of seven letters you have six numbers), but if the image was larger, the savings would be more substantial.

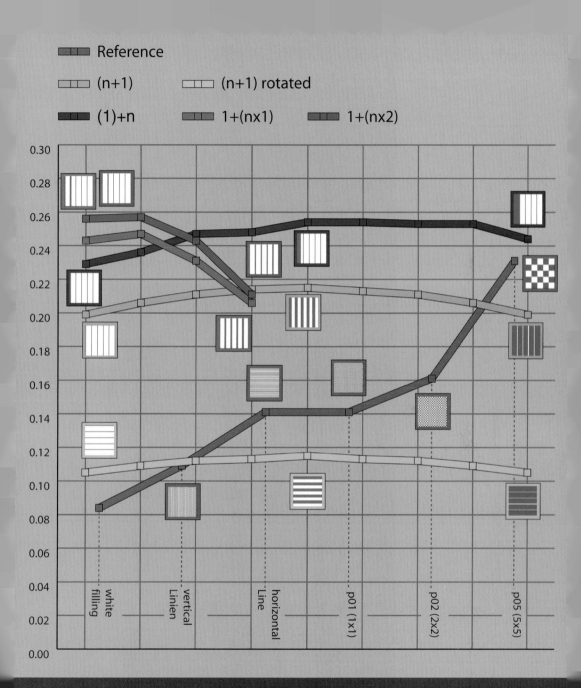

Legend

- **Reference**
- (n+1)
- (n+1) rotated
- **(1)+n**
- 1+(nx1)
- 1+(nx2)

Vertical axis values
0.30 · 0.28 · 0.26 · 0.24 · 0.22 · 0.20 · 0.18 · 0.16 · 0.14 · 0.12 · 0.10 · 0.08 · 0.06 · 0.04 · 0.02 · 0.00

Horizontal axis labels
white filling · vertical Linien · horizontal Line · p01 (1x1) · p02 (2x2) · p05 (5x5)

▲ To get a better feeling for the LZW algorithm, look at this comparison of a group of one-bit GIFs that all are variations on patterns. See the next two pages for the individual graphs.

1+(nx1)	KB
01+2x1	0.243
01+3x1	0.247
01+4x1	0.231
01+5x1	0.206

1+(nx2)	KB
01+2x2	0.256
01+3x2	0.257
01+4x2	0.243
01+5x2	0.211

▲ The width of the five vertical lines was continuously increased by one pixel.

(1)+n	KB
01+1	0.229
01+2	0.236
01+3	0.247
01+4	0.248
01+5	0.254
01+6	0.254
01+7	0.253
01+8	0.253
01+9	0.244

▲ For reference, only the first red line was widened by one pixel until it measured 10 pixels in width.

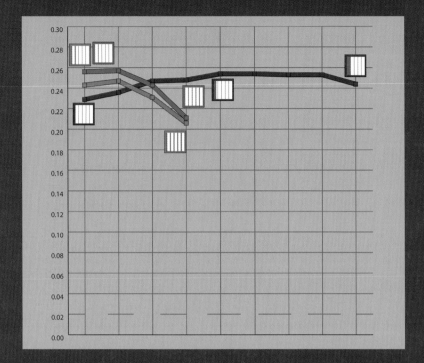

Now that we have gone through this explanation of LZW compression, can you see why an image with horizontal lines compresses better than one with vertical lines? Look at the comparison chart on page 197: the image with vertical lines requires more memory than its rotated version. This makes sense, since same-color runs create fewer patterns than if pixel colors alternate.

But there are exceptions to this rule. If you look at the chart on the top of page 219, you will see that a pattern with one-pixel vertical lines requires less memory than its rotated counterpart with horizontal lines. It's a bit confusing, but the reason is that after LZW has indexed the patterns and written all the index numbers, it compresses the resulting byte patterns. To simplify this, just imagine that while earlier we looked for horizontal patterns, now we are looking for vertical patterns. The image with the horizontal lines is much more complex in that respect, and it therefore carries more data.

What does all this mean to our work? Not much, really, since you don't want to design an image on the basis of how well it compresses. But it will help you to make a more educated choice when you need to decide which format will yield the best results and what compression settings to use.

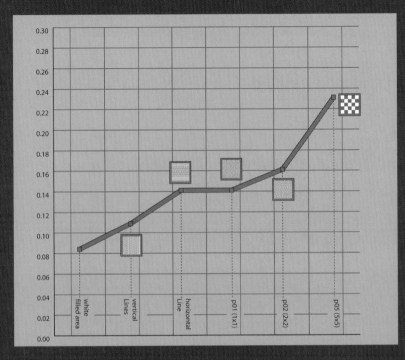

Reference	KB
white	0.084
vertical lines	0.109
p01 (1x1)	0.141
horizontal lines	0.141
p02 (2x2)	0.161
p05 (5x5)	0.231
Noise**	2.900*

*(-0.76 kByte for the CLUT)
** not shown in graph

▲ I created several files as references. As expected, the white file is the smallest, and the Noise file, created with the Add Noise filter, is the largest (not shown on the graph). Strangely enough, the file with vertical lines is smaller than the one with horizontal lines—this has to do with final byte compression (see the previous page for details).

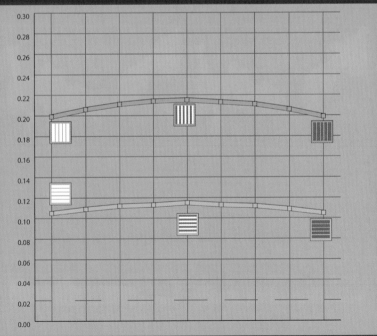

	vert.	horiz.
01	0.199	0.105
02	0.206	0.109
03	0.211	0.112
04	0.214	0.113
05	0.215	0.115
06	0.213	0.113
07	0.211	0.112
08	0.206	0.109
09	0.199	0.105

▲ A red vertical line with a width of 1 pixel is repeated every 10 pixels. With every instance, the line is widened by one pixel. As expected, the file size decreases as soon as the line width surpasses five pixels. Rotating the files to make the lines horizontal decreases the file size.

This table focuses on color depths of 3 bits to 5 bits (8 to 32 colors), which is commonly the range used for saving GIF images. Images that require more than 32 colors should be saved as JPEG. I applied the Adaptive palette to Image A and the Web-safe palette to Images B, C, and D. Compare the file sizes of the images and my own subjective quality scale, a Q value of 0 to 5, with 5 being highest quality.

8 COLORS

	Dithered	Non-Dithered

IMAGE A

9451 bytes	Q=5.0	6689 bytes	Q=4.0

IMAGE B

11,643 bytes	Q=4.0	7411 bytes	Q=2.0

IMAGE C

7739 bytes	Q=4.0	6424 bytes	Q=7.0

IMAGE D

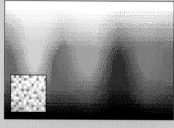
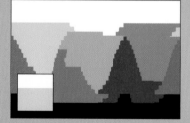

8695 bytes	Q=6.0	1579 bytes	Q=1.0

16 COLORS

| **Dithered** | **Non-Dithered** |

13,311 bytes   Q=7.0

9736 bytes   Q=5.0

13,488 bytes   Q=6.0

8189 bytes   Q=2.0

13,450 bytes   Q=9.0

9769 bytes   Q=6.0

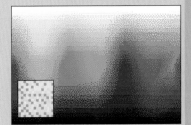

11,524 bytes   Q=6.5

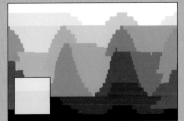

2412 bytes   Q=1.5

▲ The JPEG comparison chart on page 238 features this image, labeled Image C, as an example of when GIF would produce the smallest file with the best quality.

If you're interested, here are the GIF results for the image above:

WITHOUT DITHERING	
Colors	**Size**
8	4,465
16	5,277
24	5,733
32	6,092

WITH DITHERING	
Colors	**Size**
8	6,127
16	6,463
24	6,875
32	6,875

All images measure 264 pixels (width) x 180 pixels (height). Uncompressed file size is 140KB.

24 COLORS

Dithered	Non-Dithered
IMAGE A	
15,576 bytes Q=8.0	12,378 bytes Q=6.0
IMAGE B	
15,635 bytes Q=7.0	9499 bytes Q=3.0
IMAGE C	
16,600 bytes Q=9.0	10,005 bytes Q=6.0
IMAGE D	
12,466 bytes Q=6.5	2757 bytes Q=2.0

32 COLORS

Dithered	Non-Dithered

| 17,182 bytes | Q=9.0 | 13,752 bytes | Q=6.0 |

| 16,609 bytes | Q=8.0 | 9754 bytes | Q=3.0 |

| 16,975 bytes | Q=9.0 | 10,005 bytes | Q=6.0 |

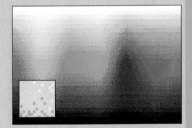

| 13,679 bytes | Q=7.0 | 3311 bytes | Q=2.0 |

DITHERING
COMPARISON CHART

The graph to the right shows the file size of the four images A, B, C, and D, saved with dithering (line graph). For reference, the quality values are displayed as well (column graph).

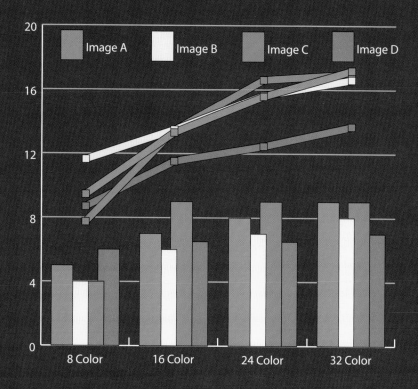

These graphs show how much the dithering affects the file size of each image.

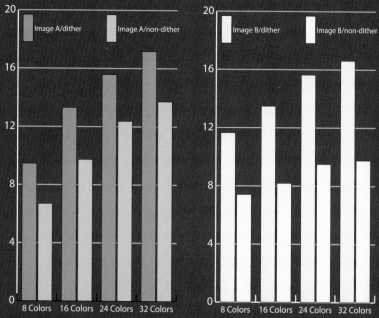

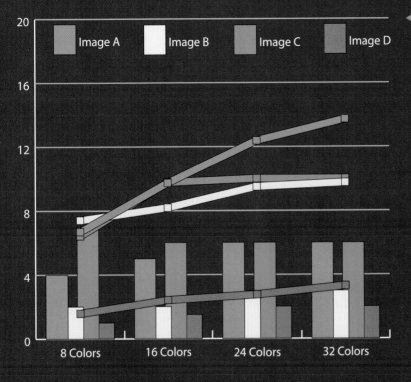

This diagram shows the file sizes of the four images from the GIF comparison chart (beginning on page 222) saved *without* dithering. They are significantly smaller than the dithered files on the previous page. For reference, the quality values are displayed as well (column graph).

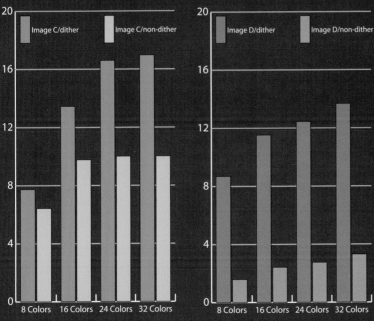

THE LOSSY OPTION

To interpret the graphs, look for dots that represent the same number of colors in each of the three files (they're connected with narrow yellow lines). The vertical axis in each chart is the file size, and the horizontal axis represents the quality; dots in the lower-right corner of the charts indicate the best images.

Both the Save for Web command and the Optimize palette in ImageReady offer the Lossy option. This option reduces file size by replacing pixels with already indexed patterns (as explained on page 194). The result can look either like a pixel storm, in the worst case, or like a dithered image, in the best case.

To get a better idea of the effects of Lossy on file size and image quality, I compressed a photo (Image A), a photo with graphics (Image B), and a spectrum (Image D), with a Lossy setting of 30%, which is pretty much the upper limit if you want to obtain good results. I also used a regular GIF with an adaptive palette as a reference image. Each image was compressed with various CLUT sizes between 2 and 256 colors. First I looked at the quality of the images compressed with the 30% Lossy setting, then I looked at each of them again with a Dithering setting of 100% and a Lossy setting of zero and gave them a (subjective) quality value (between 1–10 with 10 being the best).

I left out the graphic image used in the GIF comparison chart (Image C) because it consists mostly of areas of flat color; the Lossy option has no effect on the quality, and its file size stays pretty constant no matter what the Lossy setting is.

▲ The chart shows that with Image A, the photograph, Lossy achieves the best results between 16 and 64 colors. With 64 colors, the Lossy GIF is 45 percent smaller than the regular GIF while maintaining the same image quality. The 16 color version shows 30 percent less quality with Lossy, but it's also 1KB smaller than the regular GIF. These results suggest that a photographic image saved as a GIF can greatly benefit from the Lossy option.

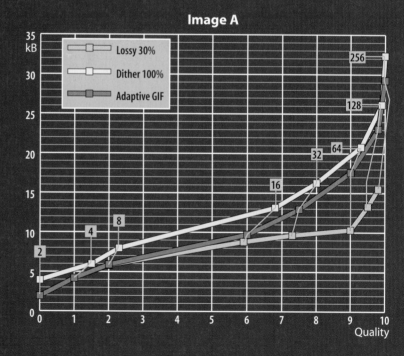

Image B

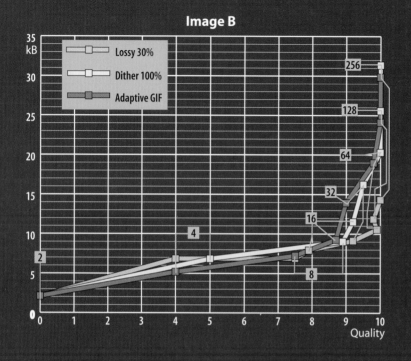

▲ Image B is a photo-illustration, which is easier for LZW to compress. The results in the chart are similar to those of Image A; the difference is that the three GIFs are much closer to each other in file size and quality. The best ratio of file size reduction/image quality occurs between 32 and 64 colors.

Image D

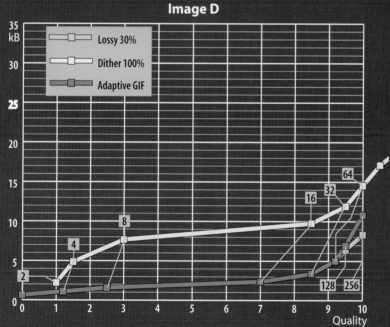

▲ Image D is the color spectrum, just about the worst kind of image for a GIF. Although the graph shows quite high marks for quality, keep in mind that these are just relative assessments; they're not meant to be compared with the quality of the other two images. You really need at least 64 colors to get a decent result with this image. Dithering improved the results quite a bit, which is why a couple of the results are actually better than 10.

▲ This image was saved with the Adaptive palette setting, 8 bits, and diffusion dithering.

▲ This image, the reference image in our comparative example, was saved with the Adaptive palette setting, 8 bits, and no dithering.

I saved each of the files with four different levels of color—with 8, 16, 24, and 32 colors. For the photograph (Image A), I used the Adaptive palette, which allows site visitors with a monitor card that supports thousands or millions of colors to see a much better image. It's important to test images that use the Adaptive palette in a browser with a 256-color monitor, but it's worth the effort. For Images B, C, and D, I used the Web-safe color palette.

At each color depth, I experimented with dithering. Many people avoid dithering a GIF because so doing limits the effectiveness of LZW compression. And while it's true that dithering does result in a decreased compression ratio, it is an important tool for simulating intermediate colors. The increased file size isn't as bad as you might think, and the drawback of the larger file is often offset by the improved image quality, particularly if you choose Noise Dithering in the Save for Web dialog box. If you want the best of both worlds, you can consider partially dithering an image. I'll explain how to do that later in this chapter.

In a printed book it is difficult to see the subtle color differences in the various GIF settings, due to the conversion of the indexed RGB color space to CMYK. Some colors that can be displayed in RGB just aren't available in print; also, dot gain and rasterizing cover up a lot of fine artifacts. So to give you a better idea of the quality differences, I included a quality value—a number between 1 and 10, where 10 is the best quality—next to each image in the chart. While this is definitely a subjective evaluation, I hope it's a useful point of reference.

CREATING GIFs

As I've said, the most effective way to create a GIF in Photoshop is to use the Save for Web command. On certain occasions, which I will address later in this chapter, you may want to prepare a GIF by converting an RGB file to indexed color in the Image > Mode submenu. The options presented in the Indexed Color dialog box are similar to those in the Save for Web dialog box, but the latter offers more features for maximizing quality and minimizing file size. Here is an overview of the options you have when saving GIF images for the Web in Photoshop.

➤ Color-Reduction Algorithms

First you must decide which colors to include in the CLUT. This is a difficult task because each image is unique and requires an individual setting. Photoshop offers the following choice of color-reduction algorithms, also called palettes, and CLUT templates accessible from both the Indexed Color and Save for Web dialog boxes (I've listed them in order of their importance for your work):

● Adaptive

I personally favor the Adaptive color palette and believe that it is perhaps the most important palette for GIF images. It lets you reduce the size of the CLUT to 32 colors or fewer and still achieve excellent results. As its name suggests, this palette adapts to the colors in the image, meaning that it picks the most frequently-occurring colors for the CLUT. Since those colors are rarely in the Web-safe color palette, you will always have some additional dithering or color shifting when Adaptive images are viewed on systems with 256 or fewer colors. Luckily, the Web Snap button in the Save for Web dialog box gives you some control by letting you shift individual colors to their closest Web-safe alternative (Web-safe colors are marked with a diamond dot in the color table).

● Selective & Perceptual

Adobe, however, believes that Selective is the best choice for Web design and uses it as the default setting in the Indexed Color and Save for Web dialog boxes. The Selective color table is similar to the Perceptual color table, but it favors broad areas of color and the preservation of Web colors. Perceptual gives priority to colors for which the human eye has greater sensitivity. You can check this out if you set the Web Snap slider to 25% and then switch between the **Selective, Perceptual,** and **Adaptive** palettes. The Selective

▲ This image was saved with the Web palette and diff. dithering.

▲ This image was saved with the Web palette setting and Pattern dithering.

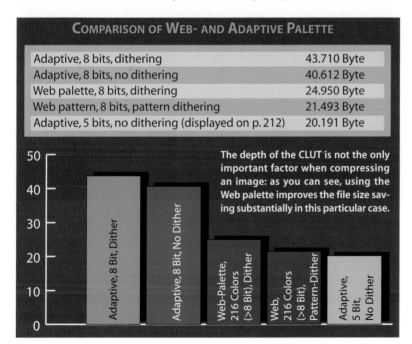

COMPARISON OF WEB- AND ADAPTIVE PALETTE	
Adaptive, 8 bits, dithering	43.710 Byte
Adaptive, 8 bits, no dithering	40.612 Byte
Web palette, 8 bits, dithering	24.950 Byte
Web pattern, 8 bits, pattern dithering	21.493 Byte
Adaptive, 5 bits, no dithering (displayed on p. 212)	20.191 Byte

The depth of the CLUT is not the only important factor when compressing an image: as you can see, using the Web palette improves the file size saving substantially in this particular case.

Bar chart values: 50, 40, 30, 20, 10, 0

Bars labeled: Adaptive, 8 Bit, Dither; Adaptive, 8 Bit, No Dither; Web-Palette, 216 Colors (>8 Bit), Dither; Web, 216 Colors (>8 Bit), Pattern-Dither; Adaptive, 5 Bit, No Dither

▲ This image was saved with the Adaptive palette setting, 5 bits, and no dithering.

reduction algorithm usually generates more Web-safe colors than Adaptive or Perceptual.

The best way to learn how the different color algorithms work is to create a full-spectrum gradient test blend and save it as **Perceptual, Selective,** and **Adaptive**, as I've done here. In the screen shot below, each version of the file has 16 colors, but each color-reduction algorithm renders a different range of hues. That's why it's important not to use the Selective color algorithm just because it's the default setting. For best results, you should consider the colors in your image and choose the palette accordingly: for more detail in dark areas, use **Selective**; for more detail in lighter colors, use **Perceptual** or **Selective**; for more detail in the red spectrum, use **Adaptive**.

● **Web**

The advantage of the Web palette is that all 216 colors display almost identically on all platforms. The different Gamma on each platform will still create slight shifts, but using this color table ensures that for the most part, what you see really is what you get, with no additional dithering or color changes. In real life, however, this color table is not used very often because it means saving your image in the worst possible color mode just to be sure it will look good on 256-color displays.

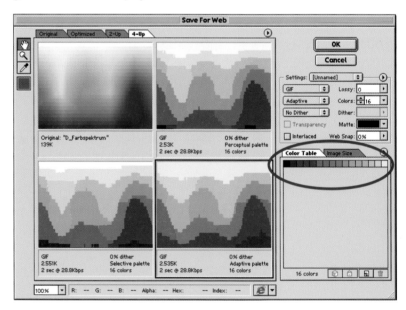

▲To get a better feel for the three color-reduction algorithms, optimize an image with each one and then use the 4-Up option to display the results and compare their color tables.

Using the Adaptive color palette and a reduced CLUT (maximum five bits) is a better, albeit more labor-intensive, way to get predictable colors and better results on high-end monitors. As I explained previously, because the color table is adaptive, it picks the colors that occur most frequently in the image, giving you the best possible display. The only drawback is that you have to view the image in each browser and on each platform, with a monitor display setting of 256 colors, to be sure that your image looks decent under those viewing conditions. Using ImageReady, you can get an idea how the image will look by selecting **Browser Dither** in the **View > Preview** menu, but that is just an approximation.

Even though using an adaptive CLUT requires more work, it is more rewarding because you get the best-looking image on high-quality displays and you can rest assured that the image also looks good on low-end monitors. Use Web only on graphics that you have created that contain mostly Web-safe colors.

● Exact
This mode is available in the Indexed Color dialog box in Photoshop, and only if the image contains fewer than 256 colors. The CLUT is built of all the colors in the image, so it makes sense that the dithering option in the dialog box is not selected.

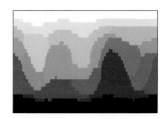

▲ PERCEPTUAL
The Perceptual palette is more detailed in the brighter parts of the image, so bright colors are differentiated more than in the Adaptive color palette. Both the Perceptual and Selective palettes emphasize the yellow part of the spectrum.

▲ SELECTIVE
The Selective palette shows more detail than the Perceptual palette in dark areas, and it favors the preservation of Web-safe colors.

▲ The Save for Web dialog box lets you display the image in the browser. This is important when you don't use the Web safe color palette because Netscape and Explorer adjust the CLUT quite differently on monitors with 256 colors.

▲ ADAPTIVE
The Adaptive palette's spectrum offers less differentiation between the bright and dark parts of the image, but it yields more detail overall throughout the spectrum (for instance, look at the magenta).

● Mac OS and Windows Systems

These choices let you save the image with a platform-specific color table. These two modes are most important for multimedia designers who might want to optimize the images for specific computers. For Web design, neither palette has much significance unless you really need to optimize your images for one specific platform.

● Custom

Custom allows you to create or import your own CLUT, which can be helpful if you want to use a common palette for all your images. There are two situations where you might create and use your own palette. The first situation occurs if you save every image on your page with its own adaptive palette; if you do this, you might run out of video memory on 256-color displays. For example, if you had 10 images with 32 colors each, then the total number of colors would be 320—which means that 64 colors on your page would shift. To prevent unpredictable color shifts or dithering, you might consider using one custom palette for all your images. But don't worry too much about this, because most images probably share many similar colors, and this type of color shifting only affects Web pages when you have a lot of very different pictures.

The second situation where you might want to use a custom color table is if your page contains many images with different shades of a single color, such as yellow. If you were to optimize each image individually, you would end up with many different CLUTs, because the frequency of certain yellows would vary in each individual image. This might mean that the same color would shift differently in the individual images. In cases where the images are adjacent (for example, in an image table), this can be a problem.

● Previous

The Previous option, which is available only in the Indexed Color dialog box, does exactly what it says: it applies the color table used most recently, which is a simple way to apply the color of a sample image to additional images without having to go through the process of saving the color table and reimporting it.

● Uniform

According to Adobe, the Uniform palette is created by distributing the available colors evenly over the whole color spectrum. You can see the effect best if you open a photo and index it with 16 colors. This will shift all the colors in your image and the result will be an image that looks posterized. If you use 256 colors, you end up with the Web-safe color palette, and you are free to choose the number of colors in your image. But to be honest, I haven't found even one useful application for this palette.

➤ Dithering

In addition to selecting the CLUT, you can also define the dithering in the Indexed Colors and Save for Web dialog boxes. Dithering improves the visual quality of an image by taking two colors from the color table and calculating a missing intermediate color. In general, dithering makes GIF compress less efficiently (it creates bigger files), but you can usually reduce the overall number of colors in the image by increasing the dithering percentage. Most of the time, reducing the number of colors is the key to producing smaller files. Therefore, you should reduce the number of colors to a point just before you can see a substantial drop in quality, then use the Dithering slider to improve the display, all the while keeping an eye on the file size. The example on pages 230 to 232 shows that there is virtually no visual quality difference between an 8-bit version of the sample image with an Adaptive palette (page 230) and the 5-bit version (page 232), but the chart on page 231 reveals that the 5-bit image is half the size of the 8-bit image. Dithering the 8-bit version didn't add much to the image's file size; this image contains so many colors that it is hard for the LZW algorithm to find any patterns (in fact, this image should really be saved in JPEG format). Finally, indexing this particular image with the Web-safe color palette (page 231) produced great results because the palette disregards all the subtle color changes and many adjacent pixels get flattened to the same color, which improves the pattern recognition.

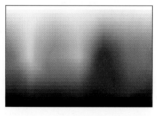

▲ What dithering does can best be seen in the reference image: without dithering, the spectrum gets reduced to flat color areas; with dithering, the colors blend gradually.

Photoshop and ImageReady let you choose from three dithering options: Diffusion, Pattern, and Noise. Pattern dithering mixes the two adjacent colors in a regular pattern that's easy for the eye to see, so you should avoid it. Diffusion and Noise dithering, which use similar algorithms, yield much better visual results. In my experience, Noise dithering does a better job, but Diffusion dithering is nice because it lets you set the amount of dithering via a slider. Remember that although dithering increases file size, the increase is usually offset by the improved image quality, and you can always counteract the file-size increase using the Lossy slider.

➤ Lossy

The Lossy option works miracles with many GIF files. It uses the patterns found by the LZW algorithm (a lossless scheme, see page 194) and stores them in a compression table. Then you can use the Lossy slider to specify how much you want to reuse those patterns in the image, thereby improving compression further. For more details, see page 228.

➤ Transparency and Matte

Photoshop's Save for Web dialog box and ImageReady's Optimize palette both offer a Transparency option; in Save for Web, this option is grayed out when there are no transparent parts or layers in the image.

You can use transparency to let the background color of your Web page show through transparent pixels in a GIF image so that the GIF blends nicely into the background of a page in a browser. But as you may recall, transparent GIFs can have "halos" if the Web page background doesn't match the background pixels in the image. That's where the Matte option comes in. Matte lets you select a color—the background color of your Web page—and blend it with the transparent pixels.

To get a better idea of how this works, choose the **Text** tool in Photoshop and write some text on its own layer, then hide the background layer by toggling off **Visibility** in the **Layers** palette. Choose **Save for Web,** check the **Transparency** box, and select a **Matte** color that matches the color of your HTML page background; it will look like a halo in the **Optimized** preview, but it will blend seamlessly with the background in a browser.

➤ Interlaced

The Interlaced option is important when you have many images on your Web site. As you know, if you don't limit the number of images and the total file size, the page will take so long to load in the browser that you may lose visitors. (If you're lucky, they'll just go make coffee and then come back.)

Because interlacing rearranges the pixel rows when you're saving a GIF or JPEG image, browsers can display a low-resolution "preview" of the image while downloading the remaining data. (Some browsers, such as Internet Explorer, actually display interlaced GIFs line by line.) Gradually, the resolution gets sharper and clearer until the image is finished downloading. Because

In order to use the Transparency option in the Save for Web command, the background layer needs to be transparent. A transparent layer is displayed as a gray-checkered pattern.

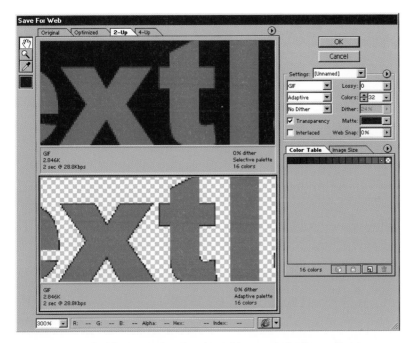

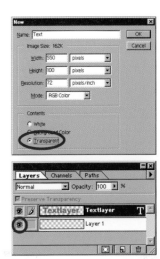

▲ You can either create a new document with a transparent layer or hide the background layer later before you call up the Save for Web dialog box. Activate the Transparency option in the Save for Web dialog box and select a matte color.

▲ As you can see, the blue matte gives the edges of the text a halo effect against a transparent background. But if you place it in an HTML document with a blue background, the text blends seamlessly. If the background color changes, just change the matte color.

visitors can see the image take shape as it's being downloaded, they get the impression that the process is faster than waiting for a whole image to appear, but in fact, an interlaced image actually takes slightly longer to download than noninterlaced images.

GIF interlacing works by transmitting every eighth row of the image (1, 9, 17, and so on) on the first pass. The second pass sends every fourth row (5, 13, 21, and so on), the third pass sends the remaining odd row numbers (3, 7, 11, 15, and so on), and the final pass sends the remaining even-numbered rows (2, 4, 6, 8, and so on).

While GIF interlacing always uses these four passes, JPEG interlacing lets you choose between three to five passes. Interlacing also affects the file size of the two formats differently: a GIF will increase slightly in size because the scrambled rows reduce the number of patterns that the LZW algorithm can use, but an interlaced JPEG is generally smaller than a noninterlaced JPEG.

It's important not to use interlacing and transparency in the same image, because unwanted pixels may display in transparent areas when the image

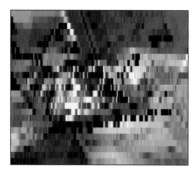

▲ The Interlaced option will encode an image in multiple passes. GIF uses always four passes—you can see how the first three passes are displayed in a browser. Some browsers, like Internet Explorer, will display it line by line instead.

is viewed in a browser. This happens because some browsers use the first data pass to display a low-resolution preview that stretches the rows to the full size of the image, which may cause colors to appear in areas that will later become transparent. And since not all browsers refresh, those pixels may remain visible. You won't always encounter this problem, but check the browser (older browsers in particular) to be on the safe side.

➤ Web Snap

Not many designers use the Web-safe color palette for their images because it subjects visitors to the worst display quality regardless of how many colors their monitor can display. The Adaptive and Perceptual palettes produce much better results on monitors that display millions of colors, while still producing decent image quality on 256-color displays. The Web Snap option in Photoshop's Save for Web dialog box and ImageReady's Optimize palette are handy if you're using these color-reduction algorithms because they let you refine the colors produced so that you can improve the quality of these images in 256-color mode. By adjusting the slider, you can specify a tolerance for shifting colors to the closest Web-safe equivalent. If you only need one or a few colors brought into the Web-safe spectrum, use this technique instead: click the color in the image with the **Eyedropper** tool (Shift-click to select additional colors), which selects the hue or hues in the color table. Then click the cube icon at the bottom of the **Color Table** palette to shift the selected colors to their closest Web-safe match; a dot in the color swatch indicates that it's Web-safe.

After you specify the colors that you've snapped to the **Web palette**, you can preview how the image will look on a 256-color display by choosing **Browser Dither** from the **Preview** pop-up menu (the right-pointing arrow at the top right corner of the image window) in the **Save for Web** dialog box. In

ImageReady, click on the **Optimized** tab and choose **View > Preview > Browser Dither**.

OPTIMIZING A CLUT

Since the goal of creating GIF images is to minimize the number of colors used while maximizing final image quality, it's important to understand how to make good use of the Color Table palette. Here are some important techniques for optimizing a CLUT using the color table.

First, select **Sort by Popularity** from the palette's pop-up menu, which places the most frequently-used color at the top left of the table and works down to the least-used color at the lower right corner. Look for adjacent colors that are similar, and chances are that you can delete one of them without a significant detrimental effect on overall image quality. When you're doing this, it's a good idea to start with less popular colors—those at the bottom of the table. To delete a color, click it in the table and then click on the **Trash** button. Keep in mind that you can't undo this command: if you make a mistake, you'll have to start over again by pressing the **Reset** button, which replaces the **Cancel** button when you press **Option/Alt**.

If you choose to reduce the number of colors in an image by increasing the Web Snap factor and you want to keep certain colors from shifting, lock them first. To do this, click on the color in the table and then click on the lock button to prevent it from being dropped if the number of colors is reduced and to prevent the color from dithering in the application. A small white square in the corner of the color swatch indicates that the color is locked.

Unfortunately, sometimes color-reduction algorithms drop colors that are important to an image; they analyze the histogram and select the most common colors in an image, but since they can't actually see the image, sometimes a color in an important detail is lost. In the image on the next page, for example, the yellow traffic light and the cars' red brake lights were dropped when the Selective palette was applied.

 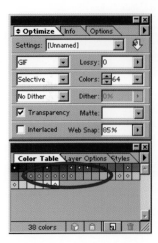

▲ Web Snap, shown here in the ImageReady Optimize palette.

THE ART OF OPTIMIZING GIFs

Welcome to the art of optimizing a GIF. Using the word art probably makes this sound more complicated then it is, and compared to optimizing a JPEG, it is complicated. There are far more choices and possibilities and it requires much more experience and expertise to get a great result.

Before you start optimizing, you may want to consider making a selection of the areas of the image that are most important. The reason is that with Photoshop 6.0, you can control the application of the color-reduction algorithm, diffusion dithering, and the Lossy option by making selections that are saved as alpha channels. It is very important to understand how you should create your selections in order to get the best result:

If you want to create a channel for the color-reduction algorithm, use the **Lasso** tool and circle areas in the image that are very important in terms of color, but might not necessarily be the dominant colors in the picture. Take, for example, the red lips of a face. While they're only a small part of a photo, they might be more significant then the colors of a background. While pressing the **Shift** key, select all these areas with the **Lasso** tool and save them as a channel (**Select > Save Selection**).

If you would like to control the dithering in your image, select all the areas that should get the least (!) amount of dithering. Later, when using a channel to modify the dithering, the selected pixels represent the areas for the Minimum slider, while the unselected pixels represent the areas for the Maximum slider.

▲ Use the Zoom tool to see more details and move the image with the Hand tool. Use the Eyedropper tool to select a matte color or to make changes to the CLUT.

The same is true for the Lossy command. The selected pixels represent the part of the image that gets the least amount of lossy, while the unselected pixels represent the part that gets the most. So when creating your selection for the Lossy command, pick the most important parts of the image and then save the selection.

In the **Save for Web** dialog box, you can view both the original image and one or more optimized views, which show you how your image will look after it is compressed. After you click on the **Optimized** tab in the upper left corner, it will take Photoshop a moment to produce the result; you'll see a progress bar at the bottom of the window. Since it's always easier to make a decision if you can see the original and the compressed image simultaneously, you can also choose between 2-Up and 4-Up. These tabs will present either two or four views at the same time and thus allow you to select compression settings independently for each view.

If you work with the 2-Up or 4-Up views, you may not be able to see the entire image at once, so use the **Hand** tool to move to the part of the image that you want to see. You will also find the Zoom tool and the Eyedropper tool in this window. The **Zoom** tool allows you to magnify the view; you can see the exact percentage in the lower left corner. The **Eyedropper** tool shows you the selected color within the color table, which is usually visible on the right side of the dialog box.

Photoshop and ImageReady can assist you in optimizing the image. Click the triangle next to the **Settings** pop-up menu, where you'll find one of the most helpful commands: **Optimize to File Size**. This command lets you designate a final file size, and Photoshop or ImageReady will choose the appropriate settings automatically. You can tell the application to try to use your current settings (**Start With: Current Settings**) or to select GIF/JPEG automatically. If you have to use a specific format, choose **Current Settings**. For example, suppose that you have to save an image as a GIF because you want to use transparency. Select GIF from the pop-up menu in the **Save for Web** dialog box (or **Optimize** palette), set your desired dithering, color table, and other options, and then activate **Optimize to File Size**, entering the desired size in kilobytes and choosing the **Current Settings** option. Photoshop will automatically reduce the number of colors until it can match your file size. It does not experiment with the other settings, however, so don't rely on the Optimize to File Size command too much. It's helpful in some cases, but

▲ **Photoshop can suggest some settings: with Optimize to File Size, you can enter a desired file size and Photoshop will adjust the settings accordingly.**

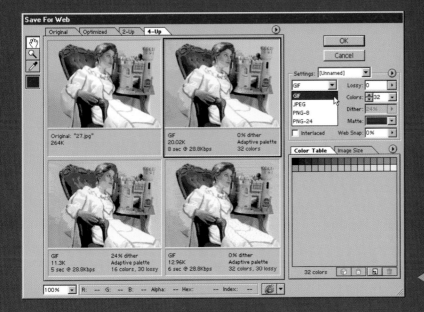

◀ **Activate the second view in the 4-Up Optimized window.**

▲ In the color table of the Save for Web command in Photoshop or in the Optimized palette in ImageReady (shown here), the selected color of the Eyedropper tool will be outlined. The buttons at the bottom let you (from left to right) shift selected colors to the Web-safe color palette, lock a color to prevent it from shifting, add a new color, or delete a color.

Reduce the colors until there is a noticeable decrease in image quality, then use dithering to compensate for this effect. If this doesn't result in the desired improvement, increase the number of colors and reduce the dithering.

an experienced Web designer can get better results by adjusting the parameters manually. A typical procedure might look like this:

1. Choose 4-Up and use the second view (upper right) to select the number of colors you think your image requires. A GIF should not use more than 32 colors; if you feel it requires more, you should probably save the image as JPEG (if you have a choice). Pick one of the color-reduction algorithms; the default is **Selective**, but when you choose the number of colors for your CLUT later on, also try **Adaptive** or **Perceptual**. If you saved an alpha channel for the color-reduction algorithm, click on the **Channel** button next to the text field.

2. Try reducing the number of colors even more using the arrows in the **Colors** box. You can also either choose a standard number (16, 32, 64, and so on) from the drop-down menu, or enter a number in the field. The fewer colors the better, but at some point you will notice a sudden drop in quality.

3. Now select a dithering method. Try **Noise** first, although it usually results in a larger file size. (The file size is always shown at the bottom of each display.) Alternatively, use **Diffusion** dithering, which has the advantage that you can set a value between 0-100%; the quality of the image will improve with dithering, and you can experiment with decreasing the number of colors until you see another quality leap (in that case, increase the number again).

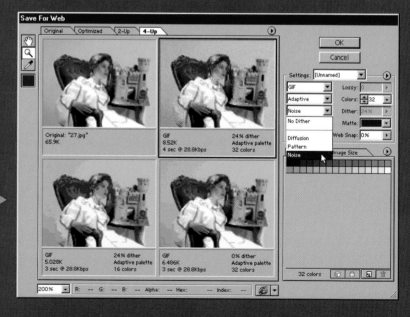

On the left you see the image with a 16-color Adaptive palette, on the right the same image with Lossy set to 50%. Used moderately (10–20%), the effect looks a little bit like dithering, but when it's increased, the visual quality goes downhill.

4. Use the Lossy option if the current quality of the image is still good enough and you need to reduce the file size. Note that the Lossy option is only accessible if Interlaced is deactivated. Lossy can be a big file-size saver! However, using the Lossy option too much creates an effect that looks like a pixel storm: the pixels appear to have been blown from left to right across the image. To get a good idea of what the best settings for the Lossy command are, see the chart on page 204. This chart shows how the Dithering and Lossy commands affect the file size.

5. Finally, activate the Browser Dither option from the **Preview** pop-up menu (hidden behind a triangle on the top right corner of the view area). Browser Dither simulates how the image will look in the browser on 256-color monitors. However, this only gives you a rough idea, and you still have to check the image in both Internet Explorer and Netscape Navigator. Use the **Browser Preview** button in the lower right corner of the **Save for Web** dialog box (in ImageReady, use **File > Preview In**). Set the color depth of your monitor to 256 colors and then compare the image in both browsers at the same time. Then you will clearly see the difference.

By now, you should have a version of the image that looks decent and is still compact. Use the other two views in 4-Up to create variations of those settings and compare them. In particular, go through the outlined steps again, this time using any saved alpha channels to control the amount of dithering and lossy. To activate those selections, click on the button next to the Value field and a dialog box will appear. Here, choose one of the channels from the pop-up menu and you'll see a small preview of that channel. The white areas in the preview represent the Minimum slider (to the left), the black areas the Maximum (to the right).

▲ The Browser Dither option gives you a rough idea of how the GIF will look in browsers and monitors when they are set to 256 colors, but remember, you still need to check the final image in the browser.

Here's how to retrieve lost colors: click on the **2-Up** or **4-Up** tab so that you can see both the original and the compressed images. Click to select the original image, and use the **Eyedropper** tool to select the color you want reinstated in the CLUT, then click on the **Optimized** version of the image, and click on the **New Color** button at the bottom of the palette. Voila, the color is added to the palette and locked in. Of course, you may want to drop another, less important color in the table. If you accidentally delete a popular color and significantly alter the quality of the image, you'll have to reset the CLUT using the **Option/Alt** key, allow a greater number of colors in your palette so that the reinstated color can be included up front, and then carefully delete unimportant colors.

CREATING CUSTOM (MASTER) PALETTES

Now that you can optimize a CLUT for one image, you're ready to learn the secrets of creating a custom CLUT optimized for several images. Such custom, or "master," palettes are useful when preparing multiple banner ads, especially when all of the ads include a company or product logo whose colors cannot shift. If you convert each banner ad with a Perceptual or Adaptive 16-color palette, you might run into problems if the logo isn't dominant in the color scheme of some of the ads. In such instances, it's quite possible that the logo color might be dropped, and the logos would look different in various banners.

▲ The color table has its own menu that you can access by clicking on the triangle in the upper right corner.

This is undesirable (to put it mildly), and the only way to avoid it is to create a custom palette that includes the logo color. It's a rather laborious process to do this in Photoshop: first you have to pick a couple of the most important ads, index them, and save their color tables. Then you combine those color tables into one, delete duplicate or unwanted colors, and save it. When you've done this, however, you can apply the custom palette via batch processing for a consistent look for all your images. Here's how:

1. Open one of the banner ads and optimize its CLUT in the **Save for Web** dialog box. You have two choices: either use the CLUT of one banner ad as the master and add a few colors from the other banner ads, or index several banner ads and combine them. If you do the latter, don't bloat the table with excess colors. If you would typically use 16 colors, try going with only 8. There is no one right way; what you do depends on the situation. To save a color table, use the **Color Table** palette's pop-up menu.

2. After you have saved several CLUTs, you need to combine them—and since the Color Table palette menu doesn't offer this option, you have to do

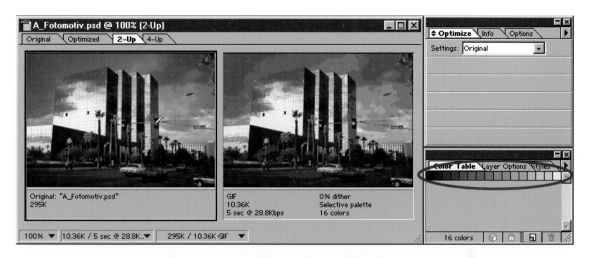

it via the Swatches palette. Choose **Window > Show Swatches**, and select **Load Swatches** from the **Swatches** palette's pop-up menu. Load the saved CLUTs one by one. (Note: the **Load Color Table** command in the **Color Table** palette's pop-up menu replaces the current table, but **Load Swatches** in the **Swatches** palette's pop-up menu actually appends the new colors to the existing palette.) Now you probably have more colors than you need, so delete extras by pressing **Command** (or **Control** in Windows) to bring up the **Scissors** cursor and then click on the swatch that you want to delete. To add a color, select it from the image with the **Eyedropper** tool, then move the mouse cursor over a free spot in the **Swatches** palette and the **Paint Bucket** tool appears. Click to add the color to the palette.

▲ When you choose a color-reduction algorithm, many of the colors in your image get dropped, such as the yellow traffic light here. To force this color back into the color table, select the color with the Eyedropper tool in the Original view, then click on the Optimized view and the Add Foreground Color button at the bottom of the Color Table palette. The color will be inserted and locked (marked with a dot in the lower right corner.)

▲ If you want to batch process a series of banner ads where it is important that certain colors are always included (such as the red of the logo), you have to create a Master palette.

3. When you've refined your swatches to include the colors for your Master palette, choose **Save Swatches** from the palette's pop-up menu, and append the file with an .act extension. Then load the palette in the **Save for Web** dialog box via the **Color Table** palette's pop-up menu, and the color-reduction algorithm automatically switches to **Custom**.

4. Now it's a snap to optimize a whole slew of banner ads so that the logo colors are consistent. Just record an action that optimizes one of the ads using the **Custom** palette, and choose **File > Automate > Batch** to process the rest of the ads automatically. (For more details on the Actions palette and batch processing, refer to the Photoshop manual and read Chapter 3, "Optimizing Photoshop.")

Creating custom palettes is much easier in ImageReady, which has a handy little command called Make Master Palette.

The essential information here is that you can combine color palettes in the Swatches palette. The way you optimize a CLUT for batch processing depends on the images itself, so this step-by-step guide might not work for other scenarios.

1. Open an image and switch to Optimized view. Choose **Image > Master Palette > Clear Master Palette** (the command will be grayed out if it's already been cleared; if this is the case, just skip to the next step). Then select the color-reduction algorithm and specify the size of your color table (for example, a 16-color **Selective** palette) in the **Optimize** palette. Then choose **Image > Master Palette > Add to Master Palette**. Repeat this process for the most important and representative images. Choose **Image > Master Palette > Build Master Palette**, and then choose **Save Master Palette**. ImageReady prompts you for a name and saves the palette in the **Presets > Optimized Colors** folder in the Photoshop 6.0 folder. Now this palette can be accessed by ImageReady and Photoshop.

2. To edit your new color table, open an image and select it from the **Color-Reduction Algorithm** pop-up menu; you can then see it in the **Color Table** palette. Colors that seem very close are probably redundant and can be deleted by selecting them and clicking on the **Trash** button at the bottom of the palette.

3. Finally, create an action in which you index an image with your master palette, and then select **Batch Options** from the **Actions** palette's pop-up menu to automate the process for other files.

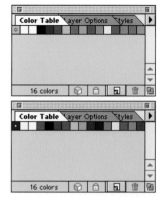

▲ These are the color palettes of the banner ads on the previous page.

WEIGHTED OPTIMIZATION

Photoshop 6.0 has added a completely new way to address the color shifts I described earlier—those caused when color-reduction algorithms lose important image details such as eye colors in a portrait. You can now use alpha channels to tell Photoshop to favor colors in certain parts of an image before you choose **File > Save for Web.** This is called *weighted optimization*.

Use the **Lasso** tool to draw a marquee around the part of the image that contains the important colors. The selection doesn't have to be precise; it's sufficient to roughly circle the main area or areas. (In most cases there are multiple areas that need to be included; hold the **Shift** key to add to the selection.) Then save the selection as an alpha channel in the **Save Selection** dialog box (choose **Select > Save Selection**).

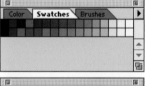

▲ To combine the color palettes from the top two images, you have to use the Swatches palette. Click on the colors while pressing the Command/Control key to delete redundant colors.

When you go to the **Save for Web** dialog box and specify a GIF file format, the **Channel** button appears next to the **Color Reduction Algorithm** pop-up menu—it's a small vertical rectangle with a white circle in the center. Click it to choose the alpha channel that you created previously, and the color table instantly weights the optimization accordingly. Try experimenting with the color-reduction algorithms to find the best one for the image.

APPLYING LOSSY TO PART OF AN IMAGE

Photoshop 6.0 also lets you use alpha channels to control the application of lossy compression. Previously, you had to apply the Lossy command to an entire image, something that often had a negative effect on its overall quality because not all areas of an image necessarily benefit from this. Being able to apply lossy compression to parts of an image affords a whole new realm of control: only areas in an image that have a very dithered texture, such as beaches and streets, can benefit from lossy compression, as can dark areas where the human eye is less capable of distinguishing hues.

▲ To force certain colors into the color table in the Save for Web command, make a selection of all the important areas in your image and then save the selection into an alpha channel.

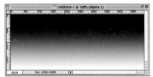

▲ To illustrate the effect of partially dithering an image, I filled a new document with this color gradient. I then filled an alpha channel with a grayscale gradient.

To select the parts of an image where you'd like to use an alpha channel with the Lossy option in the Save for Web dialog box, you could use the Magic Wand or Lasso tool, but Photoshop offers an even better way: the Threshold command, which provides a histogram of the luminance levels of the pixels in the image and allows you to you adjust that threshold with a slider.

But first, you must create the alpha channel. To do this, duplicate the document by choosing **Image > Duplicate**. Then choose **Select > Select All** and copy the selection to the Clipboard with **Edit > Copy**. Switch back to the original image and create the alpha channel by clicking on the **Create New Channel** icon at the bottom of the **Channels** palette. Finally, paste the contents of the **Clipboard** in this new channel by choosing **Edit > Paste**.

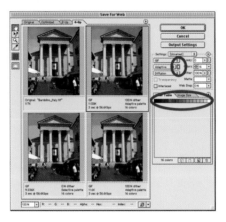

▲ The alpha channel was used to modify the color-reduction algorithm for the upper right view. Without this, the red color of the man's shirt would have been dropped as in the other two views at the bottom.

Now apply the **Threshold** command: with the alpha channel active in the **Channels** palette, choose **Image > Adjust > Threshold**. You can accept the default level or adjust it; when you're satisfied with the results, click **OK**.

Click on **RGB** in the **Channels** palette and then open the **Save for Web** dialog box and click on the **Channel** button to the right of the **Lossy** option text box. In the Modify Lossiness Setting dialog box, choose your alpha channel and adjust the sliders. Usually if it's applied to the entire image, the maximum lossy value lies around 30, but you can use a maximum value of up to 60 for your alpha channel without much visual deterioration. This means that you can greatly reduce file size without compromising bright parts of an image (if the dark areas in your image take up half of the image).

DITHERING PART OF AN IMAGE

As I've explained previously, dithering increases file size, but it can also substantially improve the quality of an image. An excellent way to minimize file size increases is to use dithering only on areas that really need it and keep the rest of the image dither-free. As with weighted optimization and the application of partial lossy compression, you do this through an alpha channel.

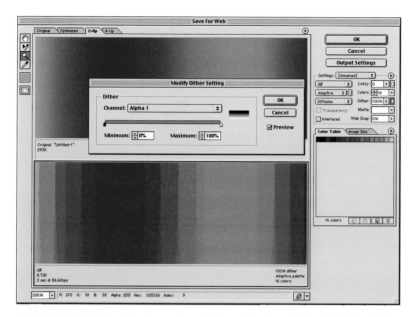

▲ In comparison, here is an alpha channel with just black and white areas.

▲ You can see how the alpha channel gradually modifies the amount of dithering in the view at the bottom.

In Photoshop 6.0, use the **Lasso** tool or any other selection tool to marquee all of the areas in the image that you do not want dithered, or that you'd like only minimally dithered. This is counterintuitive, but what can you do? That's just the way it is. Then save the selection by choosing **Select > Save Selection** and **New** from the **Channel** palette's pop-up menu. Then, when you go to the **Save for Web** dialog box and select **Diffusion** dithering for your GIF, you can limit dithering to the areas outside the selection by clicking the button next to the **Dither** text box, choosing the alpha channel, and adjusting the sliders.

If, however, you are already using an alpha channel to weight the color-reduction algorithm, you need to make a different type of selection with regard to partial dithering: use the **Magic Wand** tool or the **Color Range** command (**Select > Color Range**) to select the most important colors in the image. The logic behind this is that these colors need less dithering because they are already favored in the CLUT. Then go through the regular steps of saving the selection as a new channel and specifying that channel in the **Modify Dither Setting** dialog box, which appears when you click the **Channel** button next to the **Dither** text box in the **Save for Web** dialog box. Use the right (white) slider to set the amount of dithering for the areas that need it the most.

But if you are already using an alpha channel to apply lossy compression to part of an image, you don't need to make a second alpha channel for your partial dither; you can use the existing channel for partial dithering. Dithering can mask the lossy effect, which bloats the file a bit, although not enough to detract from the enhanced quality.

Finally, if you are using alpha channels for both the color-reduction algorithm and lossy compression, the selection for your dithering channel should be a combination of the areas for these two commands: for the color-reduction algorithm you've selected the areas of the image that are important in terms of color; for the lossy alpha channel you've probably selected areas with a busy texture, which makes the lossy effect less noticeable. The selection for your dithering alpha channel should be a combination of the areas that are less important in terms of color (and are not featured in the alpha channel for color reduction) and the areas that are in the lossy alpha channel.

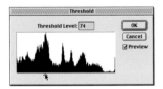

▲ To determine the cutoff point, use the slider in the Threshold dialog box.

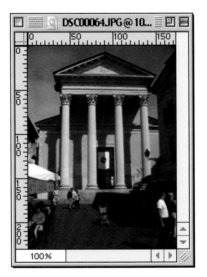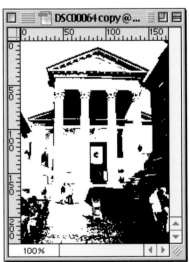

▲ The easiest way to create an alpha channel for the dark parts of an image is to create a duplicate of the image and then apply the Threshold command.

CREATING EFFECTIVE ALPHA CHANNELS

The best part of being able to modify the color-reduction algorithm, dithering, and lossy compression with an alpha channel is that the alpha channel is based on a grayscale mask. That means you can not only apply minimum and maximum values, but in-between values as well. This is most helpful for dithering and lossy compression, because it's unlikely that just the minimum and maximum values are enough.

Before creating any alpha channels, it is important to determine which settings you would like to apply. Since everything depends on the color-reduction algorithm, first optimize your image with regard to color. Open the **Save for Web** dialog box, choose **No Dither** and set **Lossy** to 0. Choose a color-reduction algorithm and perhaps use the **Eyedropper** tool to add colors that were dropped. After you've optimized the color table, press **Option** (Alt) and click on **Remember**, which appears in place of the **OK** button. Now experiment with different dithering and lossy compression settings. Take note which areas look best with a particular setting and then click **Cancel** to close the **Save for Web** dialog box.

You might have a list of settings like this: Area 1: 30% Lossy, 75% Dithering; Area 2: 60% Lossy, 0% Dithering; Area 3: 0% Lossy, 40% Dithering. Here's how to create one alpha channel for all of these lossy conditions, and one for all of the dithering conditions.

First click the **Create New Channel** button in the **Channels** palette to create a channel that is called, by default, Alpha1. Switch back to the RGB channel and select the areas of the image that require 30% lossy compression. With the selection still active, switch back to Alpha1 and then click on the background color field in the **Tool** palette. In the **Color Picker**, deselect the option **Only Web Colors** and then do some math: 255 - (x * 2.55). If x = 30 (the desired amount of lossy compression), the result of the equation is 180; enter this value in the R, G, and B text fields in the **Color Picker**, and click **OK**. Then press **Delete** and the selection will be filled with the background color (gray).

For the image areas in our example that require 60% and 0% lossy compression, select each area in sequence, make the background color calculation in the **Color Picker**, and fill each area in Alpha1 with the appropriate shade of gray. When you're done, this alpha channel can be used in the **Save for Web** dialog box to modify the **Lossy** option.

Now repeat this procedure to create an alpha channel for dithering, making the appropriate selections, background color calculations, and fills. Keep in

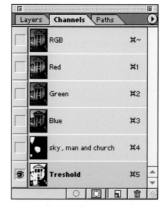

◀ After manipulating the duplicate with the Threshold command, everything needs to be selected and then copied to the Clipboard. A new channel is created in the original image into which the contents of the Clipboard are pasted.

▲ One way of combining several channels is the Calculations command.

mind that since the value in the Modify Dither Setting dialog box comes directly from the channel itself, you should always set the Modify sliders to 0 percent for Minimum and 100 percent for Maximum.

Is it overkill to use multiple alpha channels to optimize lossy, dithering, and color-reduction commands, and even use grayscale alpha channels to differentiate these even more? Certainly it is for a personal home page that hosts just a few visitors a day, but consider that 5 KB more on a Web site that gets 1000 visitors every day is 5 MB more data per day that your server has to transfer. That is 150 MB per month, 1.8 GB per year. So it is very important for designers of professional Web sites to optimize images to the greatest extent possible.

SIMULATING MULTIPLE LEVELS OF TRANSPARENCY

The GIF format has only one level of transparency, which is nothing like the 256-level alpha channel transparency available in PNG format. Still, it is possible to simulate a multi-level transparency with GIF. The trick is to use a transparent pattern; to demonstrate, I'll create a headline with a transparent drop shadow.

1. In Photoshop, create a new 2 x 2-pixel file with a transparent background (**File > New**). This new file will be our transparent fill pattern. Depending on how much transparency you want, you might need to start with a larger pattern; A 2x2-pixel pattern lets you create either a 25 percent, 50 percent, or 75 percent transparency, whereas a 3x3-pixel pattern allows increments of 11 percent and so on. (The rule of thumb is that the percentage equals 100 divided by the number of pixels, but this is just a guideline. Not all combinations are useful, nor will they all give you the desired effect, so there is a limit on how many levels of transparency you can achieve.)

▲ The 50 percent transparency trick is used to simulate the plastic of the CD.

2. Magnify your pixels as much as you can and use the **Pencil** tool to draw a pattern like the one in the example (see top picture). The color black is going to dim the underlying background, so leave the other pixels transparent.

Select the entire pattern with **Select > All**, and then choose **Edit > Define Pattern**.

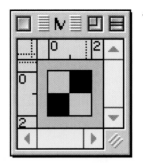

◀ This is the Shadow fill pattern. Some of the pixels must remain transparent, otherwise it is impossible to use the Save for Web command for the export.

3. Create another new image with a transparent background, and on a new layer, place all the elements for which you want to create drop shadows. Activate this layer in the **Layer** palette, and click with the **Magic Wand** tool in the transparent area. The selection should include all transparent areas. Invert the selection via **Select > Inverse**. Add or subtract any areas that didn't get selected—hold down the **Shift** key to add to a selection, or hold the **Option/Alt** key to subtract from a selection while you're working with the **Magic Wand** tool.

4. If you did everything correctly, you should now have a selection around the objects and elements that you placed on the new layer. To create the drop shadow, select the layer beneath the current layer. Use one of the **Marquee** tools (or the arrow keys on your keyboard) to move the selection to the desired position, then fill it by choosing **Edit > Fill (Contents: Use: Pattern)**.

▲ When saved as a GIF with transparency, the image can be combined with different backgrounds in the browser. If the pixels of the shadow don't blend well enough, try using a color of the background (mixed with black) as your shadow color.

5. Now call up the Save for Web command and select the **Transparency** option and **Matte: None**. Save the GIF and import it into GoLive. If you have a background image, you will see how this drop shadow seems to blend with the background; if the black pixels in the transparency pattern are too apparent, try using a color other than black. For a bright background, you might want to use a combination of the background color and black.

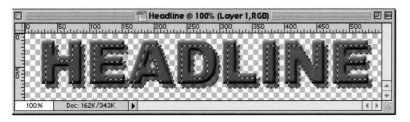

▲ With the selection being in the background layer, fill it with the transparent shadow.

Illustration: Michael Baumgardt

JPEG

JPEG—Joint Photographic Experts Group

For digital movies, MPEG is equivalent to JPEG. JPEG is used for stills only.

JPEG is currently the single most important format for photos and images requiring more than 256 colors. In the future, we may see JPEG losing ground to PNG, which offers some advantages such as lossless compression and alpha channel transparency. But for now, and certainly for the next few years, JPEG will remain an extremely popular and important format.

➤ DCT Compression

JPEG uses a compression algorithm called the Discrete Cosine Transform, or DCT. DCT compression is based on the fact that the human eye is less sensitive to changes in color than to variations in brightness. While most image formats for the Web save the RGB color value for every pixel, JPEG actually splits color and brightness information and compresses each individually. The JPEG algorithm works on a block of 8x8 pixels at a time: first it calculates the DCT, which is then quantified, and finally, a variable length code compression scheme is used on it.

Text in an image is pretty much the worst thing for JPEG; if you place text in front of a background and compress it with a very low setting, you can see the effect clearly.

Fortunately, you don't have to understand this to work with JPEG images, but it does explain why JPEG works so badly for images with extreme color changes: DCT tries to interpret the image as the sum of frequencies, and while this works pretty well for smooth color changes, such as gradients, if an image includes abrupt changes and high contrast it can be a serious stumbling block for the algorithm. The DCT technique is also the reason why blurring a photo improves the ratio of the compression: blurring smoothes color changes in the image.

➤ Transparency

Unlike the GIF image format, there is no transparency feature in JPEG—which makes sense, since JPEG is a lossy compression technique. Every time you save a JPEG image it actually changes the image and shifts colors (which made it impossible for the JPEG developer to use the chroma-key color technique).

➤ JPEG is not Lossless

When I said JPEG changes the image and shifts colors every time you save it, I really meant it. Every time. So even if you open a JPEG image, make no changes whatsoever, and save it again, it will lose quality. You can limit this effect by using the same settings under which the image was initially saved, but the difference is marginal.

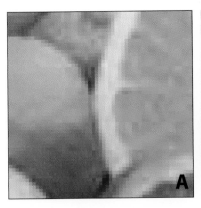
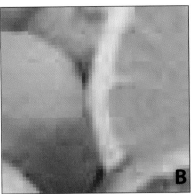

At one point there was an initiative to create a lossless version of JPEG called JPEG-LS, but it never succeeded because its compression rate was only 2:1. And by now, PNG is the preferred solution.

➤ Progressive JPEG

The JPEG standard has seen one important improvement over the years: because of the growing popularity of the Web, you can now save your JPEG in progressive format, which works pretty much the same way as GIF's interlaced format. With progressive JPEG, the image starts to appear in the browser while it is still downloading. At first it's a blurry preview of the image, then it gets more detailed as the stream of data comes in. While GIF is limited to four passes, you can choose between three and five passes for a progressive JPEG image.

HOW WELL DOES JPEG COMPRESS IMAGES?

You're probably wondering how much space you can save with JPEG compression. Compared with other methods, it is actually quite impressive. The best lossless compression methods can reduce the amount of data for a 24-bit image by about half, or 2:1. By comparison, JPEG can compress the same image between 10:1 and 20:1 (high quality) without visible loss, which is why most stock photos on CDs are saved as JPEG images. After all, this means that you can store a 20MB high-resolution image in only 2 MB of disk space.

At a compression rate of 30:1 to 50:1 (medium quality), you will start seeing some visible shifts, which are generally quite tolerable. Only with the maximum (low quality) setting will you end up with a serious loss in visual quality, but the benefit is a whopping 100:1 compression ratio.

▲ To demonstrate the cumulative negative effect that the JPEG algorithm has on images, I saved the above image multiple times with different JPEG settings and compared the results. I saved Image A 10 times with a rather low Quality (20) setting each time, and the image degradation is quite visible. I saved Image B 10 times, changing the compression settings each time (4 times with a Quality of 20, 3 times with a Quality of 30, and 3 times with a Quality of 40). You would think that image B should have the better visual quality because it was saved with higher quality settings most of the time, but that is not the case. As a matter of fact, image B is even slightly worse in quality than image A.

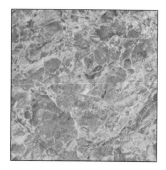

Dimensions Pixels	TIFF Size	JPEG Size	Coeff. Size
224	151.1	13.5	11.2
225	152.4	14.1	10.8
226	153.8	14.3	10.7
227	155.1	14.4	10.8
228	156.5	14.4	10.8
229	157.9	14.5	10.9
230	159.3	14.6	10.9
231	160.6	14.6	11.0
232	162.0	14.5	11.2
233	163.4	14.9	11.0
234	164.8	15.1	10.9
235	166.2	15.2	10.9
236	167.6	15.3	11.0
237	169.1	15.3	11.0
238	170.5	15.4	11.1
239	171.9	15.4	11.2
240	173.4	15.4	11.3

▲ I took the above image, originally a 240x240-pixel file, cropped by one pixel increments (in height and width), and then saved each version as JPEG and TIFF (uncompressed) to find out how the 8x8-pixel blocks used by the JPEG algorithm affect compression. The above chart shows the file sizes for each, in KB. For a graph of this data, see the next page.

THE JPEG FILE STANDARD

For a long time JPEG didn't even have a file standard; it was simply a series of compression algorithms. The JPEG committee wanted to develop a global file standard, but because of internal disagreement in the International Standardizing Organization, it was a long time before they agreed on the SPIFF standard. Because it's impossible to exchange images without a common file standard, programmers initially created their own format; consequently, the JPEGs of many programs back then were incompatible. Thanks to the efforts of the programmers at C-Cube Microsystems a quasi-standard emerged. These standards are:

● **JFIF (JPEG File Interchange Format)**
This is a simple format that only saves the pixels without much additional information.

● **TIFF/JPEG, also known as TIFF 6.0**
An extension to the Aldus TIFF format; it stores all additional information with the image.

JFIF became the pseudo-standard for the Internet, because of the need for files to be as small as possible. The TIFF 6.0 definition, designed to be integrated with JPEGs, did not succeed, because it suffered from a few significant weaknesses.

For color photos there's no question that JPEG is the way to go. With grayscale images, however, GIF may yield better results. That's because JPEG does most of its compression on colors, not on luminance (brightness) information.

How noticeable are the differences in quality between different compression settings? To answer this, I saved three images (a regular photo, a photo with text, and a graphic) in nine different compression settings in Photoshop, then I viewed all the JPEGs and compared the quality. Unfortunately, it wouldn't help much to show the images here, as a lot of the subtle shifts in quality are lost in the printing process, so you'll have to trust the subjective assessments I've made based on my experiment.

JPEG is really excellent for use on the Web. It produces astonishingly small files, and while you will see slight degradations in quality, they are really quite acceptable. In the worst case, quality might decrease by 20 percent. In the graphs on pages 266 to 267, you can see that the compression rate is most effective with a setting of zero to four with Photoshop's Save a Copy command, and with zero to 40 with the Save for Web command.

Personally, I always use a setting of 20 to 30 with the Save for Web command because it seems to offer the best compromise between quality and file size. Images look great, without major distortion, and the file sizes are usually small enough for my needs.

THE CORRELATION OF COMPRESSION AND 8X8-PIXEL BLOCKS

As already mentioned, JPEG's compression algorithm divides the image into blocks of 8x8 pixels. But what if the dimensions of the image are not exactly divisible by eight? Does this have an impact on the file size? And does the algorithm create additional overhead? To answer these questions, I cropped a 240x240-pixel image gradually, by one pixel at a time. I then saved the image as

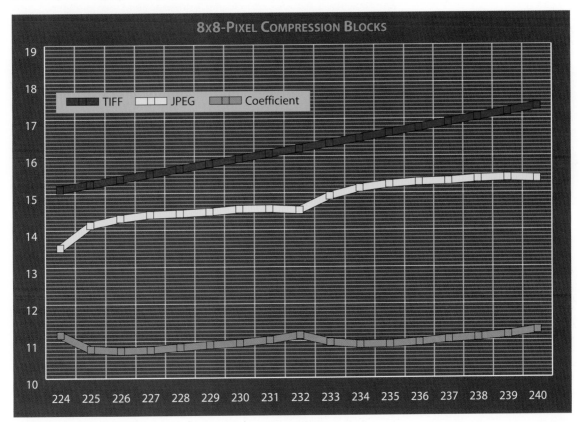

▲ To determine the correlation between image size and JPEG's 8x8-pixel compression blocks, I gradually cropped a 240x240-pixel image by one pixel at a time in both directions and saved the files as TIFF and JPEG. The height and width of the images are recorded along the x-axis here, and the file size in KB on the y-axis. (TIFF values were divided by 10 for easier viewing.) Compression blocks do appear to create some overhead, so whenever possible, image dimensions should be in multiples of eight.

JPEG and as TIFF (without LZW compression). The TIFF was my reference to ensure that potential variations in the file size weren't caused by the motif itself.

As you can see from the graph on the previous page, there is indeed a correlation between the 8x8 blocks and compression. In the graph you can clearly see a notch at every eighth pixel in the JPEG curve (yellow line), while the TIFF curve (red line) is linear. (Note: The file size of the TIFF was divided by 10 in order to display both lines closer together).

The notches also appear in the coefficient that was derived from both values (blue line). As you can see, the possible savings in file size are between 2 percent and 4 percent—not very much. Still this is useful to know, especially for images that you use as background in the browser. Keep their dimensions to a factor of eight to optimize the file size.

JPEG OR GIF?

For larger photographic images, you will definitely get better compression with JPEG. But the question remains, where is the threshold where it becomes more efficient to use GIF? This question is particularly important when you're slicing an image or using small navigational elements like buttons. To answer this question, I cropped an image and saved it as GIF and JPEG with different quality settings.

My results suggest that large photo images should always be saved as JPEGs. Even with low-compression/high-quality settings, you will get a smaller file size than with GIF, and the visual quality of the JPEG will be better. However, this doesn't hold true for images with an original file size of 10K to 25K (roughly 900 pixels in total, such as a 15x60-pixel image) that require a color depth of 8 to 32 colors. In such cases you'll get better results with a GIF than with a JPEG, as you can see from the graph on the following page.

Since this test is only based on one image and is therefore not conclusive, your results might vary, but that's OK. What's important to know is that the smaller the image, the smaller the benefit of the better format. Keep this in mind when exporting and optimizing: Always use the 4-up view in the Save for Web dialog box when you're optimizing small images and compare the results of JPEG vs. GIF.

Original Size Pixels/KB	GIF 8 Col.	GIF 16 Col.	GIF 32 Col.	GIF 256 Col.	JPEG 30 Qual.	JPEG 60 Qual.	PNG 8 Bit	PNG 24 Bit
100x150 / 78.8	3.1 KB	4.2 KB	5.8 KB	11.8 KB	2.4 KB	4.4 KB	11.9 KB	32.4 KB
80x120 / 51.1	2.2 KB	2.9 KB	4.1 KB	8.2 KB	1.8 KB	3.1 KB	8.3 KB	22.0 KB
60x90 / 28.7	1.3 KB	1.9 KB	2.6 KB	5.4 KB	1.3 KB	2.2 KB	5.4 KB	13.7 KB
50x75 / 19.9	1.0 KB	1.4 KB	2.0 KB	4.1 KB	1.1 KB	1.8 KB	4.1 KB	10.1 KB
25x38 / 5.1	0.4 KB	0.5 KB	0.7 KB	1.7 KB	0.6 KB	0.9 KB	1.9 KB	3.2 KB
12x19 / 1.3	0.2 KB	0.2 KB	0.3 KB	1.1 KB	0.4 KB	0.5 KB	1.1 KB	1.1 KB

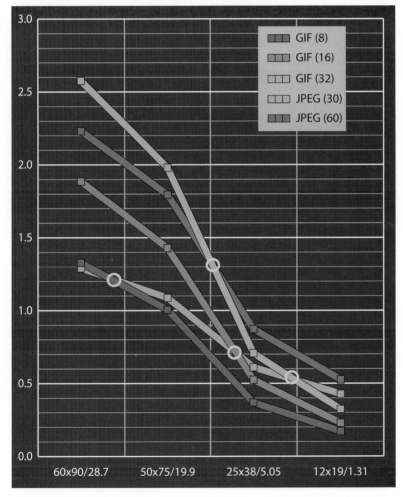

◀ FROM THE GRAPH, YOU CAN SEE THAT:

● For images smaller than 25KB, an 8-color GIF is smaller than a JPEG with a Quality setting of 30.

● With images of 12KB, a 32-color GIF is smaller than a JPEG with a Quality setting of 60.

● With images of around 7KB, a 16-color GIF produces a better result than a JPEG with a Quality setting of 30.

● With images of 3KB, a 32-color GIF is smaller than a JPEG with a Quality setting of 30.

▲ Wherever the red lines (GIF) cross one of the blue lines (JPEG), the file size saving with GIF surpasses that of JPEG.

For all of you technophile readers, here's an overview of how a JPEG encoder works. This will give you some understanding of the complex process that goes on behind the scenes.

1. Separation of Brightness/Color

The JPEG baseline compression algorithm works in several steps. For the first step it is irrelevant whether the RGB or CMYK color model is used, although a CMYK JPEG is larger than its RGB counterpart (for use on the Internet, the image should, of course, be saved as RGB). You can make JPEGs from grayscale images, but since the algorithm mainly compresses the color information, the compression factor in grayscale images is significantly less.

▲ This is a JPEG as it is displayed in the browser or in Photoshop. If it were possible to see how a JPEG stores the information, the result would look like what you see on the right: an image that includes only color information and one that contains only gray-scale information. This separation makes sense, because for the human eye, the difference in luminance is more important then subtle changes in hue.

2. Reduction of the Color Space

When saving, the encoder has the option of reducing the color space by a horizontal and vertical factor of 2:1. The encoder can also scale only the color information on the horizontal axis and leave the vertical unchanged (1:1). Both options leave the brightness information, with its resolution and measurements, untouched. This compression step is used by only a few programs.

3. Compilation in 8x8 Blocks

The pixels in the image are divided into 8x8-pixel blocks and then analyzed with the Discrete Cosine Transform (DCT) algorithm, which is closely related to the Fourier analysis. In the process, the higher color frequencies are deleted, while lower frequencies, containing the significant color changes, are retained.

4. Quantization of Color Frequencies

In every block, each of the remaining 64 frequency components is divided by an individual quantization coefficient, and then rounded to the next integer.

This step creates the biggest savings. The higher the quantization coefficient, the more data will be truncated. Even the lowest possible quantization coefficient—1, which equals Quality 100 in Photoshop's Save for Web command—will change the color information, because the DCT doesn't generate integers.

Due to the larger coefficient, higher frequencies are quantized less accurately than lower ones—it's okay, though, because the eye can't perceive those subtle differences anyway. Brightness information (luminosity), however, is quantized with a much higher level of accuracy (64 possible values) than the color information (chroma). The quantization table can be set by the JPEG encoder, but most encoders only use the simple, linear scaling that is set by the JPEG standard. The quality level that the user sets in the encoder defines the scaling factor of this table.

This quantization table is responsible for the different qualities between some of the JPEG encoders, because JPEG's standard table works well only with medium-quality settings, not so well for high or low levels. So you can get a smaller file size with an encoder optimized for low-quality settings, which are necessary for the Web (this explains the differences between the Save As and Save for Web commands).

5. Arithmetic or Huffman Encoding of Coefficients

This step is lossless. Although arithmetic encoding generates 10 percent better compression, its Q Encoding is patented. Therefore, Huffman encoding is usually used instead.

6. Inserting the Correct Header and Saving the File

All compression parameters are saved with the image, so the decoder can reverse the process accordingly. These parameters contain the quantization table and the Huffman encoding table, for example. The specification also allows you to omit this information, which saves several hundred bytes. However, the image can then only be decoded if the decoder itself contains the required tables.

▲ The image is divided into 8x8-pixel blocks. The color frequencies are rounded, which results in a loss of detail that you can see here. The top image is the original image, the middle image is an enlargement of the original image, and the bottom image is the enlargement after compression.

▲ I treated this original image (290x470 pixels, 400 K) with various filters to see how they affect JPEG compression.

▲ I applied the Despeckle noise filter here and then saved the image as a JPEG. (See the next page for more examples.)

QUALITY DIFFERENCES AMONG JPEG DECODERS

You may never have considered it, but the way a JPEG image looks will vary in quality from one program to another. A good JPEG decoder will try to adjust and smooth the edges of the 8x8 blocks to make them less visible. This is totally dependent on the program; it is not built into the JPEG standard.

Another trick that a JPEG decoder uses is saving processor power by doing a "fast" decompression. This basically involves rounding values, and similar tricks exist for color mode conversion. (This is not really applicable to Web design, but if, for example, you want to save your JPEG image in CMYK mode, the browser would have to convert it to RGB in order to display it. The accuracy of this conversion depends on the decoder.)

All this means that you should view your JPEG images in both browsers to get an idea of how they are really going to look. Don't rely on Photoshop or ImageReady, since their decoders differ from those in Internet Explorer and Netscape Navigator.

IMPROVING COMPRESSION WITH BLURRING

One of the best-known tricks for reducing the file size of a compressed JPEG image is to apply a Gaussian Blur to an image before saving it. With JPEG compression, sudden color changes cause artifacts—visual flaws—but a **Gaussian Blur** addresses this problem by looking at each pixel and adjusting the colors of the pixels that surround it, thereby minimizing those sudden shifts and increasing compression. Of course you must be careful because this improved compression sometimes reduces image quality: text in an image, for example, is particularly vulnerable to reduced quality when blurred and compressed.

But while you can learn this trick from pretty much any book on Web design, I'll bet you didn't know that there are alternatives to applying a Gaussian Blur to maximize JPEG compression: you can use a Smart Blur filter or a Despeckle noise filter as well. What is the difference between these techniques?

A Gaussian Blur filter blurs a selection by an adjustable amount, adding low-frequency detail and creating a hazy effect. The Blur option in the Save for Web dialog box actually applies a Gaussian Blur.

Smart Blur offers a bit more control: first, it allows you to specify a radius. All pixels within the radius will be adjusted, not just adjacent pixels. This sometimes creates a graphical effect because it makes the area within the radius look flat.

The Smart Blur also offers a **Threshold** slider that lets you adjust what the filter should recognize as an edge. If the Threshold is set to 100 (the maximum), all subtle color changes disappear. Finally, you can specify a blur quality (low, medium or high) and a mode (normal, edge only or edge overlay).

Despeckle (**Filter > Noise > Despeckle**) detects areas where significant color changes occur and blurs all of the selection except those edges, which has the effect of removing noise while preserving detail.

I applied a Gaussian Blur filter to the left image and a Smart Blur filter to the right image and then saved each as JPEG. Even in print, the difference in visual quality is apparent. ▶

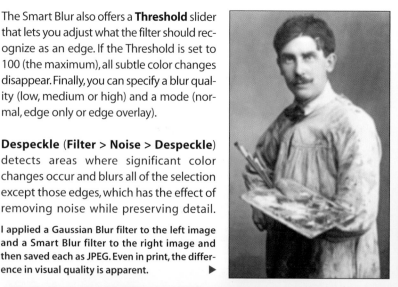

	Original	D1	GB 0.3	D2	GB 0.6	D3	GB 0.9	D4	GB 1.2	Smart Blur
Q 70	50.8 KB	41.7 KB	42.7 KB	38.3 KB	37.7 KB	36.0 KB	33.0 KB	34.5 KB	29.2 KB	42.1 KB
Q 30	19.3 KB	16.3 KB	16.6 KB	15.1 KB	15.0 KB	14.3 KB	13.3 KB	13.7 KB	11.9 KB	16.5 KB
Q 0	8.5 KB	7.8 KB	7.8 KB	7.5 KB	7.4 KB	7.2 KB	6.9 KB	7.2 KB	6.4 KB	8.0 KB

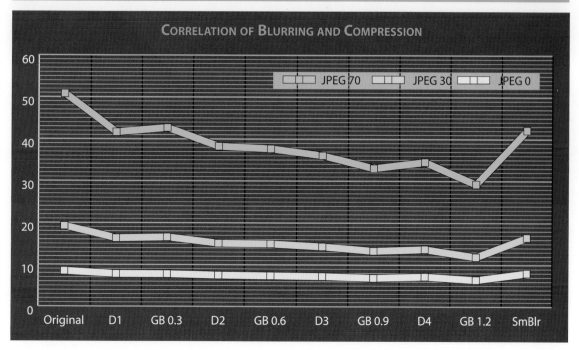

JPEG Comparison Charts

These charts compare the file size of our usual test images: a photograph (Image A), a photo illustration (Image B), a graphics file (Image C), and a color spectrum (Image D). See page 228 for more on Image C, and note that Image D is almost a best-case scenario for JPEG compression and is therefore an excellent reference. All images measure 256x180 pixels, require 140KB uncompressed, and were saved using both the Save for Web and Save As commands.

Although the Save for Web command offers quality values of 0 to 100 and the Save As command offers settings of 0 to 12, settings above 80 (or 8) are never used in Web design, so I excluded them here. In reality, only quality levels up to 40 are ever used with Save for Web (up to 5 with Save As), because the

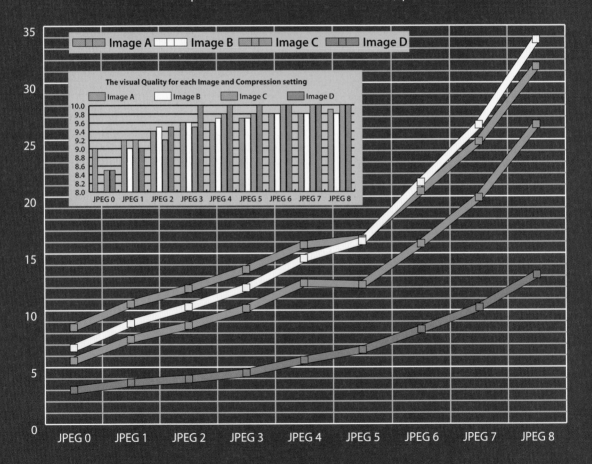

JPEG algorithm delivers excellent and sufficient results at these lower quality settings. Only quality levels of 0 to 10 introduce a deterioration in quality. (Because the nuances between these quality levels would be difficult to discern in print, and the differences aren't dramatic anyway—especially compared to GIF—there was no point in showing them here.)

As you can see, Save for Web (right) achieves better compression than Save As (left). Also notice the flatter slope of the curve between quality values 4 and 5 in the Save As chart: This is because Save As uses the standard JPEG quantization table, while Save for Web uses a quantization table that better optimizes these low- to medium-quality JPEGs for the Web. That's why you should always use the Save for Web command to save your JPEGs; it also gives you the option of blurring the file and attaching an ICC profile.

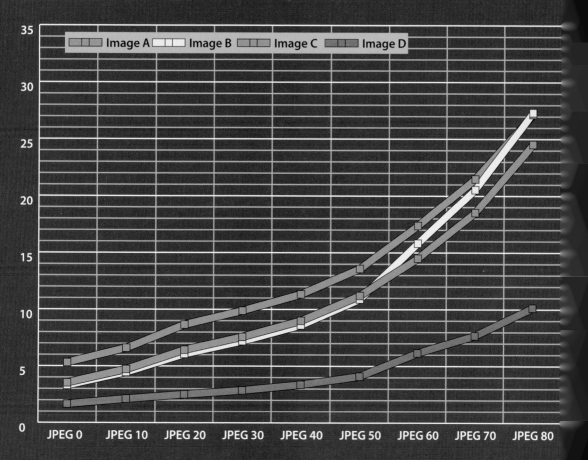

▲ Because JPEG has an 8x8-pixel block compression, a selection should always be a little larger. In this example, the selection was expanded by 8 pixels with Select > Modify > Expand; otherwise, the lower Quality setting for the outer area would have created some artifacts at the edges.

Since Despeckle always works with a fixed value, you sometimes have to apply it several times until you achieve the desired level of blurring.

So just how much savings do these filters actually buy? To find out, I applied a Gaussian Blur (with values ranging from 0.3 to 1.2 pixels), a Despeckle filter (applied between one and four times), and a Smart Blur filter (Radius 3.7, Threshold 11.9, Quality: High) to the same image in various combinations and then compared the results.

▲ To modify the quality setting with an alpha channel, click on the button next to Quality.

As you can see from the results printed on these pages, applying these filters to an image before saving it as JPEG does make a difference, but more filtering is not necessarily better. A Gaussian Blur of 0.3 or a Despeckle filter applied once rendered the best results. An increase in the Gaussian Blur from 0.6 to 1.2 and multiple applications of Despeckle from two to four times don't result in proportional file size savings—and the visual quality drops substantially. For a Gaussian Blur of 1.2, the decrease in quality is (subjectively) about 50 percent, and for four applications of Despeckle, it's around 30 percent.

What's nice is that you can apply the Despeckle and Smart Blur filters before going to Save for Web. Then, if you like, you can apply a Gaussian Blur with the Blur option. When you do that, you get the greatest file savings (roughly 20 percent) for higher quality settings. The lower the image quality, the less can be gained (10 percent). The bottom line: You can get smaller image files if you use a Gaussian Blur, a Smart Blur filter, or a Despeckle noise filter before saving a JPEG image, but don't overdo it. You'll get the best compression-to-quality ratio if you blur as little as possible. Using Despeckle and Smart Blur in combination with Blur in the Save for Web dialog box is great, but if you do that you can use a smaller Blur setting because most of the work has already been done.

OPTIMIZING SAVINGS THROUGH AN ALPHA CHANNEL

The Save for Web command lets you set the quality level of JPEG compression on a scale of 0 to 100, where 0 results in the best compression, but the lowest image quality. With Photoshop 5.5, you had to compromise between quality and compression if the image had areas with a lot of details, but not so with Photoshop 6.0. Now it's possible to modify the quality level with an alpha channel.

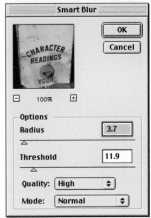

Before opening the **Save for Web** dialog box, select (for example with the **Lasso** tool) the area or areas to which you want to assign the **Maximum Quality**. Remember that JPEG uses 8x8-pixel blocks in its compression algorithm, which means that you should not (!) make a tight selection, because the edges of the two different quality settings will be more obvious. Ideally, it is possible to have the edge of the selection run through a darker area, because this is going to mask it. If you are unsure about where to put the edge of the selection, study your image first in the **Save for Web** dialog box. Use zero as your quality setting and zoom in. The 8x8-pixel blocks should be easy to distinguish and they'll give you an idea of how to draw your selection. Then cancel out of the **Save for Web** dialog box, make your selection, and save it by choosing **Select > Save Selection**.

Now open the **Save for Web** dialog box and click on the **Channel** button next to the **Quality** text field. In the **Modify Quality Setting** dialog box, choose the alpha channel that contains your selection. The channel is visible in a thumbnail: the white areas represent the **Maximum** slider (marked in white) and the black areas represent the **Minimum** slider. When adjusting the **Maximum** value, don't go overboard: the **Maximum** value should be 30 (plus or minus 10) and the **Minimum** should be 10 (plus or minus 10), otherwise the file will grow too much. The idea behind this feature is not to save the JPEG with a higher quality value than you would usually do, but rather to squeeze out the last bit of savings where possible.

▲ Smart Blur lets you define a radius within which it equalizes the colors of all pixels. With Threshold, you can set the level of details. In the image at the top it is easy to see the effect: the rust on the vintage Future Teller almost vanished.

As with GIFs, you can use a grayscale alpha channel to modify the quality gradually, but this is rather redundant and offers little real-world gain. You're better off specifying a Blur value in the Save for Web dialog box (this reduces edge artifacts and color shifts and also improves the compression), or applying a Gaussian Blur, a Smart Blur filter, or a Despeckle noise filter before saving for the Web.

Illustration: Michael Baumgardt

PNG

PNG—Portable Network Graphic Format

The PNG (Portable Network Graphic) format was supposed to be the next-generation image format for the Web. It was developed to bring the best of two worlds together: it has many of the benefits of JPEG and GIF, but it transcends some of their limitations.

PNG is based on a compression technology also known as deflation, which was developed by Jean-Loup Gailly and is also used in ZIP file compression.

PNG allows lossless compression with 24-bit color, which yields more than 16 million colors. It comes in two flavors: PNG-24, which you can use for photographic images in lieu of JPEG, and PNG-8, which is an alternative to GIF. Like JPEG, PNG supports interlacing; unlike GIF, it does not support Lossy. PNG stands apart from both formats in a couple of ways. First, PNG-24 provides 256 levels of transparency through a dedicated Alpha channel, which lets you create transparent drop shadows that blend seamlessly with the background; PNG-8 supports one level of transparency. JPEG doesn't support transparency at all, and transparency can be problematic with GIF, where you sometimes get a halo effect with anti-aliased images.

PNG saves the Gamma along with an image, but that doesn't necessarily mean that the browser (or the plug-in) will interpret this information and adjust the image. I am not aware of problems with any browsers, but that doesn't mean that there aren't any.

That's not all. PNG saves a Gamma curve along with the image. As you may recall, the Macintosh uses a different Gamma than Windows, so images that are optimized for a Mac will appear darker on PCs, while images created on a PC look too bright on Macs. PNG solves this problem by saving the Gamma, so regardless of which computer you use to create the image, it will look the same on both platforms. (By the way, ImageReady lets you see how your images will look under different Gamma settings by switching between Macintosh Gamma and Windows Gamma in **View > Preview**.)

Does this mean that JPEG and GIF are obsolete formats, and PNG is about to take over the Web? Not anytime soon. For one thing, some PNG files are substantially bigger than their GIF or JPEG equivalents. Take an image saved as PNG-24 and JPEG with Quality 100: they'll be of comparable visual quality, but the PNG version will be twice as big. Likewise for an image saved as PNG-8 and GIF. The size difference is not quite as drastic, but usually the PNG-8 file will be 20 percent to 30 percent bigger than a GIF version of comparable visual quality. So although PNG's lossless compression pays off in terms of visual quality, you pay for it in terms of file size.

Other factors holding back the PNG format's widespread acceptance are that it doesn't support animation, and it isn't universally and seamlessly supported by browsers. Microsoft Internet Explorer 4.x browsers for Windows can display PNG without a plug-in, but Macintosh Internet Explorer 4.5 and Netscape Navigator 4.08 cannot. You can view PNG files in either browser on the Mac via Apple's QuickTime plug-in, but QuickTime doesn't support PNG transparency.

Internet Explorer 5 and Netscape 6 (Mac and Win) support PNG, including the most important feature: the alpha channel for transparency. So if you don't care about backward compatibility, you can use a PNG image in your design. However, you should be aware that there are still many users, who have older browsers and to them, the design will look much different (the transparency for example will be rendered as a white background). Creating a browser switch with JavaScript would be one way of solving this problem, but it would require you to create two versions of your web site, just to be able to use PNG. Because of this, I wouldn't advise you to use PNG until most users have made the switch, which will be probably towards the end of 2001.

SAVING PNG IMAGES WITH SAVE FOR WEB

Since GoLive 5.0 and the latest browser support PNG, it can't hurt to experiment with it and enjoy 256 levels of transparency while you wait until the latest browsers are being used by enough people.

➤ Saving an Image as PNG-24

To experiment with PNG-24's 256 levels of transparency, create a new image in Photoshop, type in some text using the **Text** tool (which places the text on its own layer), and apply an effect such as a **drop shadow (Layer > Layer Style >**

According to the official PNG Web site (www.libpng.org/pub/png/pngstatus.html), Internet Explorer 5.0 for Macintosh has "near-perfect" support for PNG (including Gamma and alpha), but it only uses QuickTime to display PNG if the Object tag is used. Netscape 6 for Mac and IE 5 for Mac support all the same PNG features, whereas IE 5.5 for Windows supports PNG and Gamma, but not alpha. According to WebSnapshot.com, those browsers currently account for 30–40 percent of Web page viewing, so it looks like using PNG is really becoming a possibility.

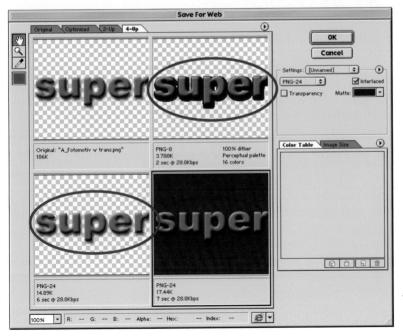

◄ PNG-24 offers 256 levels of transparency; PNG-8, like GIF, has only one transparency level.

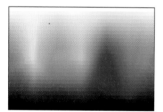

▲ These are the Images A–D that were used to compare PNG with JPEG and GIF.

▲ The best way to experience PNG-24 is to open a file in GoLive 5.0. Here is a PNG-24 image with a drop shadow and transparency; here you can see that the drop shadow blends seamlessly with the background.

Drop Shadow) to spruce it up. Make sure that your text is large enough and that the drop shadow is very soft and blurry so that you will be able to see the effect clearly in GoLive. Then hide the background layer in the Layer palette (**Windows > Show Layers**) by clicking on the eye icon; the checkerboard grid indicates that the background is transparent. Now choose **File > Save for Web**, and in the dialog, select PNG-24 as your file format. **PNG-24** doesn't offer many options: you can specify only Interlaced, Transparency, and Matte color. Interlaced lets the browser display the image while it is still streaming from the server; for our experiment it's not important, so deselect it. Do check the **Transparency** option so that the transparent background doesn't get filled with a **Matte** color. Now click on OK, and in the **Save Optimized As** dialog box save the image with a ".png" extension. After you place this image on an HTML page in GoLive, the drop shadow will blend seamlessly with the background color or pattern.

➤ Saving an Image as PNG-8

Go back to Photoshop and the image you just created. Call up the **Save for Web** dialog box again and this time select **PNG-8** from the **File Format** pop-up menu. You have the same options for optimizing PNG that you do for GIF, except for the **Lossy** command, as noted earlier. Select a color reduction algorithm, pick the number of colors you want to use, and choose your dithering method, if any. Check the **Transparency** box again, but keep in mind that PNG-8 offers only one level of transparency, just like a GIF. The similarity between GIF and PNG-8 becomes very apparent here, especially if you use the

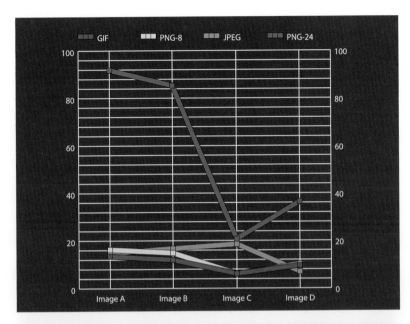

	Image A	Image B	Image C	Image D
GIF	13.450	11.930	6.104	9.616
PNG-8	16.290	14.850	6.100	10.100
JPEG	14.880	16.680	18.540	6.963
PNG-24	91.830	85.320	20.740	36.450

The results of this graph (left) should not be regarded as universal. After all, this is a test with just four images, so it is possible that different images would produce smaller file sizes with PNG. The folks at the PNG Web site, for example, claim that PNG-8 files are, on average, smaller than GIF files. They say that displaying an image in the 4-up window to compare a GIF with a PNG-8 is not sufficient. True, the 4-view display doesn't take the CLUT compression into account the way that PNG does when the image is saved. However, the maximal size of a CLUT is only 768 bytes, and when I compared file sizes via the desktop, the GIF still turned out smaller than the PNG. So, at least for this set of images, PNG-8 didn't work very well.

4-Up view to compare the GIF and PNG-8 side by side. With identical color reduction algorithms, color tables, and dithering, there is no difference between the two formats except for file size (PNG will be larger). Now view the PNG-24 version in one of the 4-up windows and you'll see the benefit of 256 levels of transparency—seamless blending with no halo effect.

Comparing PNG, GIF, and JPEG File Sizes

The chart above compares the size differences of our four test images, each of which is saved in four formats: GIF, PNG-8, JPEG, and PNG-24. All four PNG-8 images are at least 20 percent bigger then their GIF equivalents (both are saved with an Adaptive palette, 100 percent dither, and 16 colors). The difference between the PNG-24 and JPEG images is even more dramatic: the PNG-24 images are as much as 400 percent bigger than their JPEG counterparts (saved with Quality 60). PNG-24 was particularly efficient for Image C, where the PNG-24 file was only 11 percent larger than the JPEG version.

GOLIVE BASICS

GoLive Basics

In this chapter, you will see how to make the transition from Photoshop/ImageReady to GoLive. I won't explain all the design features of GoLive in detail, but if you have some knowledge of HTML or even GoLive, this chapter will help you work efficiently and understand how all the applications come together.

Once you and your client have finalized the main page and the design concept for all the body pages in Photoshop and/or ImageReady, it's time for you to move everything into GoLive and re-create the Web site as HTML documents.

Instead of designing the Web site page by page, you want to take advantage of GoLive's ability to automate and manage your assets. This requires the creation of a site, which is essentially a collection of folders and a database that keeps track of your files. The next step would then be to export all your images and rollover buttons from Photoshop/ImageReady to the site folder and to start creating your stationery files. With these stationeries you then build the whole structure and architecture of the site, and after that, the pages get filled with content.

The tutorial in this chapter walks you through such a scenario and illustrates the typical steps. But since the tutorial can't cover everything, I would like to explain some of the most common techniques and describe problems that you might encounter when creating your own Web site.

STATIONERY AND COMPONENTS

One of the most important features of GoLive is the capability to save HTML documents as stationery and components. This feature is the key to working efficiently, but it is often overlooked by designers who have just started working with GoLive. So let me take the time to explain this concept and how it can help you.

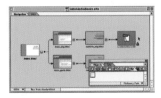

Stationery allows you to easily create the structure of your Web site. After you have saved a stationery file, choose Stationery Pads from the pop-up menu in the Site Extras tab and then drag the page into the site (Design > Navigation View).

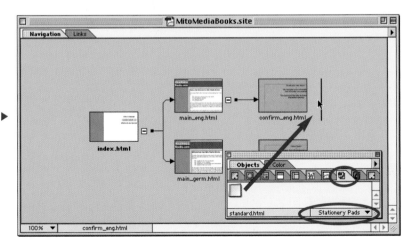

Stationery refers to a predefined page that you can drag and drop into your site structure. If you have worked with layout programs such as Adobe PageMaker or InDesign, you are probably already familiar with this concept; layout programs use the similar concept of master pages or templates. However, while master pages are linked to subsequent pages in a layout document, the pages that you create in GoLive's site structure are not linked to the stationery. Therefore, if you make changes on a stationery page, they won't show up on the pages in your site that uses this stationery. GoLive stationery is, in fact, nothing more than a copy of a page; the only way to change something globally is if, for example, you overwrite an image that is used by every page. If you need to create elements that are dynamically updated, you have to create a component.

▲ The Site window lets you manage the mirror site as well as other aspects of your Web site. On the Extras tab, you'll find a folder for stationery and components.

A component is an element on a page that will be updated if the original component is changed. Usually it is a good idea to save a navigation bar as a component. If one of the links changes, all you have to do is open the component, change the link, and save it. GoLive will then replace every occurrence of the component on the site with the new version.

◀ A component is dragged from the Objects palette onto the document. In this example, the navigation component has only two buttons. To extend it, double-click on the placed component.

◀ A third button is added and the component is saved.

Since components can be placed on stationery, you can make GoLive mimic the way master pages are handled in a layout program. For example, you could create a component for navigation and place it on your stationery page. You could do the same thing with a company logo, a banner ad, or the text link navigation that usually comes at the bottom of every page. These items make ideal components. But that's as far as you can go with stationery: it is not possible to change a background color or link color globally. The only way to do this is to do a manual search for the HTML code and replace it with the new color.

Components also have limitations. For example, what do you do if you want a navigation bar that always displays the current section, for example, an inverted Home button when the user is on the home page and an inverted Products button when the user is on the products page? This requires you to create multiple copies of the component, and if the links change, you have to go through all the copies of the component. This really isn't anything major,

▲ When saving the modified component, GoLive displays which documents the component is used in. After updating, every occurrence of the component will display three buttons.

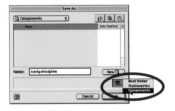

▲ When saving a component, use the shortcut in the lower right corner of the Save As dialog box to locate the Components folder.

but it can cost you some time. One useful improvement in GoLive 5.0 is that you can nest components within one other.

Creating stationery or a component is simple: create a new page with **File > New**. Place your elements and then save the page in either the Components or Stationery folder of the Web site. GoLive offers a shortcut in the **Save As** dialog box that lets you locate these folders by clicking on the button in the lower right corner. Be sure not to strip the document of the ".html" extension, otherwise it won't show up on the **Site Extras** tab of the **Objects** palette (**Window > Objects**). To switch between stationery and components (and custom, which are just snippets of HTML code or other elements), use the pop-up menu in the lower right corner of the **Site Extras** view.

CREATING HTML TABLES

Even though most browsers today support HTML layers, tables remain the most reliable way of laying out Web pages. To create a table in GoLive, just drag a table icon from the **Basic** tab of the **Objects** palette onto a document. By default, GoLive creates a table with three rows and three columns; the **Table Inspector** appears automatically, showing the table's dimensions and other attributes. The biggest problem you'll have when working with tables is making sure that they work with different browsers. Here are some guidelines for creating effective HTML tables.

1. Make the table invisible. For a table to be invisible, the Border, Cell Pad, and Cell Space attributes must be set to 0. If the Table Inspector isn't visible, access these attributes by clicking on the border of the table in the GoLive document.

2. Vertically align to "Top." The default vertical alignment for content in each table cell is centered, but it's better to align content to the top of the cell; otherwise, you might end up with a gap between the content and the edge of the cell (for example, if you're creating an image table). You can't change this universally, but you can do it by row. Click with the mouse cursor to select a table cell and then switch to the **Row** tab of the **Table Inspector**. Set **Vertical Alignment** to **Top** and then use the arrow keys on your keyboard to move to the next row, and repeat.

3. Set the proper height and width. If you're placing an image in a table cell, it is important that the height and width of the cell equal the image's dimensions. The best way to ensure that the cell fits the image it contains is to first set the width and height of the entire table and then go through each cell that contains an image and set its height and width individually.

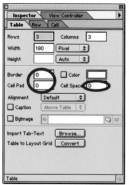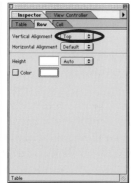

◀ To set up a table so that it appears invisible, Border, Cell Pad, and Cell Space must be set to zero (far left). By default, the vertical alignment of the table cells is set to centered. You can change this row by row (middle). If the table cells contain images, then the width and height of the cell must be set to values that correspond to those of the image (right) to prevent any gaps.

4. Use the spacer tag for empty cells. It is not enough to set the dimensions of empty table cells and leave it at that. Internet Explorer will obey the Width attribute and maintain the cell's width with integrity, but Netscape Navigator might "collapse" the cell. To fix this, drag the **Horizontal Spacer** tag, which is a Netscape tag used exclusively by Navigator, into the cell from the **Basic** tab of the **Objects** palette. Set the width to that of the cell itself.

5. Use Cell Pad instead of Cell Space. If you have defined a background color or you're using a background image for your table and you want the table cells to appear continuously, without gaps between them, don't use Cell Space (it creates space between cells). Use Cell Pad instead.

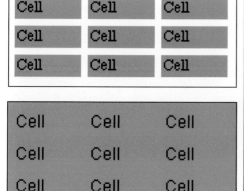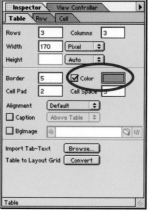

Placing a table in GoLive is as simple as dragging the table icon from the palette to the document. By default, GoLive creates a 3x3 table, but you can click the top or left edge of the table to change this. Enter the desired number of rows and columns in the Table Inspector. GoLive measures the width in pixels, but you can also specify the dimensions as a Percent or Auto. One nice feature of GoLive is its ability to import tab-separated text files into tables with the Import Tab-Text button (near left), which can save you a lot of time.

▲ Navigtor (top left) and Explorer (above left) render the table differently when the table color is set in the Inspector. Use Cell Pad instead of Cell Space to get a solid colored background.

▲ Drag a layout grid from the Basic tab of the Objects palette and adjust its size in the Layout Grid Inspector.

6. Check backgrounds. It is possible to load an image into a table as background, but Navigator handles backgrounds very poorly (see the example later in this chapter). If you intend to use images as backgrounds in tables, be sure to check them in Navigator on both platforms. Also, set your monitor to 256 colors, because Navigator treats background images differently than other images.

➤ Using the Layout Grid

An alternative to HTML tables is the layout grid, which is an invisible table that uses a "control" row and column (with spacer tags) to optimize the table's display in Navigator. Each time an object is placed on the layout grid (or moved within it), GoLive automatically generates a new table to position the objects. This table contains the fewest cells that your grid's layout will allow,

---

FIXING IMAGE TABLES IN HTML

Stitching the pieces of a sliced image together in a table doesn't seem particularly tricky, especially if you tell ImageReady to create the HTML code for you, but if for some reason you're doing this task manually in GoLive, you can end up with unwanted space between cells. It might also happen that the image table will look fine in one browser and not in another. In any case you'll have to do some troubleshooting to find the HTML tag that's causing the problem. As there are several possible causes, here is a little checklist:

1. Check for spaces in the cells. Many authoring programs (not GoLive) automatically place a space in a cell because without it, the cell will not display the cell border. Delete those spaces. If you are not completely sure that your image is the only thing in the cell, look at the HTML code. It should read as follows: <td><img= ...></td>.

2. Check justification. You can justify the contents of a cell vertically and horizontally using the VALIGN and ALIGN attributes of the TD tag. Make sure all the cells use the same justification and that there are no conflicting attributes (like VALIGN="Top" in the TR tag and VALIGN="Bottom" in the TD tag).

3. Adjust the height and width of the cells to fit the image. You can find the exact measurements of the image in the IMG tag. After you enter those values for the table cell, the table should fit the image tightly.

4. The TABLE tag may contain CELL SPACE or BORDER attributes. Remove all unnecessary attributes or set them to zero.

5. If an image is defined as a LINK, make sure it isn't defined with a border by entering the attribute BORDER=0 in the IMG tag. In GoLive, click on the image and in the **Image Inspector**, select the **Basic** tab. Select the **Border** option with a value of 0 (in GoLive 5.0, the border is 0 by default).

but when objects are not perfectly aligned vertically and horizontally, the table can become complex. And complex tables not only bloat HTML files but also may not display as expected in Web browsers. Explorer, for example, may not correctly display tables produced with GoLive's layout grid if they contain unaligned objects; it may overestimate the table's width and display a horizontal scroll bar when it isn't needed.

You may want to use a plain table instead of a layout grid for some objects, such as those that won't be the same size in all browsers or operating systems. In particular, this applies to forms—Explorer and Navigator display form elements such as text boxes and pop-up menus in different sizes. When your document's design requires that paragraphs of text stay aligned with an image, you should put the text and image in a table. That way, they'll always line up.

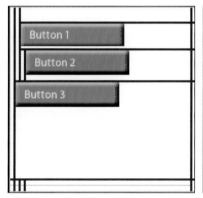

▲ This is the underlying table architecture of the layout grid (made visible by deleting the Cool attribute in the HTML code). As you can see, the table on the left is much more complex because the elements are not aligned. When working with a layout grid, always use the Align commands in the toolbar to get the best results.

▲ At the top you see a layout grid with two text boxes; below is the result in Explorer and Navigator. As you can see, they differ because of the fonts they are using. If you have a layout like this, use a table instead.

In fact, you should opt for a table instead of a layout grid any time you're working with a lot of text, since you don't really know how the length of the text will vary between the browsers. Tables are always better than text boxes and layout grids (see the example on the left) because they adjust their height according to the text flow, whereas layout grids are static.

You can actually convert a layout grid to a table to see how it's built, which can help you to ensure that all objects are aligned and that you don't have unnecessary cells. First select **Source** view and remove the Cool table attribute from the **Table** tag. This is a flag that tells GoLive to display the table with the layout grid interface. Switch to the **Layout** view to see the table.

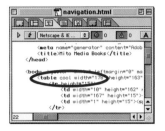

▲ The word "cool" inside the TABLE tag tells GoLive that this is a layout grid. Browsers or other HTML-authoring tools will ignore this attribute. It is possible to convert a layout grid back to a regular table by deleting this word from the code.

Don't modify it—you could very easily ruin the page. Without making any changes, return to **Source** view and reinsert the Cool attribute. When you go to the **Layout** view again, the layout grid should be back in place. Then you can make any necessary adjustments to optimize the content on the layout grid.

USING BACKGROUNDS IN TABLES AND GRIDS

Since Internet Explorer 3.0 and Netscape Navigator 4.0, designers have been able to use images as backgrounds for tables. This allows for some nice tricks; for example, the mock-up below that simulates computer paper. The great thing about using background images in tables is that (theoretically, at least) you can place your content inside a table cell and the background will always adjust to the length of the table. Before you get too excited, however, I must add that Navigator does a horrible job of using background images in tables. If you want your site to be compatible with both browsers, this automatically limits what you can do.

For example, you can't use nested tables (tables within tables) with Navigator, because the nested table uses the background of the table in which it's embedded (even though there is no background set for the nested table). Since the embedded table tries to synchronize the background with its own zero origin point, this generally creates an offset (see example on the next page). The same is true for the parent cells: the background will be repeated at zero origin for every cell, which means that you can't just define one pattern for the entire width of the table. Instead, you have to split the pattern into individual pieces and define each cell with its own piece of the pattern.

You can create elements like this computer paper by applying an image background to tables. This table contains three columns (marked in blue) and each one contains its own background image. Since Navigator handles backgrounds in tables poorly, this is the only way to render it correctly in both browsers.

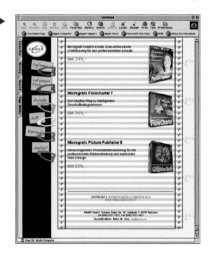

To illustrate these problems with Navigator, I created a sample Web site that consists of a 3-column table where each column uses a different background. The left column uses the left-hand guide holes, the middle column uses lines, and the right column shows the outer set of holes. Without nested tables, you are severely limited in how you can position the elements. Ultimately, it all comes down to setting the Align attribute for inline images.

The last table restriction is that you can't use patterns with transparency. Although Explorer renders them correctly, Navigator displays transparent areas as white. If this weren't the case, we could fix the nested table problem by using a transparent image as background for the nested table, but unfortunately, that is not an option. The bottom line is that you can use background images in tables only where Navigator's limitations won't be apparent. For everything else, you have to think up a workaround and test it before you can even start designing in Photoshop. In particular, be sure to test how the background will look on 256-color monitors, because Navigator (for Mac, and probably also for Windows) handles the colors of an image serving as a table background differently from the rest of the page.

Layout grids can display a background image; after all, they are tables. Since GoLive doesn't offer such an attribute in the Grid Inspector, the path to the image has to be inserted manually into the code inside the TABLE tag Background attribute. Of course, the same restrictions that I explained before apply, and GoLive will not display the background image in the Preview—it can only be tested in the browsers.

▲ An invisible table (containing the computer images) was nested inside another table with an image background. Although Explorer displays it correctly (left), Navigator 4.x repeats the background pattern inside the invisible table, making it visible (right).

How do browsers handle background images that use transparency? Navigator 4.x doesn't display the transparent color (right), while Explorer 4.x does so with no problem (bottom right).

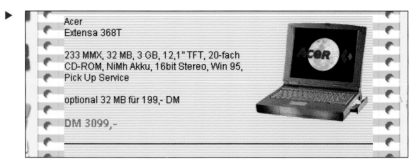

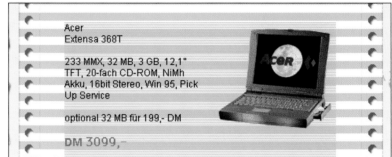

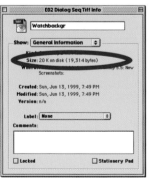

▲ A background image that uses only 20KB on the hard drive can eat up several megabytes of memory when decompressed in a browser.

IMAGE INFLATION

A significant problem in designing a Web site—especially one that uses backgrounds—is that browsers can crash when they run out of memory. You may think this is unlikely, since all those image files are so small, but you'd be wrong. Although a background saved as a JPEG or GIF may be only 10KB, it will be decompressed to full size in the browser. This can amount to 1MB, 2MB, or more. Take the effect of image inflation or decompression seriously, and check the exact memory requirement of your image in Photoshop or ImageReady by looking at the lower left area of the image window. (If your Photoshop document displays something different, click on the triangle icon and select Document Size.) In this example, the decompressed background requires 3.75MB even though the file takes up only 19.3KB on the hard drive. Visitors with low-end computers usually don't allocate enough memory to their browsers, and if they view your page, the browser may reach its memory limit and crash.

Image inflation is mostly a problem with backgrounds because of the additional width that they require so that users won't see a repetition. If all the additional pixels on the right consist of a plain color, using an invisible frame on the right side of the page might be the solution. This trick was once used very effectively on the David Bowie Web site designed by Marlene Stoffers and Ben Clemens from N2K (unfortunately, that version of the site is no longer live). Because the site used a large background image (roughly 500 pixels in height), the designers had to limit its width to avoid the risk of a browser crash due to image inflation. On the right side, the background image faded to black and Stoffers and Clemens used an invisible frame with a black background. For this trick to work, it's important that the right-hand frame is set to **Scale** in the GoLive **Frame Inspector**. Here is a step-by-step guide to accomplishing this:

1. In Photoshop, create a background with a width of 600 pixels and select a color from the Web color table (to avoid dithering) to fill the rest of the image on the right side. Use the **Airbrush** tool to blend the image with the background color if necessary (in the example on the next page I used just a gradient fill to illustrate the principle). Save the finished background as a GIF or JPEG.

2. In GoLive, define a two-frame vertical frameset by dragging that icon from the **Frames** tab of the **Objects** palette into the **Frame Editor** document view. (The **Frame Editor** is the tab in your document window between the **Layout** and HTML **Source** Editors.) Then load the HTML document with the background image in the left (main) frame and load an HTML document with a solid-color background in the right frame. In the **Frame Inspector** make the left frame 600 pixels, and set the right frame **Size to Scale**. If you switch to the HTML Source Editor, the HTML code for this frameset would look like this: <FRAMESET COLS="600,*">.

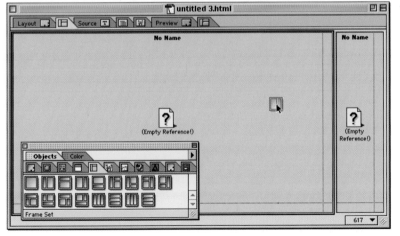

◄ Switch to the Frame Editor, then drag a frameset from the Frame palette to the document window.

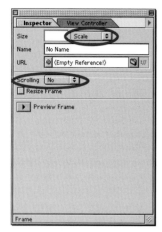

▲ To set the Size attribute, click inside the side frame and set it to Scale. The main frame needs to be set to the size of the background image.

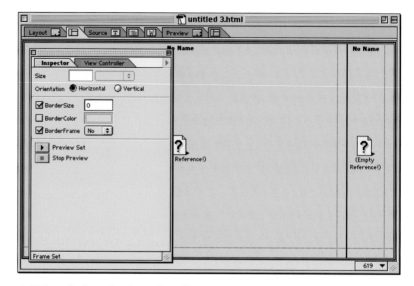

▲ Click on the frame border to show the Frame Set Inspector, where you need to set the BorderSize to 0 and the BorderFrame to No. Next, create two HTML documents, one with the image background (for the main frame) and one with a black background (for the side frame.)

When you switch to the Frame Preview, the two frames will appear to be one background. The dotted line here shows where the two frames meet, but as soon as there is some hidden content, a scroll bar will show up in the main frame. So unless you have to be backward compatible to a non-CSS browser, use CSS to solve the repeating background image problem.

▶

Unfortunately, this simple solution isn't perfect, and isn't suitable for every scenario. As soon as you place more text on the main page than can be displayed in the window, a scroll bar will appear on the right side of the main frame. If you don't need to be backward compatible, use cascading style sheets (CSS), which allow you to repeat a background pattern only along the vertical or horizontal axis. You can do this locally (for one page) or globally (for several pages at once). (If you want to do it globally, create an external Style Sheet document and link all the pages to it.) Here's how to do it locally:

1. Creating a cascading style sheet: in the **Layout Editor**, click on the Open **CSS Interface** button in the upper-right corner of a document (the icon looks like a staircase) to access the CSS window.

2. In the CSS toolbar, click on the **New Element Selector** (< >) button. In the **Basics** tab of the **Inspector**, type BODY in the name field. (What we are basically doing is overwriting the HTML marker BODY.)

◀ Click on the New Element Selector in the Options palette to insert a new element in the cascading style sheet. In the Inspector, this style must be named like the HTML tag that it is supposed to overwrite.

3. Switch to the Background tab, check the **Image** box and then browse for the background image. Choose **Repeat x** from the **Repeat** pop-up menu to repeat the background horizontally, or **Repeat y** to repeat it vertically. It's even possible to have the background repeated only **Once** or to have the background stay at a fixed position by selecting **Fixed** from the **Attach** pop-up menu. After you have saved this document, open it in Navigator or Explorer to see the effect, because you can't preview it in GoLive.

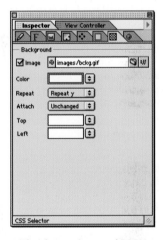

ALIGNING FOREGROUND WITH BACKGROUND

▲ The element is named BODY (like the HTML tag) on the first tab of the CSS Inspector. To change the background, use the Background tab and browse for the image. It is important to use Repeat y to have the background repeat only vertically.

When you use backgrounds in a design, you may discover that it's difficult to align objects in the HTML page with the background. This problem is caused by the browser offset, which unfortunately is not only different for Navigator and Explorer but also varies for different computer platforms. Browser offset is the distance that content is placed from the upper-left corner of the browser window. In the early days of HTML and the Web, it made sense for the browser to display the content with an offset so that it wouldn't crash into the upper right corner of the window. But when the background image function was introduced to HTML, this browser offset became problematic: since the background is positioned without an offset, you can't be exactly sure how a foreground graphic element will align with the background. Back in the "old" days (with the 3.0 browsers) Web designers had to use JavaScript to detect which browser the visitor was using and then compensate for the offset by loading different background images. Luckily this isn't necessary anymore. Netscape and Microsoft fixed this problem, and all

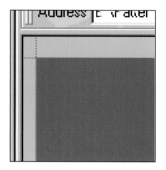

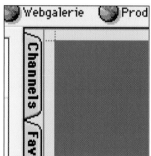

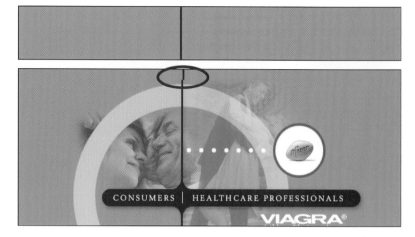

▲ The old Viagra Web site (designed by Andreas Lindström; Nicholson NY) uses a background image (see top) that needs to be aligned with an image in the foreground, which can be done by setting the browser offset to 0.

4.x or later browsers let you set the offset by including some additional attributes in the BODY tag. However, since this was an extension to the official HTML specification, each company used different attributes, so in order to set the offset to 0 for both browsers, you have to use a combination of those attributes in the BODY tag: <BODY leftmargin= "0" marginwidth="0" topmargin="0" marginheight="0">.

In GoLive 5.0 you don't have to type these attributes in manually (in GoLive 4.0 you did). All you need to do is click on the **Page** icon in the upper-left corner of your document and set **Margin Width** and **Height** to 0 in the **Inspector**.

▲ Use the Page Inspector to set the browser offset.

▲ From top to bottom: the browser offset in Explorer 3.0 for Windows, Explorer 4.0 for Macintosh, and Navigator 4.0 (Mac).

WORKING WITH TEXT

In Web design, the possibilities for formatting text are limited. You can either use the FONT tag or cascading style sheets (CSS), but both require the viewer to have the font installed on their computer. This limits you to the serif combination Palatino/Times or san serifs Helvetica/Arial, because these fonts come with the Macintosh and Windows operating systems. It is possible to embed a font in a page, but that requires special software to convert a regular font to what's called a *dynamic font* (more about this later). Still, it's important to format the text on your page; otherwise, you cede control to site visitors, and if they set the standard font in their browser preferences to something exotic, the text on your page might run longer or shorter than you originally intended, which can cause your layout to break apart.

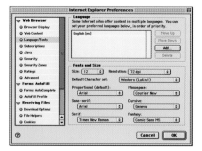

◀ Visitors can set font preferences in Navigator and Explorer (left). If they choose something exotic or in a very large size, your design can break apart. You can control this by using the FONT tag or cascading style sheets.

➤ Using the FONT tag

The FONT tag predates cascading style sheets and is therefore understood even by older browsers. To format text with the FONT tag, you first need to create a font set (**Type > Font > Edit Font Sets**). In the **Font Set Editor**, click the **New** button underneath the Font Sets list to create a new set. Specify fonts that you want

◀ With GoLive, you can create font sets that are specific to a page by clicking on Page in the left column. Then create new font sets by clicking on New and adding fonts in the Font Names column (using the pop-up menu).

to be part of the set using the pop-up menu under the **Font Names** list. Specify more then one font in case your first choice is not installed on the visitor's computer. I recommend that you create two font sets, one for serifs (including Times and Palatino, in that order) and one for sans serifs (Arial and Helvetica, also in that order). After you have defined your font sets, they are available in the **Type > Font** submenu and you can apply them to selected text in HTML documents.

As you probably noticed, GoLive already has predefined font sets (similar to the one we just defined), but they include too many alternatives, and every time you apply a FONT tag to text, the entire tag gets placed into the HTML code:

```
<font face="Arial,Helvetica,Geneva,Swiss,SunSans-Regular">This is an example</font>
```

As you can see, this FONT tag uses more characters than the actual text in this example, and the HTML code gets quite bloated. Even though this doesn't cause much of a problem for browsers, it is extra data that needs to be transmitted and it makes editing HTML source code all the more tedious.

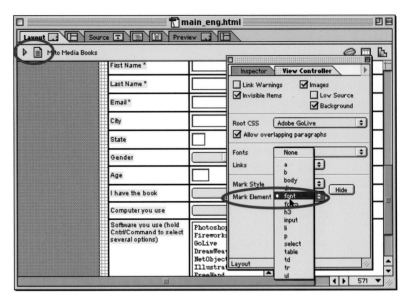

▲ This is a great feature when testing and checking your Web page for bugs: in the View Controller (the tab next to the Inspector), the Mark Style and Mark Element pop-up menus let you highlight the text that is using certain cascading styles or HTML tags. Here all the text formatted by the FONT tag is highlighted.

Still, the FONT tag, as applied in GoLive's font set feature, is a convenient way to design Web pages. If you're working with text-intensive pages and you want to verify that you have formatted all the text properly, try this trick: click on the **View Controller** tab next to the **Inspector**. Choose **Font** from the **Mark Element** pop-up menu, and GoLive highlights all of the text that has a FONT tag applied to it. You can also identify text that has body, paragraph, or anchor tags applied.

➤ Using Cascading Style Sheets

Nowadays, most browsers are capable of reading cascading style sheets, which are a better choice than the FONT tag. The CSS extension was included in the HTML specification to give designers more formatting capabilities then the FONT tag offers. From setting the font, color or white space to background images or borders of your text, cascading style sheets seem to fulfill all the designer's needs—at least in theory. Unfortunately, the incompatibilities among the browsers are a disaster, and if you use anything beyond the basics (such as font, size, and color) you will have to check your page in all browsers. In particular, it is difficult to predict how CSS-formatted text will behave in tables. Some older versions of Navigator will not expand a table cell when a line height has been set, so the text will actually extend beyond the border of the cell.

But otherwise, cascading style sheets have a lot of advantages. You can, for example, use one external CSS document for all your HTML pages, which lets you change the appearance of an entire Web site by editing just one document. Another great feature of cascading style sheets is that you can over-write the browser formatting of standard HTML tags. If you wanted all your headlines to be in a bold Arial font, for example, you could just name a Style <H1>. Even if the browser doesn't understand cascading style sheets, it will interpret the structural tags as usual. (The creators of cascading style sheets didn't want to simply create additional HTML text-formatting tags; they wanted to ensure that HTML would remain a structural language.)

▲ The best way to use cascading style sheets is as an external document. This way the style sheet can be referenced in all documents.

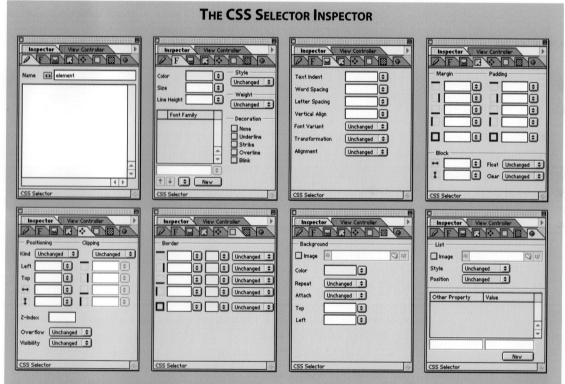

THE CSS SELECTOR INSPECTOR

The cascading style sheet specification is very complex. In order to set all the attributes, the CSS Selector Inspector palette has many tabs (from left to right): after typing in the HTML tag, you can set the font size and style. On the third tab, you can set paragraph formatting characteristics like alignment or text indent. The fourth and fifth tabs allow you to define the appearance and position of the box that surrounds each element. On the seventh tab, you can determine the background, including how often it should be repeated. Because the background can be set for every tag, it is even possible to give a headline a textured background. On the last tab, you'll find the properties for lists and all unsupported properties.

There are three ways to implement style sheets: besides linking pages to an external CSS document as I just described, you can also use embedded styles or inline styles. Embedded styles define a document structure in the same way as a linked, external document, but they are placed at the beginning of a document and apply to that specific document only. Inline styles, meanwhile, are for local formatting of single words or lines of text in a document. There is a hierarchy to these style sheets: embedded styles overwrite any definitions of a linked style, and inline styles overwrite embedded styles. So if for example you are using an external style sheet in which the paragraph tag is defined as Helvetica, but the embedded paragraph style in a linked document is Palatino, the paragraphs will appear in Palatino. If you've applied an inline style to one sentence of one paragraph of the document to make it Arial, then that sentence will appear in Arial.

THE TEXT STYLE TAB

When selecting text and switching to the Style tab of the Inspector palette, you can choose between four columns named Inline, Par, Div, and Area to apply a style sheet to the text:

Inline is used to format selected text in a paragraph.

Par stands for paragraph and will automatically format the entire paragraph.

Div stands for division and disconnects the paragraph from the normal flow of HTML. The effect seems the same as using Par, but the CSS syntax is different.

▲ The classes of style sheets can be applied to text using the Style tab in the Inspector (elements are applied automatically and IDs are not supported in GoLive).

Area applies a style sheet to the body section of a page, meaning that the entire page with all the text will be formatted with this style sheet. If you use cascading style sheets to control an image background in your browser (CSS lets you repeat a background image along just the horizontal or vertical axis) and you need a different background for each page, create an internal style and click on Area to apply it.

The three types of style sheets are often used together so that child styles modify the display of the parent style as described above. This is similar to style-tagging text in page-layout software, where you can format a paragraph, but give individual words a different appearance. For example, in the linked style sheet, the paragraph tag might be defined as Arial. If the font color in the embedded style sheet is red, then the text in the document will be displayed in a red Arial font. You might then use an inline style to make text bold or give it a background color. Marking a paragraph <P STYLE="background: #660033">Top Ten</P> would highlight the words "Top Ten" without affecting any of the other formatting. You can find more on cascading style sheets in the GoLive manual or at www.w3c.org.

Cascading style sheets and browser incompatibilities could fill an entire book; I'd rather show you how to use them to format text as a replacement for the FONT tag. The most effective way to do this is to create a linked external style sheet in which you define all the standard text tags that occur in your document, such as <P>, < A>, and <H1> through <H7>. Unfortunately, there are always cases where the style sheet will not have any effect. For example, if the first paragraph in a table cell is not marked with a paragraph tag, this text will not be formatted. Since almost all the text on your page will be placed in a table cell, this is a problem, but luckily not a major one. You could fix it by inserting the paragraph tag manually in the HTML source code or including a CSS definition for the table data cell tag (<TD>). Neither way is optimal; it is easier to create a class definition and apply it to the text or to the whole page by checking the Area column on the Style tab. Classes work reliably in all the CSS-capable browsers and you can apply them using the Inspector without having to edit the HTML code.

➤ Creating and Linking External Style Sheets

1. Choose File > New Special > Style Sheet Document. Save this file in your Site folder.

2. Click on the New Element Selector button in the **Toolbar** (marked with angle brackets). This lets you change the browser formatting of the HTML tags. To change the formatting of paragraphs, for example, enter P in the **Name** field of the **Basics** tab in the **Inspector.** Click on the **Font** tab of the **Inspector** and change the font family, size, and color as desired. The Style, Weight, and Decoration attributes will also be interpreted by most browsers, but the attributes that you can specify on the other tabs in the Inspector need to be checked in all browsers and on all platforms. To see what you've specified for the paragraph tag, click back on the **Basics** tab of the **Inspector.** Then define attributes for heading (<H>), unnumbered list (<UL>), and ordered list (<OL>) tags.

▲ Since an external style sheet is a separate document, you'll need to create it using the New Special command in the File menu.

After clicking on New Element Selector, you can name the new entry and change its settings. ▶

3. Click on the New Class Selector button in the toolbar (marked with a dot). This will let you format (later) all of the first paragraphs in table cells. It is important that the name of the class is preceded by a dot (for example, ".paragraph"). Apply some of the same attributes that you used for the paragraph tag. When you're done, save your .CSS document.

4. Now open an HTML document that you previously created for your site and click on the CSS button in the upper right corner of the document window; an untitled .CSS document appears. Click the **New Style Sheet File** button in the toolbar and an **External** folder with an empty reference appears. In the **Inspector**, link the external style sheet that you just created to this document by browsing and selecting it in the **Reference** field. Now all the text in your document should adjust according to your external style sheet—except the first paragraphs in tables. To format those, select the text and click on the **Style** tab of the **Inspector**. The .paragraph CSS class that you previously created should be listed; now just check the **Par, Inline,** or **Area** box to apply it to the text.

After clicking on New Element Selector, you can name the new entry and change its settings. ▶

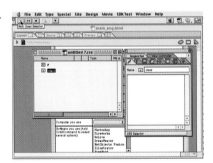

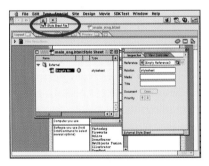

▲ Click on the New Style Sheet button to insert a new external style sheet reference.

➤ Troubleshooting CSS Designs

As I mentioned before, it is important to apply cascading style sheets to all the text on your page. Otherwise, the visitor's browser preferences might cause some text to appear differently. It is a good practice to test your page in a browser after you've set the default font size to an extreme value, such as 36 points. If you have applied CSS to all the text on your page, nothing should happen, but if you missed some text, your design will probably break apart. GoLive offers a helpful feature for troubleshooting pages with cascading style sheets: click on the **View Controller** tab next to the **Inspector** and use the **Mark Style** pop-up menu to select a particular style; GoLive highlights all text in the HTML document that has been tagged with that style.

USING DYNAMIC FONTS

To use dynamic fonts, you need to download Explorer 4 (or higher) for Windows or Netscape 4.03 (or higher) for Windows, Unix, or Macintosh. If you are using Explorer for Windows, you should also download the Microsoft Font Smoother. Font Smoother is included with Windows NT 4.0, and is a free download for Windows 95/98 users. In some ways, Explorer for Macs has not been developed as completely as the Windows version, so dynamic fonts will not work in IE for Macs.

Before you can even use dynamic fonts, you have to declare the PFR MIME Type "application/font-tdpfr" for the browser. Also make sure that the font files have the extension ".pfr". More importantly, talk to your ISP's system administrator, because the Web servers must also be set up to recognize the PFR MIME type.

It is possible to use dynamic fonts that are located on a different server. You can, for example, use free fonts from "www.truedoc.com" and link to those. This at least ensures that the server is set up correctly and that the fonts should work. Allow enough time for the fonts to download to your browser; sometimes download times vary, depending on the size of the dynamic font and the speed of your connection to the Internet.

If you are interested in creating your own dynamic fonts, you need to have software to "burn" the PFR files. Unfortunately, most of the software to do this is no longer around because this is a niche market—it's not lucrative enough for most software companies. To my knowledge, the WebFont Wizard from Bitstream (www.bitstream.com) is the only commercially-available software. You can get it for a reasonable price (there are two versions of the product: one includes hundreds of fonts and is therefore a little pricier) and it is available for Windows and Macintosh.

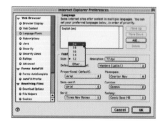

▲ To test your Web site, try some extreme font settings (like 24 points for the size) in the Preferences of your browser (here I've used Explorer). If nothing changes, then you'll know that you formatted everything correctly.

Dynamic Fonts are PostScript or TrueType fonts, that are saved in a special format, so that they can be embedded on a web page. Dynamic Fonts have nothing to do with GoLive's Dynamic Link feature or Dynamic HTML. The only reason why I am mentioning it here in the GoLive chapter is that Dynamic Fonts give designers more control over the look of a page. If you want to use Dynamic Fonts, you need a special software to convert the PostScript or TrueType fonts. Once converted, it takes very little HTML/CSS knowledge to use the fonts on a Web page.

The interface of Bitstream's WebFont Wizard is straightforward: select one font, the style and then the character set. This lets you reduce the PFR file to just those characters that are used—a big file-size saver. ▶

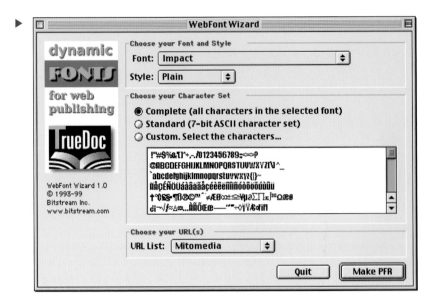

OPTIMIZING THE WORKFLOW BETWEEN GOLIVE AND PHOTOSHOP

In GoLive 5.0, Adobe has introduced a set of new functions and commands that improve the workflow between GoLive and Photoshop, Illustrator, and LiveMotion. The new functions include:

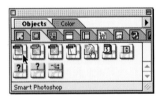

▲ The SmartObjects are listed on the Smart tab of the Objects palette. They will only appear if the software is also installed on the computer.

Smart Objects, which allow you to directly place into a GoLive HTML document a Photoshop, Illustrator or LiveMotion file that is saved in the Site folder as GIF, JEPG, SVG or even Flash. Any changes made to the original file or to the dimensions of the Smart Object will automatically create an updated version of the HTML document, making it much easier to work in GoLive.

Tracing Image, which allows you to load a Photoshop file and display it in the background, making it easier to re-create a design in GoLive. You can even use the Crop tool to slice the image, automatically importing the cropped areas.

Import Photoshop as HTML, imports every layer of a Photoshop document and places it in an HTML layer.

These features make it much more convenient to work with Photoshop files and other page elements in GoLive, and beg you to find new, more efficient ways to work. Let's look at how you can put these features to best use.

➤ Working with Smart Objects

To access a **Smart Object**, click on the **Smart** tab in the **Objects** palette. The first three icons are **Smart Photoshop**, **Smart Illustrator**, and **Smart LiveMotion**, which let you position files created in those applications in your GoLive HTML page. (Only icons for installed applications will appear.) Drag, for example, a **Smart Photoshop** placeholder onto a page and select your Source image from the **Basic** tab of the **Inspector**. GoLive presents you with the **Save for Web** dialog so that you can optimize the image's GIF or JPEG settings, so do that and then click **OK**. GoLive prompts you for the name of the **Destination** file; specify the image folder of your mirror site. Now if you edit the original file (double click on it to launch Photoshop), the **Smart Object** is automatically updated in GoLive. If you scale the **Smart Object** in GoLive, the application creates a new file with those new dimensions under the destination's file name. The original file is left untouched.

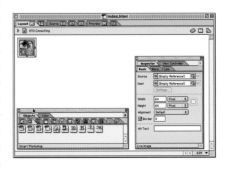

Smart Objects allow you to work in GoLive much as you would in a layout program like InDesign. Theoretically, you could design your entire interface this way, but that is not advisable. It is still more efficient to design the interface in Photoshop and to use Smart Objects when designing the content of the pages.

➤ Using Tracing Image

The **Tracing Image** command makes it easy to load a Photoshop file as a backdrop and trace it so that you can easily re-create a design. As with Smart Objects, this command is best for "converting" a mock-up of a content page; it is not necessarily the best tool for importing your interface design, mostly because it doesn't support rollover effects.

To use this feature, choose **Tracing Image** from the **Window** menu to access the palette. Check the **Source** box and browse to select the Photoshop file that you want to use. The image will be dimmed when loaded; adjust it using the **Opacity** slider. To reposition image, you can either type in **Position** values to offset it from the upper left corner of the page, or drag it with the **Move Image** tool. You can then eliminate parts of the image by dragging the

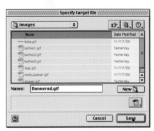

▲ The four steps for placing a Smart Object: after dragging it into the document from the Objects palette, the Save for Web dialog box appears for the optimizations settings. Then you must specify the target file before the element is displayed.

The Tracing Image palette allows you to adjust the opacity of the image in the background. Positioning the image is easy with the Move tool, and the Cut Out tool lets you import parts of the image into a layer. ▶

Cut Out tool to select an area and then clicking the **Cut Out** button. GoLive will display the **Save for Web** dialog box, and after choosing an image format and the optimization settings, you can save the file in your **Site** folder.

➤ Importing a Photoshop File as HTML

If you plan to use layer-based animation, GoLive's capability to import Photoshop files as HTML (**File > Import > Photoshop as HTML**) is particularly handy. This command does exactly what it says: after selecting the Photoshop file and choosing a destination folder, GoLive displays the Save for Web dialog box for every layer in the image, letting you choose each one individually. One limitation of this feature is that it does not render any layer effects, and it includes hidden layers. So if you have a Photoshop file with 20 layers but you only want to import some of them, it is not enough to hide those layers by toggling off their visibility in the Layers palette. Another tip: the layer names in Photoshop will become the names of the layer's corresponding floating box in GoLive. Some browsers have difficulty handling floating boxes if their name begins with a number, so it's important to name the layers properly in Photoshop: don't begin a name with a number, or use exclusively numbers in the name.

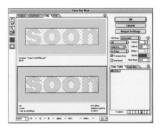

➤ Converting Layers into Layout Grids

The Photoshop as HTML command places image layers in GoLive documents as floating boxes. (So does the Tracing Image feature, when individual elements are extracted using the Cut Out command.) But unless you have to use HTML layers (for animations, for example), it is better to use HTML tables instead. Luckily, converting HTML layers to HTML tables is a snap: in the GoLive **Floating Boxes** palette (Window > Floating Boxes), choose **Convert to Layout Grid** from the palette's pop-up menu. If the command is grayed out, then the selected layers are overlapping. Fix this by selecting the layers individually and repositioning them so that they don't overlap. After using the **Convert to Layout Grid** command, GoLive re-creates the layout in a new HTML document. Either overwrite the original document (after closing it) or copy and paste the layout grid into the original file.

▲ After selecting a file and a destination folder, the Import as HTML command goes through each and every layer displaying the Save for Web dialog box.

▲ The Convert to Layout Grid command only works if the layers in GoLive don't overlap.

▲ This is the Site folder with all the subfolders: one for the mirror site and one for the site data, which contains the components.

Select the folder in which to save the Web site. Use the Create Folder option to have GoLive place the information inside a subfolder. The Site window appears (bottom) with the first page (index.html). Click on the icon in the lower right corner to split the window and reveal the Extras tab.

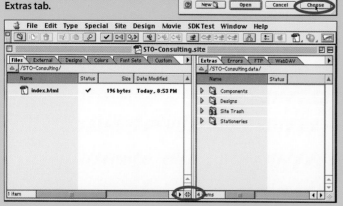

TUTORIAL: HTML AUTHORING

At first, creating a Web site may seem difficult and complex. Indeed, you have at your disposal two of the most complex and powerful tools that are available for designers—Photoshop and GoLive—and reading through the manuals is an almost impossible task (even though Adobe has considerably thinned the manual for GoLive 5.0). But when you know what to do and which buttons to press, you can create a Web site—from the design phase to the actual HTML authoring in GoLive—in just a few hours. Efficiency is essential: a simple mistake like creating the stationery and the site architecture before setting up the cascading style sheet can be time-consuming to fix. But all this will come together when you work through this tutorial, which is designed to show you the most efficient workflow and it is a good outline for all your projects.

1. Setting up a new site: choose **File > New Site > Blank** to create a new site. In the **File Selector** dialog box, select where you want to place your project folder (use the **New Folder** button if necessary), then name the site and check the **Create Folder** box, which places a project folder inside the selected folder. GoLive puts the site management document (".site") and two subfolders in this folder. The folder with the extension ".data" holds four subfolders called **Components, Designs, Site Trash,** and **Stationeries.** The other folder in the project folder has the site name without any extension; it represents your actual site. It is the local copy of the site (mirror site), which will later be uploaded to the server. You can create folders inside it to organize your files; if you do, you should get into the habit of using the Go-Live **Site window** for this. GoLive keeps track of all the files and folders in the local site folder in its internal database; if you place any documents or folders in your mirror site via the desktop, GoLive won't have a record of them. This can be confusing for new GoLive users since a folder or document (one that was created using the operating system commands) will not appear in GoLive's Site window. If this is ever the case, simply fix it by using the **Site > Rescan** command.

2. Creating the first stationery: In the Site window, double-click the index.html page to open it. An empty white page will appear. Change the page title from "Welcome to Adobe GoLive 5" to your desired title. Because most search engines put a lot of weight on the title when indexing a document, be sure to use descriptive keywords. If your site is about music, for instance, you may want to include keywords like music, CDs, MP3, or songs.

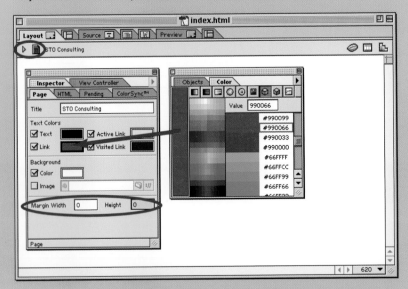

▲ Make sure to change the default "Welcome to Adobe GoLive 5" title. Way too often, such default titles end up in final sites (try using the keyword "untitled" in a search engine and you will get thousands of hits for pages where the designer overlooked this detail).

◄ Click on the Page icon to bring you to the Page Inspector, where you can set the colors and the browser offset.

Next set the colors and background for your page. Click on the **Page** icon next to the document title to view the **Page Inspector**. Open the **Color** palette via **Window > Color Palette** (**View > Color Palette** on Windows), choose a color for **Text, Link, Active Link,** and **Visited Link,** and drag to the color fields in the **Page Inspector**. GoLive automatically activates them (the checkboxes will be marked). Also very important: set the Margin Width and Height Attribute to 0.

3. Exporting images and rollover buttons: at this point we need to export all the images and rollover buttons for our design (see "Tutorial: Creating Slices and Rollovers" on page 197). But first, create an image folder in the **Site** window by clicking on the **New**

◄ As your very first step, create an image folder for your site.

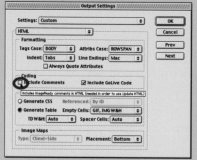

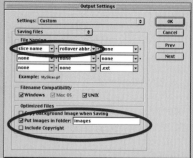

▲ Name the file: use "HTML and Images" for Format and "Selected Slices." Also, check the option "Include GoLive Code."

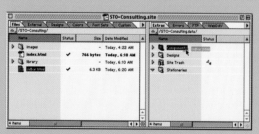

▲ Move the HTML file to the Components folder, and GoLive displays the Move Files dialog box.

Folder button in the toolbar and name it Images. Then open the tutorial design in ImageReady and select all the slices for the sidebar navigation (slices 12 and 13 through 17) by pressing the Shift key and using the **Slices Select** tool. Use the **Save Optimized As** command and look for the root folder of the mirror site (that is, the one that contains the "index.html" file). Name the file (preferably something sensible like "sidebar.html"), choose **HTML and Images** from the **Format** pop-up menu and **Selected Slices**, as well as the **Include GoLive Code** option. To set the output settings, click on the button (see the screens, above, for the appropriate settings). Make sure to deactivate **Include Comments** and the **Include Copyright** option. After confirming with **OK**, the images are saved into the **Images** folder and the HTML is saved inside the root folder, but they won't appear in GoLive's **Site** window until you rescan the **Site** folder (**Site > Rescan**). Drag the HTML file (sidebar.html) over to the **Components** folder and confirm the **Move File** dialog box. Usually components are created by saving the HTML file directly to the Components folder, but since we are exporting so many images (all the buttons consist of two images), it is much easier to save to the root folder and only drag the HTML file to the Components folder.

It would be logical to use the same procedure for the vertical rollover buttons, but we can't because all the buttons use one shape layer instead of individual ones, which causes some problems. Whenever we create a rollover state for one of the buttons, the areas in the other button slices change, too, and ImageReady notes this. When exporting the buttons along with the HTML code, it seems to work fine in GoLive at first, but when viewing it in

Explorer or Navigator, all the buttons change simultaneously. This is actually not a bug: ImageReady can trigger several image changes with one rollover, and that is exactly what is happening (the only "bug" is that GoLive interprets the code differently than the browsers do). Because we are using the inner shadow effect, we can't split the shape layer into several smaller pieces. Luckily, what seems to be a major problem has a very simple solution: just export the slices without the HTML and create the component with the rollover buttons in GoLive. So in the next step, we select all the remaining slices (1 to 9, 18, 20, and 22) and export them. Since the images are saved without an HTML file, use **Format: Images Only** and save them into the **Images** folder (otherwise they will be saved in the root folder). Now that all the images are exported, use the **Rescan** command again and create the component for the vertical navigation in GoLive.

4. Creating a component in GoLive: for the vertical navigation, we need a new document in which we place a table with one row and six cells. In the **File** view of the **Site window**, select all the buttons and drag them into your document (this is easier than using the **Image object** and then linking to the image). Place each button in its own cell and adjust the width and height of the table so that the buttons are tightly packed (this is important; otherwise,

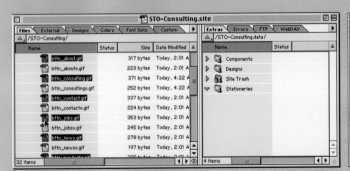 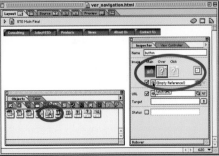

you will have gaps. We could leave out the table completely, but that would create some problems later with the display in GoLive: the last button would be wrapped and displayed underneath the others. The HTML code would still work correctly in the browsers though). Then drag a **Rollover** icon from the **Smart** tab of the **Objects** palette onto each button to convert it to a rollover object. Select each rollover button: in the **Inspector**, click on the **Over** state, then use the **Point-and-Shoot** feature to locate and link to the file in the **Site** window. After all the rollover buttons are done, save the file using the **Save As** command. In the lower right corner there is a pop-up menu with a shortcut to the **Components** folder. The component appears in the **Objects** palette

▲ Drag the button images from the Files window into the document. Then place them in a table and drag the Rollover icon onto them. Click on the Over State and then use the Point-and-Shoot tool to link to the image file for the over state.

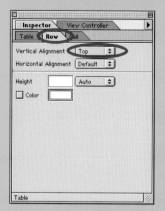

▲ All table cells should be aligned vertically to the Top. This is done row-by-row on the Row tab of the Table Inspector.

on the **Extras** tab as soon as you have saved the file. Make sure that **Components** is selected in the pop-up menu in the lower right corner.

5. Creating the master table: as I mentioned in the ImageReady tutorial, this design could be re-created in GoLive with frames as well as with tables. We will do this later on for the simple reason that it is a more difficult, not to mention that frames are somewhat unpopular nowadays due to the problems with search engines.

Place a table in the document with four rows and three columns and make the border invisible by using zero for the **Border** (also set **Cell Pad** and **Cell Space** to 0). There are two reasons why we are using a table and not a layout grid: for one, we are using an image background for some of the cells, and for the other, we need some areas to adjust dynamically to the size of the browser window. You can only do this with a table because the nature of the layout grid means that it is rather static.

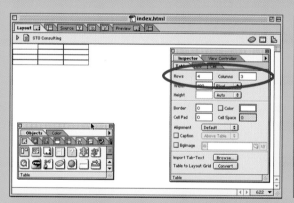

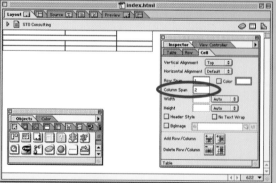

▲ After a table object has been placed, the number of rows needs to be increased by one, and two cells need to be merged in order to create a table that can function as the container for all other elements.

Merge the first and second cells of row 2 by using **Column Span 2** in the **Table Inspector**. The third cell of row 1 must be merged with cell 3 of row 2 by using **Row Span 2** (see the screen shots or the tutorial on page 197). Then go through each row and choose **Vertical Alignment: Top**.

6. Placing the images, components and backgrounds: now comes the fun part. Drag the black image of the upper left corner for the **File** window into the document and place it in the upper left table cell. Click first on the image and remember its dimensions, then click on the border of that particular cell and switch the dimensions from **Auto** to **Pixel** and enter the values for the image. This might be a little tricky since the border is so close to the border of the image—you know you have the table when the **Inspector** changes. Then

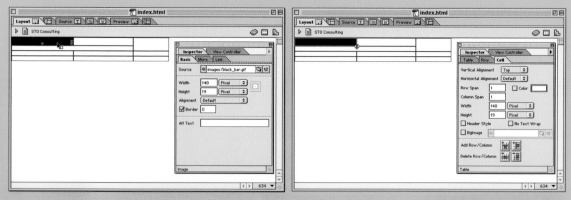

place the vertical navigation bar (ver_navigation.html) into the second cell and adjust the size of that cell (its width is 461 pixels). In the first cell of the second row, place the logo (with the arch), but don't change any dimensions of the table cell. It is not necessary to do so because we set the dimensions of the table cells above, but most importantly, the value in this merged table cell will always reflect the value of the first cell and it will not be the sum of both cells. Now place the component for the sidebar in the first cell of the third row.

▲ The different image slices and elements need to be placed in the table cells. It is important to first check the size of the image (above left) and then adjust the table cell accordingly (above right).

The page is starting to come together, but the most crucial part is still ahead. On the right side, we want the design to continue up to the edge of the browser. Since the size of the browser window always changes, we can't just place an image and give it a fixed size. We have to use a trick that is not that

▲ The next step is to place the components in their locations. On the left you can see what the layout looks like before an image background has been defined for the table cells.

well known, but has been around for quite some time: use a table with cell that adjust to the width of the browser and define for those cells an image background. How do you do that? The first step is to set the width of the table to 100 percent. Since two of the table cells in a row have a fixed size in pixels, the third cell is set to 99 percent width. Are you surprised? Did you expect that Auto would be the right setting? It isn't, because Auto always adjusts to the content of the cells and that won't work here, but 99 percent does (welcome to HTML, newbie). But this makes sense in a way: since this cell is set to almost the maximum, it will always try to fill the entire space. If it can't, it

will adjust. However, we are still not done. If you preview the page in a browser after you have selected the cells and used the BgImage option to load an image background, you won't see a background in Navigator (in Explorer, you do). Navigator simply doesn't display a cell background if the cell is empty. To fix this, place a transparent GIF in the cells and that's it.

The only thing left to do is to select the sidebar cell and load an image background for that, too. And by the way, your page in GoLive might look like it has gaps in almost every cell (left), but it will look correct in the browser.

▲ After the background for the table cells has been selected, the layout looks like this. The gaps between elements are caused by GoLive and will not appear in the browser.

That is something you just have to live with. This happens because GoLive adds extra space around elements like components in the Layout view. One more thing: If you are using a background image, pick a background color that comes close to the overall color of the image. That way, if the background image can't be loaded (due to a network error, for example), the page will at least look as close as possible to the way it is supposed to look.

▲ At the very end, a layout grid is placed in the main cell. This layout grid will later hold the content and a layout text box.

7. Placing the layout grid: the next step is to place a layout grid in the main table cell (the one that is later going to be used for the content). The layout grid is the first element in the palette (**Window > Palette**). When you place the grid in your document, the **Inspector** changes to the **Layout Grid**

Inspector, which allows you to set the dimensions of the grid. The default setting of 16 pixels for the horizontal and vertical spacing can be changed to a more useful value of 5 pixels. In order to place text on a layout grid, you have to place a layout text box, which is the second object in the **Objects** palette. You should also insert some text for the next steps.

8. Setting up the FONT setups: as you know by now, fonts are a problem when it comes to designing for the Web. In the early versions of HTML, you had no choice whatsoever in defining fonts. Later, the FONT tag was introduced, which at least allowed you to designate a font, but with the major restriction that this font had to be installed on the user's system. So it's almost impossible to use anything exotic; it literally comes down to using Arial, Helvetica (sans serif) or Palatino, Times (serif) combinations, since these are the only fonts that come standard on both Windows and Mac systems.

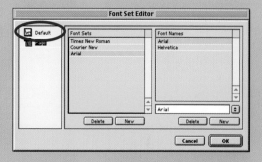

▲ Even if you don't plan to use the FONT tag, it is helpful to set up a font set. Later on, you can use it in the CSS definition. All you need to do is save the font sets using the default settings.

Even though we are going to use cascading style sheets later, there is a good reason to create font sets. They can also be accessed later in the Cascading Style Sheet Inspector, thus making the setup process much more convenient. Specify the FONT tag by using **Style > Font > Edit Font Sets**, which brings up the **Font Set Editor**. Make sure (!) that you have **Default** selected in the first column, then click the **New** button to insert an empty font set. In the **Font Names** column, choose the font from the **New** pop-up menu or just enter the name of the font in the text field. It's customary to pick a couple of sans serif fonts, so choose Arial, then click the **New** button and select Helvetica. You can pick additional sans serif fonts, but it is a good idea to just keep it down to two or three fonts, since this information is embedded every time you assign the FONT tag to text. The order in which you put fonts into your font set does make a difference by the way: if Arial is your first font, then the browser will use Helvetica only if Arial is not installed. To assign your newly created font set to text, select the text and choose the set in **Style > Font**.

9. Setting up the cascading style sheet: to create an external CSS document, choose **File > New Special > New Stylesheet Document**. The "untitled.ccs" window that appears contains Classes, Tags, IDs, Imports, and Font Faces. We will create one Class (that will allow us to format text that has no HTML tag) and the main HTML text marker (P and H1 to H6).

▲ Here's a list of elements and classes that you should create and save as an external cascading style sheet file.

Click on the **New Class Selector** button on the toolbar to insert a class in the CSS document. Enter a name, but keep the dot as the first character. Then switch to the second tab in the CSS Inspector and select **Arial Font Setup**

▲ Use the Font Setup menu to quickly apply a Font Family to the formatting.

An external CSS document is linked to this HTML page. You can see the effect right away in GoLive because it is capable of displaying cascading style sheets.

from the **Font Setup** menu. GoLive will now automatically list all the fonts of that setup in the font family; leave everything else unchanged. Later on, you can use this class to apply these fonts to selected text without changing any of the other formatting of the text.

Now define the HTML paragraph and header tags in the **CSS Selector Inspector**, and then use the various tabs to set the values that you want to assign to each HTML tag. The possibilities range from text color to having a border and a background color for text—but we will keep it simple since support for some of the features vary between browsers. All we do for now is set the font family and a font size and then save the document in the root folder of the Web site.

Since the style sheet is an external document, it needs to be linked to the HTML page. Bring the "index.html" page to the front and click the stair-shaped icon in the upper right corner of the document. The CSS window for this page will open. Click the **New Style Sheet File** button on the toolbar and an "Empty Reference" will appear in the window. This reference must be linked to the saved CSS document with the **Point-and-Shoot** tool or the **Browse** button.

GoLive will display the CSS settings even in Layout mode, but again, to avoid surprises, check your document in all browsers that your audience uses.

10. Setting up the colors: before creating the site structure with a stationery page, it's a good idea to set up the colors you want to use throughout your site. Select the **Color tab** in the **Site window** and choose **Site > Get Colors Used** to import all the colors used so far. Since we haven't yet defined many colors, you'll probably get just the colors that you used for the text, links, and background. Name them appropriately to make sure you know when you are using a link color for something else; use the link colors sparingly. It certainly is not a good idea to color regular text with the link colors since this is confusing to the visitor.

▲ Colors that you create on the Color tab of the Site window will appear as custom colors in the Color palette.

The colors that you drag in the Colors tab will appear on the right-most tab of the **Color** palette, making it easy for you to work consistently. When you're finished with the colors, save your document and use the **Save As** command to save a copy of the index.html page in your Stationeries folder (use the shortcut in the **Save As** dialog box).

▲ The Get Colors Used command on the Site menu is only available when the Colors tab is selected.

11. Creating the site structure: the last step before filling your site with content is to create the site structure. Click on the **Navigation View** button on the toolbar and a window will appear. At this point in time, this window shows only the home page (index.html). Activate the **Site Extras** tab in the **Objects** palette and drag the **Stationery** document over from the palette. As the **Page** icon comes beneath the index.html page icon, a bold line indicates that GoLive is ready to insert the page beneath the home page. To insert pages on the same hierarchical level, just bring the **Stationery** page icon close to one side of an already-placed page and drop it there.

You can even move pages around by dragging them to the new location, or you can delete them by pressing Delete. But working with the Navigation View will be much easier since you can actually see the content of the page. GoLive is able to display little thumbnails of the pages: switch to **Thumbnails** on the **Display** tab of the **Inspector**. Since all these new pages are just

▲ Before creating the site structure, save a copy of the home page in the Stationery folder. The shortcut in the lower right corner makes it easy to locate that folder.

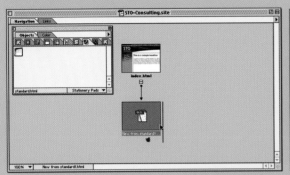

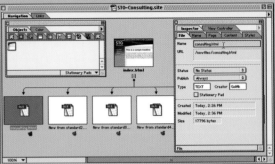

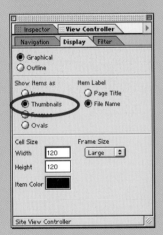

▲ After a copy of the home page has been saved as Stationery, click on the Site Extras tab in the Objects palette. Here the Stationery page is accessible and you can drag it onto the Navigation View. A bold line indicates the position at which GoLive will insert the page. After placing all the files, click on one of the page icons and rename the files in the Inspector palette.

▲ To display a page as a thumbnail, switch to Thumbnails on the Display tab of the Inspector.

named "New from …", it is time to rename the documents. You can do this either by clicking on them in the **Navigation View** and then changing their names in the **Inspector** (in the **File tab**), or you can rename them on the **File** tab of the **Site** window by clicking on the name once. All the pages that you created are in one folder named "newfiles"; since this probably doesn't reflect your desired folder structure, use the **Site > New > Folder** command to create an empty folder. Rename this folder and drag into it all the HTML files that you want here from the "newfiles" folder. A **Move Files** dialog box prompts you to confirm which files and links need to be updated.

12. Updating components: the navigational elements need to be updated now to make the site navigable. To edit a component, locate it in the **Site** window. Locating the component requires you to activate the split view by clicking on the tab in the upper right corner and then selecting **Extra**. You can also double-click on a component that is placed on a page. After the component is open, select each of the rollover buttons and create a link to the appropriate page. Use the **Point-and-Shoot** tool to point to the page in the **File** view, make the necessary changes and save the document again. GoLive will then display an **Updating Component** dialog box, which you need to confirm.

After you've set up the entire navigational structure and the hyperlinks, the pages displayed on the **Site** tab will be connected by solid lines and you can fill the site with content using Smart Objects, for example. To preview your Web site in the browser, click the **Show in Browser** button on the toolbar.

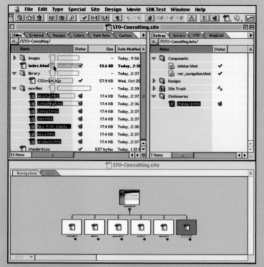

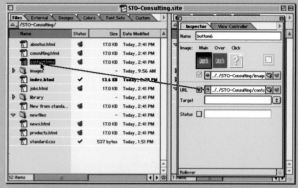

▲ After you've renamed all files, move them out of the Files folder to a new location in the site. Then open the components and link the buttons to the files. When saving, GoLive will ask you if you want to update the placed components.

13. Uploading the site: the almost last step in the Web design process is uploading the site. First you must set up the FTP connection. Choose **Site > Settings**, then select FTP and enter server, username, and password. After closing **Settings**, open an Internet connection and click on **Site > Connect to server**. The server directory is only visible if you click the tab on the upper right, which splits the window in two (select the FTP tab). To upload, you can manually drag the folder and files from the left to the right window, but Go-Live automatically synchronizes the directory of the server with your mirror site when you click on the **Upload to Server** button on the toolbar.

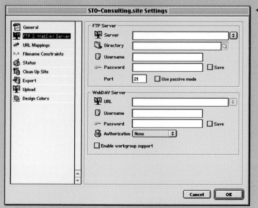

◀ After inserting the server name, username, and password, you are almost ready to upload your Web page. Connect to the Internet and then click on the server connect/disconnect button on the toolbar.

Illustration: Michael Baumgardt

VIDEO AND AUDIO

Video and Audio

If you are a designer working with GoLive, you should really spend some time with the QuickTime features. The possibilities for enhancing your Web site are tremendous, and QuickTime is widely available.

As more and more people get cable modems and DSL connections, Web designers can more energetically develop sites with richer content, such as video and audio. Luckily, GoLive makes it easy to create multimedia-rich Web sites because it comes with extensive QuickTime features. This chapter will give you all the information you need to spice up your site.

CAPTURING FORMATS

Although the Web doesn't yet allow for high-bandwidth real-time video, it's a good idea to capture high-quality content anyway. There are several reasons for this:

- Highly pre-compressed video cannot be compressed again—at least, not with acceptable results. It might not be clear why this is such a big issue, but you can now use compression algorithms—Sorenson II, for example—that produce stunning quality even for Web use. But these algorithms won't work well on already compressed images, and the image quality will deteriorate significantly.

- Aside from Web publishing, you might want to use your videos for CD-ROMs, high-resolution screen shots, or even your own movie edits that go back to video.

- You can always scale down a movie file, but you can't scale it back up without a loss in quality. This is especially important if you want to create several smaller clips designed for different connection speeds (a feature that comes standard with QuickTime and RealMedia SureStream G2). Scaling means that someone visiting your Web site with a 28kbps connection will see a movie with 160x120 resolution, while visitors with 56kbps modems will see a movie with 240x180 resolution.

- Not all compression algorithms work equally well for all purposes. Even with some experience, you might still need to test the different output options (algorithms) for your particular project.

CREATING A TWO-FRAME POSTER MOVIE IN QUICKTIME PLAYER PRO

One of the problems with embedding QuickTime movies into HTML pages is that they will start downloading immediately even if a visitor doesn't want to watch them. To avoid this, you have to either get your ISP to install Quick-

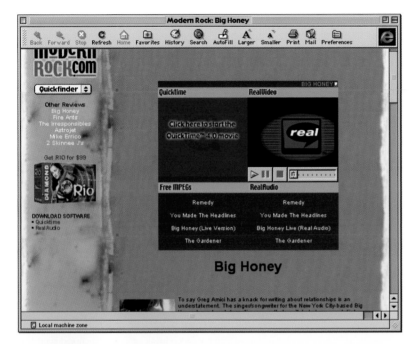

▲ These are the two images for the poster movie.

▲ Instead of using QuickTime or RealAudio Player, movies can be embedded into the HTML page. To avoid having movies download immediately to the browser cache, you can use poster movies that link to the real movies.

Time Streaming Server software, or you can use a poster movie. Technically, a poster movie can be anything from a single image to a movie trailer that acts as a placeholder. Of course, it makes sense to keep the poster movie as small as possible; I'll show you how to create a poster movie with two frames, which will ensure that there is some animation in the movie itself.

First, create two images with the same resolution as the movie file for which the poster movie will be used (in this example, 160x120 pixels). Quick-Time has some movie controllers that are always displayed at the bottom of the screen; if you want to hide the movie controllers, add an additional 16 pixels to compensate. This is important, because later on you will position the poster movie in GoLive, and if it doesn't have the exact measurements as the movie itself, you'll end up with a squeezed movie. You could display the controllers for the poster movie, but visitors may be confused about where to click. (For a poster movie to load the real movie, users have to click inside the poster movie.) I recommend including a message such as "click here to start the movie" in your poster movie, as in the example above, in which I created the effect of flashing text.

▲ Save the movie and click on Options to set the codec.

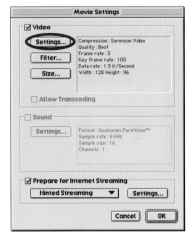

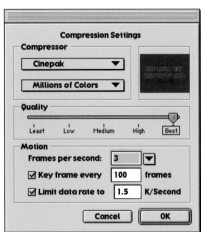

▲ In the Options dialog box, click on Settings to access compression settings. For a poster movie, use Cinepak as your Compressor and select a motion frame rate. In this example the two frames will flash in intervals of 0.66 seconds because the frame rate is set to 3 frames per second.

▲ In QuickTime Player Pro, the images can be imported as PICT sequences and saved as a movie.

To do that, I created the first text frame in Photoshop and saved it as "poster1.tif," and then I applied an Outer Glow layer effect and saved that image as "poster2.tif." It's important to keep the files in a separate folder and to name them sequentially, because when you choose **Open Image Sequence** from the **File** menu, QuickTime Player Pro loads all of the images in the folder in the order that they're listed. Choose 1 frame per second as your display rate, and preview the movie in QuickTime by selecting **Movie > Loop** and pressing **Play**.

To use this as a poster movie, choose **File > Export;** in the dialog box that appears, click **Options** to select a compression method. Cinepak yields the smallest file size but shows visible degradation. The Animation codec yields good results but generates bigger files; since file size is an issue in Web design, I suggest you stick with Cinepak. This example ended up using 20KB, which is quite a lot, but it's still better than having an entire movie embedded.

Given GoLive's capability to create "sprite" tracks in QuickTime movies, you can divide poster movies into different sections, like image maps, to provide links or trigger other actions. For example you could click one section of the poster movie to open the movie in a new window, and click another to open it in the original window. A third area could open the movie in QuickTime Player, and a fourth section could open a universally compatible version of the movie that runs on all systems. You can make all options accessible from one poster movie.

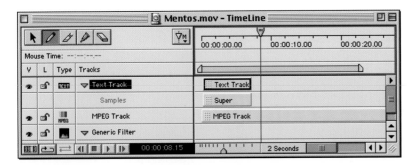

▲ The interface for the QuickTime TimeLine was updated extensively in GoLive 5.0. Here, for example, I've added a text track that will appear as a closed caption in the movie.

▲ Double-click on an embedded movie in GoLive to open the movie in its own window. Click on the Track Editor button in the toolbar (circled) to edit tracks.

COMPRESSING AND EMBEDDING MOVIES FOR THE WEB

Compressing your movie for publishing on the Web is the last significant step of media preparation. Although there are numerous codecs, the two most popular platforms for Web video are Apple QuickTime and RealNetworks' RealVideo. While RealVideo offered streaming technology before QuickTime did, Apple has caught up on that technological front, which has boosted QuickTime's popularity.

Apple offers QuickTime Player Pro and FinalCut Pro for compression. RealNetworks offers several versions of RealProducer with different feature sets (RealProducer, RealProducer Plus, RealProducer Pro).

▲ GoLive's QuickTime palette contains icons for all of the objects and modules that can be used by the Track Editor. To insert a video track, just drag the icon (circled) into the Track Editor.

Although both of these products are inexpensive, consider buying Terran's Media Cleaner Pro if you plan on using video frequently on your Web sites. Media Cleaner Pro is a dream when it comes to encoding video and audio. It costs quite a lot more, but it is worth the higher price tag. It supports the highest-quality compression codecs, such as Sorenson Developer Edition, Qdesign2 Professional Edition, Real G2, and original source MP3. These formats are all becoming increasingly important on the Web; if you've ever seen the amazing results that you can get with Sorenson II, you'll understand why. And since Media Cleaner Pro also does batch

◄ This is RealPlayer, which launches automatically when a RealAudio or RealVideo file is linked to a Web page. It can be downloaded from www.real.com.

▲ In the left column, Media Cleaner Pro lists all the available codecs and settings.

▲ For novices, Media Cleaner offers a wizard that walks users though settings and gives visual examples. Here, for example, it shows how the Sorenson video compares to a regular version.

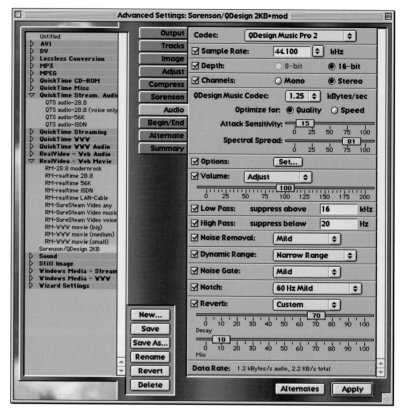

▲ Media Cleaner Pro offers an incredible variety of options, such as the audio settings of a Sorenson QuickTime video, shown here. Media Cleaner Pro's robust feature set and batch processing capability make it the best choice for professional Web video producers.

processing, you can set up a computer to do the time-consuming encoding task at night. This alone could justify the investment, but there is so much more.

The visual control and support throughout the program are excellent. The program gives you a number of settings that allow you to edit source material without having to leave the program: audio and video fades, several audio filters, and several video filters like brightness, hue, and saturation, adaptive noise, and removal. You can only access some special codec features from Media Cleaner Pro; for example, the Disable saving from WWW option prevents visitors from storing published QuickTime movies to their hard drives, thus providing copy protection for your media. This method works more reliably than the HTML QuickTime attribute, which is supposed to do the same thing.

Working with Media Cleaner Pro is very simple. A settings wizard guides you through a multiple-choice sequence to pick the right compression setting for your situation, and chances are that if you're looking for a feature, Media Cleaner Pro has it. At this point, it's certainly the unchallenged powerhouse of media preparation.

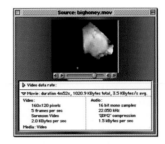

► **Which video format should you use?**

Once you've decided to use video on your Web site, you have to choose a compression standard. Since RealVideo entered the streaming media market before Apple, it's likely that more users will have RealPlayer installed (most new content is delivered in the G2 standard, however, which requires a new player that some users may not have). If you're trying to decide between RealVideo and QuickTime, here are some other factors to consider:

▲ Media Cleaner Pro shows a preview of the movie its converting, as it is performing the conversion. You can even split the screen and simultaneously view the before and after movie.

Generally, QuickTime requires less CPU overhead, is more responsive, and therefore works on even slow systems without breakups. With the QDesign Music 2 codec, it also sports better audio quality (16-bit, 44.1 kHz stereo at 3 K/s) and the data rate can be adjusted in finer increments. Video playback also works smoothly on slow systems.

RealVideo creates an impressive image quality that is sharp and crisp, but yields sluggish response on slow systems due to high demands on the CPU when decompressing images. This may result in low frame rates (one image or less per second) and net congestion errors even at local playback.

If you have Media Cleaner Pro and the Sorenson II codec (which costs almost as much as Media Cleaner Pro itself), you get the best of both worlds. QuickTime's Sorenson Professional codec offers a variable bit rate (VBR) for encoding, and the video image quality will be equal to (or even better than) that of RealVideo. If you can't decide, you probably will end up having both.

► **How to embed video in HTML**

Finally, it's time to embed your prepared media into your Web pages. GoLive is the best tool for doing this, as it supports QuickTime and RealMedia attributes. Make sure you install the appropriate plug-ins that come with the GoLive installation CD, otherwise it will be much harder to preview the media (GoLive will also not provide all the HTML features for the media type.)

▲ Sorenson II offers the best video and audio quality available to date for QuickTime. It is amazing how much Sorenson is able to compress a video/audio file. It's a must-have for anyone who wants to deliver high-quality video on the Web.

The simplest way to integrate video on your Web page is just to create a link to the file. When the user clicks on the link, the file will be opened externally

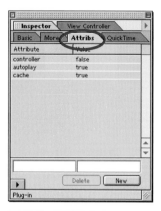

▲ Many QuickTime attributes, such as Loop and Autoplay, can be set in the QuickTime tab of the Plug-In Inspector. For a complete list, switch to the Attribs tab. This is where more exotic attributes can be manually entered.

in either QuickTime or RealPlayer. Although this technique does the job, I personally prefer actually embedding the movie in the page. But in order to have movies play directly in Web browsers, you must know at least a few attributes of the different plug-in standards. Keep in mind that since plug-ins are updated continuously, authoring software may not supply all current attributes. Below you will find several QuickTime and RealMedia attributes and descriptions of their practical use.

➤ QuickTime attributes

Before you embed QuickTime movies into your Web page, make sure that their file names end in ".mov." QuickTime movies also need to be flattened (their headers need to be removed) before they are put on the Web. Quick-Time Player Pro and Media Cleaner Pro do this automatically.

To place the QuickTime movie, just drag it into the document window or choose the **Plug-In object** from the **Palette** and press the **Browse** button in the **Plug-in Inspector**. Then set the following parameters:

● **AUTOPLAY=true:** to have the movie start automatically after the page has loaded

● **LOOP=true:** to loop the movie after it's ended

● **CACHE=true:** to cache or temporarily store the movie on the visitor's hard drive

● **HREF=[URL of actual movie file]:** With reference to the QuickTime poster movie mentioned earlier, the HREF attribute can be used to load another movie when the visitor clicks on the poster movie. HREF defines a URL that can be absolute or relative. Use the Target attribute to define where the HREF movie should play. Setting it to "_self" or "myself" will open it in the original place of the SRC movie.

● **CONTROLLER=false:** Set this attribute if you want to hide the controllers for the SRC movie. This attribute does not apply to the HREF movie. To avoid placement anomalies in the two movies, the SRC movie in the example should have a height of 136 pixels without the controllers, and the HREF movie should measure 136 pixels with the controllers (or 120 without).

You can set all of the above attributes in the QuickTime tab of the **Plug-in Inspector** by clicking on the appropriate options. As mentioned earlier, the QuickTime plug-in needs to be placed in GoLive's **Plug-in** folder for the QuickTime Inspector to appear. There are many more QuickTime attributes than are currently available in GoLive; to enter these attributes, click on the **Attribs** tab of the **Plug-in Inspector** and click **New**. Enter the attribute name in the left field and the attribute value (without quotation marks) in the right field. Press **Enter** on the keyboard to finish.

The following example will display the flashing poster movie from the earlier example in a loop and without controllers until the visitor clicks on it to load the target movie. The poster movie is 136 pixels high without controllers, and the target movie is 120 pixels high. Note that the order of the attributes has no relevance:

```
<EMBED SRC="poster.mov" WIDTH="160" HEIGHT="136" AUTO-
PLAY="true" LOOP="true" CONTROLLER="false" HREF="target.mov"
TARGET="myself" TARGETCACHE="false">
```

These are just a few examples of the many attributes available in Quick-Time. If you would like to find out more, point your browser to the URL www.apple.com/quicktime/.

➤ Embedding RealMedia

Embedding RealMedia content into Web pages is a little more complicated, but still is not very difficult. First of all, it's important to know that you need to create a metafile if you want to use Web-based streaming without a server. A metafile is a simple text file that contains the URL of the media file to be streamed. You can use a simple text editor to create such a file, or in GoLive, choose **File > New Special > New Text Document**.

RealProducer Plus and Pro allow you to encode videos in the Real-Video format. RealProducer is available at realnetworks.com. ▼

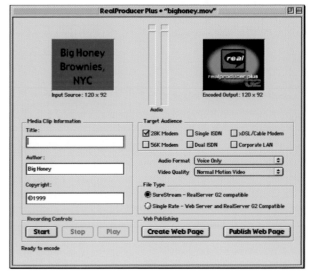

The information inside the metafile consists basically of a single text line with the absolute URL of the audio or video file. It could look like this: http://www.mysite.com/media/movie.rm.

Again, the URL must be absolute to work, which makes it a bit more tedious to preview your work locally before uploading to the server. If you'd like to preview the result in your browser

▲ RealProducer displays the before and after when converting a movie.

▲ After the conversion, Real-Producer gives detailed information in the Statistics window.

▲ To stream RealVideo, make sure that the HTML link in the browser addresses a text (meta) file with the URL of the video.

locally, the path needs to start with "file://" and must include the complete path to the destination: file://harddisk/documents/Web sites/mysite/media/movie.rm

If you create a local path, don't forget to change it to a URL before uploading, or your link will not work. Actually, it will still work on your computer but not on anybody else's, and you might not even realize it.

Another very important thing is that the name of this metafile must have the extension ".ram" or ".rpm." A ".rpm" file is commonly used to play movie or audio content inside a Web page, while a ".ram" file will play a movie or audio in the RealPlayer application. To play the ".ram" file all you need to do is create a hyperlink to it in the Web page. If the plug-in is installed on the visitor's browser, the associated MIME type will automatically direct the file to RealPlayer.

To display the video (or play audio) in the Web page, you need a few attributes; just like QuickTime media, RealMedia is embedded in the page using the Plug-In object from the palette. One major difference between RealMedia and QuickTime is that QuickTime displays its controllers as part of the video window, while RealMedia doesn't. The way RealMedia works is that you place instances of the movie in the Web page and use the Controls attribute to define what the SRC window should contain. It could be the video itself or just the controllers for it. This gives you the flexibility to display, for example, just a Start and Stop button, or you can also show a progress bar. Among the values available for this attribute are ImageWindow, PlayButton, StopButton, PositionSlider, and VolumeSlider. ImageWindow will display the movie content, the other values are self-explanatory.

You might decide to use the Console attribute to have the PositionSlider control the movie. Here is an example of a movie file measuring 160x120 pixels with associated play, stop, and position controls. The HTML code on your page should look like this:

```
<EMBED SRC="movie.rpm" WIDTH="160" HEIGHT="120" _CON-
TROLS="ImageWindow" CONSOLE="movie">
<EMBED SRC="movie.rpm" WIDTH="44" HEIGHT="26"
CONTROLS="PlayButton" CONSOLE="movie">
<EMBED SRC="movie.rpm" WIDTH="26" HEIGHT="26"
CONTROLS="StopButton" CONSOLE="movie">
<EMBED SRC="movie.rpm" WIDTH="90" HEIGHT="26"
CONTROLS="PositionSlider" CONSOLE="movie">
```

Note that the width and height values for Play and Stop buttons can't vary much from the ones given in this example. This limits your placement and design choices.

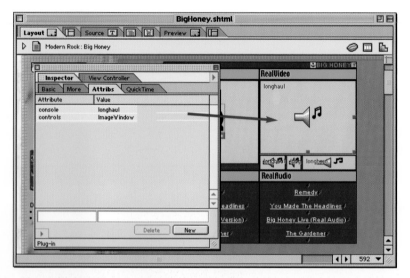

▲ To embed a RealVideo in a Web page along with its controls, you must create several instances of the video and use the Controls attribute to specify the function. For example, Controls=ImageWindow will display the movie.

▲ Switch to Preview mode in GoLive to check that your video plays correctly.

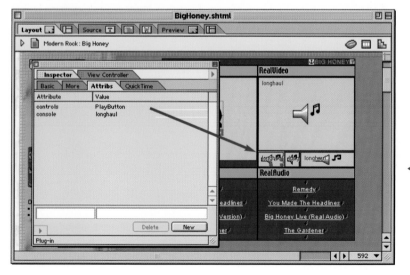

◀ To insert a Play button, I placed an instance of the movie in GoLive and used the attribute Controller=PlayButton. Console=Name is required so that this Play button only starts the movie with this name (in this example the name is "longhaul".)

▲ Most attributes for sound can be set in the Audio tab of the Plug-In Inspector. Only the more exotic attributes need to be set manually by switching to the Attribs tab.

WAV (.wav): This format is the standard audio format on an IBM-compatible computer running Microsoft Windows.

AIFF (.aiff): This is the standard audio format on Mac OS computers and is good for music and high-quality sound.

AU (.au): Developed by Sun Microsystems, this has a poor sound quality, but a small file size.

MIDI (.mid): If you are a musician, you are probably familiar with this format, because it is used to record music with a sequencer or to hook up two keyboards. Because MIDI is not an audio format, it requires that at least one of the following be installed on the user's computer: a sound card that supports MIDI playback, an external MIDI device, or a QuickTime (which provides MIDI playback in software).

MUSIC AND AUDIO

With MP3 becoming so popular and bandwidth increasing, we will probably see more Web sites using sound to enhance the online experience. There are basically two methods for delivering audio over the Web: files that have to be downloaded before playback, and audio that plays during download, which is called streaming audio.

In general, the first scenario gives you better control over the sound quality and doesn't require any plug-in. Both Internet Explorer and Netscape Navigator can play these files directly. The problem is that the download of a long audio file takes awhile. Streaming audio has the advantage that the sound starts playing even before the file has completely loaded.

➤ Implementing a sound file

There are several ways of integrating sound into your Web page, but the most commonly used is the <EMBED> tag, which both browsers understand and which can play WAV, AIFF, AU, and MIDI files. The EMBED tag is automatically placed when you drag the Plug-In object from the palette in GoLive and link it to a sound file. Here's an example of a sound file placed with an EMBED tag:

```
<EMBED SRC="music_file.mid" AUTOSTART="true"
WIDTH="144" HEIGHT="60" LOOP="1">
```

Depending on the file type, you need to use the right attributes. In this example a MIDI file is loaded and the attribute Autostart="true" automatically plays the sound after it is completely downloaded. If this attribute is set to "false," the sound will only play when the user hits the play button in the control panel.

The Loop attribute tells the browser how many times you want the sound to be played, and it can be an integer or true/false. "True" means that the browser will continue playing the sound until the stop button on the console is clicked. "False" will play the sound file only once from beginning to end.

➤ MP3 audio format

MP3, or MPEG Audio Layer-3, is an advanced audio format that provides almost CD-quality sound with reasonable file sizes. The compression ratio is up to 12:1. The resulting files are bigger than RealAudio files in best quality mode (17:1), but also superior in sound. MP3 compresses sounds by remov-

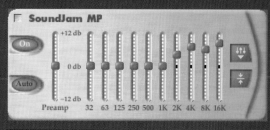

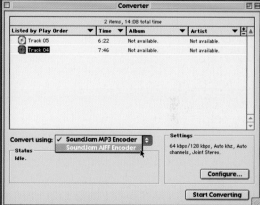

ing parts that are inaudible, while retaining the full frequency and dynamic spectrum. Streaming of MP3 files is incorporated in the file format, but requires high-bandwidth connections, such as ISDN.

If you are looking for a great MP3 player software, I strongly recommend SoundJam from Casady & Greene. This software has great features, from the ability to change the design of the user interface to nice visual effects to batch encoding of MP3 from a CD.

➤ **RealAudio**

Thanks to streaming technology, this popular file format allows almost instant access to very long sound files, such as songs, interviews or even live transmissions. The RealAudio algorithm uses high compression rates ranging from about 17:1 to 170:1, which are based on CD-quality audio. A three-minute song can be reduced to as little as 180KB, compared to about 30 MB in CD quality. There is a definite deterioration in sound quality when using these high compression ratios with slower modems. However, the resulting low data rate necessary for those files provides real-time audio access for modems as slow as 14.4kbps.

▲ SoundJam is one of the best MP3 players available. It comes with several interfaces (skins), but most important, it offers batch conversion of music directly from CD. Other converters copy the original sound files to the hard drive first, which can be a problem.

▲ The Eclipse is a spectral display in SoundJam that makes it fun to view the music.

INDEX